D0906624

MALES
AT
RISK

*To those who struggle to overcome
the effects of abuse of sexuality
childhood experiences*

MALES

AT

RISK

The Other Side of Child Sexual Abuse

Frank G. Bolton, Jr.
Larry A. Morris
Ann E. MacEachron

SAGE PUBLICATIONS
The Publishers of Professional Social Science
Newbury Park   London   New Delhi

For information address:

SAGE Publications, Inc.
2111 West Hillcrest Drive
Newbury Park, California 91320

SAGE Publications Ltd.
28 Banner Street
London EC1Y 8QE
England

SAGE Publications India Pvt. Ltd.
M-32 Market
Greater Kailash I
New Delhi 110 048 India

Printed in the United States of America

Library of Congress Cataloging-in-Publication Data

Bolton, Frank G.
  Males at risk: the other side of child sexual abuse / Frank G.
Bolton, Jr., Larry A. Morris, Ann E. MacEachron.
      p. cm.
  Bibliography: p.
  ISBN 0-8039-3236-7. — ISBN 0-8039-3237-5 (pbk.)
  1. Sexually abused children—Mental health. 2. Boys—Abuse of.
3. Child psychotherapy. I. Morris, Larry A. II. MacEachron, Ann
E. III. Title.
RJ507.S49B65   1989
616.85′83—dc20   89-10226
                                                           CIP

FIRST PRINTING 1989

Contents

1

Of Sexual Abuse and Other Things in the Night

Direction and Misdirection

It happens. Male children and adolescents are sexually abused, sexually misused, and involved with adults, peers, and siblings in ways that inhibit the development of normal sexuality. Less than a decade ago, child sexual abuse researcher and clinician Susanne Sgroi (1975) admonished clinicians in the following manner:

> . . . recognition of sexual molestation in a child is dependent upon the individual's inherent willingness to entertain the possibility that the condition may exist. (pp. 18–21)

This book does not attempt to describe a problem of epidemic proportion. For the clinician, the possibility of a single case demands preparation. This book does not suggest that males are at equal risk to females. That does not seem reasonable given available data. This book does suggest that clinicians may sometimes overlook two critical elements in serving the population of children and adolescents at risk from sexual victimization. First, it is *children* who are at risk, not only female children. Second, our present focus upon sexual abuse, one which assumes some physical contact, may have diverted attention from the equally or more damaging effects of more subtle sexual interactions. These covert interactions between adult and child which inhibit the development of sexuality must be factored into our litany of sexual victimizations directed toward children. We have described this broader sexual victimization as the *abuse of sexuality.* This inhibitor to normal development serves as a foundation here and will be described later. Finally, there are no more eloquent descriptors of clinical problems than the words of the patients who have lived them. Several of our patients have given permission to use these descriptions as case studies. The words are rough and sometimes difficult to read, but they are real. Consider the following report from a fourteen-year-old boy regarding the range of sexual victimizations he experienced with his mother, her boyfriend, and his younger sister:

It seemed like my mom and stepfather were always fighting about something. They would scream and yell and sometimes really hit each other hard. One night they were both drinking and started to argue about something stupid, I'm not sure what it was, even. One thing led to another and pretty soon they were really at it. They smacked each other around and broke a lot of stuff in the house. Then I heard my stepfather say he was leaving and I never saw him again.

A few months after that mom started coming into the bathroom when I was taking a bath. At first she said she just wanted to get something from the medicine cabinet, but I noticed her looking at me. Later she asked me if I wanted my back washed like she did when I was younger. I was embarrassed but let her do it a couple of times then it seemed like one thing led to another until she wanted to wash me all over. It felt good but I was scared. When she started dating she didn't come into the bathroom as often and she stopped asking to wash my back so I figured that it was all over. But one night she woke me up and asked me to sleep with her because she heard some noises outside and was afraid. I was so sleepy, I hardly knew what was going on, but I went to her bedroom and went to sleep. In the morning, I woke up with an erection and mom was sort of up against me with her hand on my stomach. I didn't want her to know I had an erection, so I started to move away from her to get out of bed, but she was awake already and she pulled me back. She wanted to know if something was wrong and I told her I had to go to the bathroom. She didn't let go and moved her hand down over my undershorts and I could feel her hand on my penis. She started moving her hand back and forth slowly. One thing led to another, I guess, and pretty soon she was kissing me on the lips, rubbing me more, and then she put my hand between her legs over her nightgown and moved it up and down. I was afraid but also was getting turned on. We rubbed each other like that until I came. I don't know if she came or not but we stopped then. Afterwards I felt real bad. This was my mother and you aren't supposed to do things like that with your mother. She never said anything so I figured it wouldn't happen again.

I was wrong. Things got worse. She started coming into my bedroom once or twice a week asking me to sleep with her and eventually we went all the way. I never told anybody because I was ashamed.

Then mom came home with a man late one night and woke me and my sister up saying she wanted to show us something. Mom and the guy were really loaded and I didn't know what was going on. They took us to the living room and they took their clothes off and started making love, telling us to watch. They then told me to make love to my sister, but I told them I wouldn't do it. So mom said, "Okay, then you can make love to me." I tried to stop what was going on but thought that if I did what they wanted, they would leave my sister alone. It worked. After awhile mom and this guy passed out on the floor and me and my sister went back to bed. That night, my sister told me she knew what had been going on with mom because she saw us a couple of times.

It wasn't long after that night that mom would bring this guy home and show us pornographic movies on the VCR and insist that me and my sister make love. They would get us drunk and we eventually did what they wanted. Pretty soon we were having regular orgies. We would all get drunk and I would have sex with mom while this guy and my sister watched. Then mom and I would watch this guy screw my sister. Sometimes the guy would suck me while mom and my sister watched, but I didn't really want him to do that to me. I never did it to him. I did do it to my sister while they watched. It was crazy. I'm glad my sister finally told someone and put a stop to it.

Growing Up Male: Easier Said Than Done

A male patient who was not sexually abused once reported to one of the authors, "Living through the development of male sexuality for me was like hitchhiking. It is more fun to talk about than it was to live through it." That may be one of the major difficulties of "growing up male." Everyone talks about it as though it were easy. Few males are willing to admit to the difficulties.

Male children are "typecast" to be dominant, competitive, aggressive, and "tough." To be a "normal" male is to aspire to leadership. The burdens inherent in these expectations are obvious. To be "normal" sexually as a male is to be active, knowledgeable, potent, and a successful seducer. The foundation seems to be an elusive sense of power and control. When transformed into a negative or dysfunctional element of a male's development, it is not difficult to understand the male perpetration of sexual offenses (Brownmiller, 1975; Groth, 1979; Russell, 1984). It is more difficult to conceive of males as sexual victims. But, they are sometimes just that—victims.

Male Sexual Development: Myth and Mystery

Although "tongue in cheek," the suggestion may be made that the initial form of sexual victimization of males is that of holding tightly to the myths regarding their sexual development. Few males experience the transition from childhood to adult sexuality as the fluid process described by the "boys will be boys" philosophy incorporated into popular thinking. The reality is that there are several difficult tasks.

Although viewing childhood development as a series of tasks has less currency among developmentalists now than in the past, it seems useful to retain it when thinking of the development of sexuality. For the purposes of this work the "stages" of this development are broadly defined as childhood experimentation, adolescent transitions, and adult sexuality. Each of these stages may be modified by the adequacy of information, cultural expectations, parental socialization, and peer relationships that occur from infancy through adulthood. Distortions in these areas, such as those introduced through aberrant sexual interactions, may contribute to confusion, delays in development, or overt sexual dysfunctions. Little is known about the appropriate content at each stage of development. There seems little certainty regarding facilitating or inhibiting factors. It does seem defensible to suggest that inappropriate sexual contacts with adults or peers would interfere with and "abuse" this developing sexuality.

The first task for the clinician is the elimination of some of the timeworn beliefs that may cloud his or her view of sexual development. Recent findings relative to sexual anatomy, physiology, behavior and treatment of sexual issues have placed some "common knowledge" at issue (Kinsey, Pomeroy, & Martin, 1948; Kinsey, Pomeroy, Martin, & Gebhard, 1953; Masters & Johnson, 1966, 1970).

The first concept currently in question is that sexual arousal occurs only after puberty. The fact is that, with the exception of ejaculation, sexual arousal and responsiveness have been observed from infancy forward (Kinsey et al., 1948; Kinsey et al., 1953; Masters, Johnson, & Kolodny, 1985). These findings do not refer to the reproduction-related capabilities that emerge in puberty, but the suggestion is that sexual responsiveness is an integral element of childhood development. It is not uncommon for pre-adolescent males to report first coital experiences long before the ejaculation capacity has developed. The clinician must be cautioned against the common conceptual error of equating reproductive capability with sexuality.

The second source of confusion confronting the clinician is that of "latency" periods in sexual development. The school-aged child was long thought to be at reduced risk for sexual victimization. Factually, sexual development continues essentially unabated from infancy through adulthood (Goldman & Goldman, 1982; Masters et al., 1985; Money & Wiedeking, 1980). Self stimulation of the genital area begins, with apparent signs of pleasure, when motor coordination becomes sufficient (Masters et al., 1985). This pattern continues with pleasurable genital stimulation, increasing knowledge of body parts and reproduction, and direct questions about sexual behavior. Unfortunately, these direct questions are often met with indirect answers. This is a pattern which results, according to Calderone (1985), in children "learning to keep silent and go underground" about their own sexual feelings and behaviors (p. 702). This may help open the door to potential victimization.

The point is that children are aware of the erotic and sensual nature of genital stimulation although they may not discuss it with adults. Sex play, exploration, curious contact with peers of either gender occur during this time. It may be considered within normal bounds as long as coercive or aggressive behavior is absent from it. As puberty approaches, this becomes less a game and more a deliberate activity. Physical changes no longer allow for dismissal of sexual feelings and partners are sought (Smith, Udry, & Morris, 1985). If the selection of that partner is dependent upon what has been learned to that point, the clinician must be concerned with all prior stages of sexual development.

The third, and perhaps most destructive belief regarding the developing male, is that males have a much larger sex drive than females. This seems to be a belief founded upon the greater amount of testosterone in the male. The fact is that hormonal studies have not been completely successful in predicting sexual behavior. Testosterone is considered "the principle biologic determinant of the sex drive in both men and women" (Masters et al., 1985, p. 94). Women do have lower levels. However, it is the reaction to testosterone rather than the quantity which stimulates sexual drive. Women have greater sensitivity to smaller quantities. This does not suggest that sexual hormones and androgens have no role in sex drive. This information requires the clinician to bring gender-based drive levels more into balance.

It appears that both genders share common sexual capabilities and experience continuous sexual development throughout childhood. Gender difference and changes in sexual behavior are not completely explained by biology. An equally critical variable, particularly for the clinician's assessment, seems to be the learning that has taken place within a specific sociocultural or family setting (Gilligan, 1982; Kolhberg, 1966; Maccoby & Jacklin, 1974; Masters et al., 1985; Money & Wiedeking, 1980). What the child has acquired as a sex role, familiar sexual stereotypes, and differential sexual socialization patterns are all pivotal elements to the clinician's understanding of the potential abuses of sexuality in a child or adolescent. These elements will be reflected upon in the following pages.

Sex Roles

Some sense of gender identity may become established as early as the age of three (Money & Wiedeking, 1980). The development of gender-based skills, solidification of gender identity, and learning of sex role attributes continues through childhood and well into adulthood (Kagan, 1976; Kolhberg, 1966). What is expected of both males and females is guided by these learned sex and gender roles (Maccoby & Jacklin, 1974). When that learning has been deviant, even in small ways, the "ripple effects" may be considerable.

Stereotyping is pervasive in the public view of male sexuality. Males are believed to have a greater sexual drive, to masturbate more, to be more knowledgeable about and experienced with sex, to be more sexually active at a younger age, and to be the initiator of sexual contact (Hoyenga & Hoyenga, 1979). A "real man" is a frequent sexual interactor who is also seen as being continuously willing and able to engage in a sexual interaction (Ingham, 1984). In contrast, the female is often believed to be more passive in her approach to sexuality. Stereotypical male sexuality is equated with successful and frequent performance. Stereotypical female sexuality is equated with long-term availability to a single partner within the bounds of a committed relationship. These beliefs no longer serve social reality and may be significant inhibitors to the clinician's assessment of a situation.

A summary view would find stereotypical masculinity to be linked to compulsive male sexuality. It is a crucial factor in the maintenance of masculine identity and may serve as part of the core self-definition of the male. Sexuality has a more tenuous linkage to female self-identity (Metcalf & Humphries, 1985). To be successfully masculine is to be sexually potent, competitive with other males in sexual accomplishments, and dominant within sexual interactions (Franklin, 1984). Failure here is loss of masculinity. Today, given the range of aberrant sexual interactions possible in the developing male child's environment, there are far too many ways in which he may see himself as a failure. No small part of this fragile sexual foundation is the differential socialization patterns experienced by males and females.

Differential Socialization

"Growing up" is undeniably difficult for children of both genders. The popular axiom that "it is easier to raise boys" helps to sustain the view that growing up as a male is somehow easier than growing up as a female. A view of some of the research-confirmed pressures on the male child helps to remove this perspective. Block (1983), for example, describes the following differences between parental expectations of a male child and that of a female child: greater pressure for achievement and competitiveness, greater control over affect, more independence, greater assumption of personal responsibility, more authoritarianism towards the male, and less acceptance of behaviors which deviate from the gender stereotype. This is changing as the view of female roles changes. But, this view remains largely true for children today. The male child may have a more narrow road to travel in the expression of many of his gender roles; deviations may not be welcome.

Often, it appears that male children rely more than female children do upon stereotypes to guide them. This is what Hartley has described as an "overstraining to be masculine" (1959). There is a studied avoidance of doing anything traditionally defined as feminine. The distance between this and homophobia is short as the literature is consistent in finding both mothers and fathers viewing cross-sex activities as being more likely to be associated with homosexual activities for males than for females. Boys may be boys and nothing more; girls may be tomboys without the same fear.

This same double standard is revealed in sexual development. While some researchers (Maccoby & Jacklin, 1974) do not identify different parental responses to expressions of sexuality in their male or female children, others do. Masters and colleagues (Masters et al., 1985) for example, describe a parental double standard that becomes apparent as children enter school and intensifies as adolescence nears. In this, while females are cautioned against sex play, males receive mixed messages. There appears to be some tacit permission for the males to follow their sexual curiosity as long as it is strongly heterosexual in its definition. This double standard continues during the period of adolescent sexual exploration. These parental reactions are mirrored by those of peers.

It is difficult to overestimate the impact of same-sex peers on socialization, especially sexual socialization. Sexual segregation begins in early childhood (Maccoby & Jacklin, 1987) and does not abate under the weight of cross-sex relationships until later adolescence in most cases (Sharabany, Gershoni, & Hofman, 1981). Since adolescents often acquire more sexual information from peers than from any other sources (Haas, 1979; Kallen, Stephenson, & Doughty, 1983; Kirby, Alter, & Scales, 1979; Shah & Zelnik, 1981; Smith et al., 1985), this becomes an additional target for clinical exploration.

Differential sexual socialization appears to be real. In males, it narrows the range of "acceptable" sexual experiences, increases the presumption of pathological negativity of homosexual experiences, defines masculinity as sexual aggressiveness through initiation and perpetration, and entrenches a double standard which generates a greater watchfulness and protectiveness toward female children (Calderone, 1985; V. Green, 1985; Hoyenga & Hoyenga, 1979; Maccoby & Jacklin, 1974, 1987, Maddock, 1983; Richardson, 1981). Stepping outside this pattern predicts ongoing impact in the development of normative sexuality for the male. The many abuses of sexuality and overt sexual abuses directed toward male children by adults and peers serve to wrench the vulnerable male out of this pattern and generate long-lasting effects. It is this abuse of sexuality that must be as much of a concern to the clinician in the sexual abuse case as are the more overt manifestations.

The Abuse of Sexuality Model: Preliminary Assumptions

The current knowledge about and definitions of child sexual abuse are too narrow to embrace necessary clinical applications. Definitions based upon overt behavioral indices are helpful for legal professionals who must identify a chargeable offense (Bolton & Bolton, 1987). Similar definitions are useful to researchers who must operationally define a concept to facilitate data collection. The needs of the clinician are much broader and more diffuse. This is especially true for clinicians working with males who may be experiencing emotional problems that are the result of undefined and subtle sexual abuses. In the absence of clear sexual contact deviations, the clinician may wrongly construct a case plan that does not reflect full understanding of the points of potential sexual victimization in the life of any patient, particularly male patients.

Further confusion is introduced in the treatment planning process by definitions which falsely appear to encompass both males and females. No greater example of this can be found than that of the young male who is sexually involved with the "older" or adult female. Age discrepant heterosexual contact with young females is viewed with disdain at best and sexual abuse at the worst. The same situation involving a young male may be seen as an early introduction to sexual prowess and "manhood." Not only does this negate any possible anxiety on the part of the young male, it may go so far as to find him being the victim of jealousy from age-mates and older males. Similarly, males exposing genital organs to young females are prosecuted. Should a female expose herself to a young male, the likelihood of a criminal prosecution appears quite low. The point here is not what "should be corrected in the system." The point to be made is that there may well be a double standard being applied within definitions of child sexual abuse today. The clinician must be aware that children of either gender may have their sexuality disrupted by experiences such as these. This is a distortion which occurs despite "legal" definitions or cultural expectations of the limits of sexually abusive acts.

The clinician must begin to assess sexually abusive situations from a broader perspective if the scope and impact of aberrant sexual interactions with children is to be usefully understood. Sexual abuse researcher David Finkelhor (1986) has warned that if a definition for an abusive act is too restrictive, some vital assumptions may be beyond testing. The clinician cannot allow any assumption to go untested. In balancing the breadth of a definition against the need for a definition to be usable, Finkelhor recommends Russell's strategy (1983) of applying multiple levels. Psychiatrist Renee Tankenoff Brandt and colleagues (Brandt & Tisza, 1977), as an example, have added the term *sexual misuse* to their definition of sexual behaviors between children and adults. This second category is a broad one which includes all sexual stimulation inappropriate for the child's age, level of psychosexual development, and role in the family. Building upon this, Brassard and colleagues (Brassard, Germain, & Hart, 1987) describe sexual misuse as "an experience that interferes with, or has the potential for interfering with a child's healthy development" (p. 71). The Abuse of Sexuality clinical assessment model takes these clinically-driven efforts one additional step. Here, we propose that the clinician remain open to the assessment of psychosocial and sociocultural experiences which may impact upon the development of sexuality rather than limiting clinical assessment to legal or actuarial data. The legal definitions will remain useful for those patients to which they apply. But, the expanded model will allow consideration of additional critical events in the life of an individual who is manifesting emotional distress of unclear etiology. The use of this model allows for the understanding that more male children and adolescents have been and are being sexually victimized than the more restrictive legal definitions would immediately identify.

The Abuse of Sexuality model rests upon several assumptions. First, sexuality is a constant developmental element from infancy forward. Second, developing sexuality may be either nurtured or hindered in multiple ways. Third, the hindrances to normal sexual development may reach abusive proportions at any time prior to adulthood. As such, the Abuse of Sexuality model describes a con-

Table 1.1 The Abuse of Sexuality

Developmental Environment	Degree of Victimization
1. The ideal environment	
2. The predominantly nurturing environment	Nonabusive
3. The evasive environment	
4. The environmental vacuum	
5. The permissive environment	Abuse of sexuality
6. The negative environment	
7. The seductive environment	
8. The overtly sexual environment	Abuse of sexuality and sexual victimization

tinuum of environments that range from the promotion of normalized sexual development in males and females to those which eliminate the possibility of normal development. Table 1.1 represents the model. At this time, clinicians working in the area of sexual abuse tend to focus upon the most graphically destructive end of this continuum. It is proposed here that clinical progress in the field will be facilitated through earlier consideration of the less obviously inhibiting environments. These environments are described next.

The Abuse of Sexuality Model: Environmental Characteristics

The Ideal Environment

The offering of an "ideal" is always a risk. Here the use of the term "ideal" refers to the general understanding that the child, whether male or female, should be provided the opportunity to learn about and experience his or her developing sexuality within a supportive, nurturing, understanding, and informative environment. As the child develops there should be access to accurate and useful information about sexuality—information that is appropriate to the child's level of curiosity and understanding. With each developmental milestone the child can receive facts and ideas which assist him or her in dealing with his or her present level of sexuality and which better prepare him or her for the next.

Behaviorally, the significant individuals in the child's life should provide good models for appropriate expression of sexuality and feelings. The environment should be consistent, in keeping with the religious or ethical standards sought by the family, and neither condone nor provide models for inappropriate expression of sexuality as it is generally understood. Aggressive sexuality must be completely absent. Given this environment's "ideal" responses to the child's developing sexuality, the probability of problems associated with sexual matters should be extremely low.

The Predominantly Nurturing Environment

This environment provides the child the opportunity to learn of his or her sexuality in a *mostly* nurturing, understanding, and supportive environment; however, there may be some less-than-ideal conditions. For example, one parent may be less supportive than another, a single-parent situation may inhibit maximal opportunities for communications, or religious/moral teaching may provide some area of conflict. The child in this environment is provided with more accurate than inaccurate information about sexuality, but the utility of the information may be hampered by attitudes.

Behaviorally, significant persons in this environment may model some inappropriate or restrictive expression of sexuality or feelings, but the majority of the behavior is appropriate. The child is not exposed directly to inappropriate expressions of sexuality. The pivotal factor in success here may be the independence and attitude of the child. Yet, since the exposure to inappropriate sexual information and inappropriate activity is minimal, the potential for the abuse of the child's developing sexuality is minimized.

The Evasive Environment

Often seen in tandem with the environmental vacuum, the evasive environment provides little or no accurate and useful information about sexual matters. Sexual information provided to the child tends to be in the form of myths and misinformation either purposefully or accidently transmitted.

Behaviorally, some of the individuals in the evasive environment may act out some of the myths presented to the child. This approach may range from one that is benign to one which results in unnecessary confusion to the child, especially regarding sexual anatomy and reproductive information. The danger in this environment is that it may provide little that is useful beyond alleviating the adult's anxiety about directly addressing sexual issues and matters brought forward by the child. The case of Alfonso illustrates these points:

Alfonso suddenly refused to attend school. His parents were surprised and perplexed because Alfonso always seemed to enjoy school. He was described as an intelligent teenager who earned excellent grades. Now he seemed depressed and reticent. They worried that "someone might have gotten our little boy on drugs or something." But no evidence of drugs was found. They insisted he see a therapist.

Initially, Alfonso was uncooperative and angry with his parents for "forcing" him into therapy. Gradually, however, Alfonso explained why he refused to attend school: "It had been building for a long time. The other kids were always making little jokes behind my back. And the girls would laugh at me when I would ask if I could talk to them. I didn't want a date or anything like that, I just wanted to talk. But I didn't know what to talk about except schoolwork. They would be interested for awhile then when they would talk about other things, I didn't know what to say. So I started making up things, pretending I knew about sports, cars, dating and things like that. For awhile it looked like I was getting away with it and I thought I was pretty clever.

Then one of the girls sat down next to me at lunch and eventually began to talk about sexual things. I never believed girls talked like that. I didn't know what to say because I don't know anything about sex—that's for people who are married and are going to have babies. I was very uncomfortable. What I didn't know was that she was part of a big joke planned by a bunch of her friends sitting at the other table. They were listening to me trying to talk to this girl and having great fun at my expense. When she asked me something about 'home base' I thought she was talking about softball. I said something that must have been really dumb because she really started laughing and her friends all started laughing too. They made fun of me. I never felt so bad. I was humiliated. I left school that afternoon and I will not go back."

When Alfonso was asked to describe his family's attitude about sexual matters, he gave a history of consistent evasive responses by both parents and a tendency by his mother to speak euphemistically about anything even remotely associated with sex and bodily functions. As examples he stated, "My father used to get so nervous when I asked where my baby brother came from, I quit asking. He would usually say something about being able to understand someday when I was older. One time he told me my brother came from heaven and when that confused me, he just told me not to concern myself about such things. Mother was no help either. When I would ask her questions she would tell me to ask my father. She still uses words like 'pee-pee' or 'tinkle' when talking about going to the bathroom. I simply could not get them to give me any information about sex so I decided to wait until I was old enough to understand, whenever that is."

The Environmental Vacuum

The child in this environment occupies a space that is nearly devoid of information about sexual matters. Curiosity about sexuality is met with little helpful information or with evasive responses. Models for appropriate expression of behavior or feelings are virtually absent. The child is "protected" from exposure to all types of information about sexuality. In this environment, children are essentially left to their own thoughts and interpretations of sexual matters and feelings. While some regard this "hands-off" view as harmless, there is concern here about neglecting to provide the basic information necessary to alleviate the child's anxiety about his or her own sexual feelings. Consider Michael's environment:

Michael's parents were very reserved and refrained from "open displays" of affection. "I never saw my parents hug each other, but they did kiss goodby occasionally. The kisses were more pecks than kisses though." Sexual matters were never mentioned by Michael's parents and "it was as though sex didn't exist at all for them, or for anyone else for that matter." Although his parents never told Michael not to ask questions about sexual matters, "I somehow knew not to ask about sex even though I had lots of questions to ask." Michael was naturally curious about sex but found no information available from his family. He also received little to no information about interpersonal relationships and developed few heterosocial skills.

As a teenager, he was introduced to peeping by a male friend. Michael's first view of a female undressing heightened his curiosity about sex. He began to use peeping as his only "reliable" source of information about females and sex. "I learned more about sex from watching my neighbors on one night than I ever did from my parents. But, what I learned was probably the wrong things."

Michael's friend "outgrew" peeping but Michael continued and eventually developed into a highly skilled and innovative voyeur. Curiosity shifted to sexual excitement and a compulsive pattern of peeping with ritualistic masturbatory practices was formed. As a young adult, Michael experimented with and eventually perfected a "Master Peeping Tom" routine that allowed him to "see but not be seen."

The Permissive Environment

Many adults adopt a completely nonrestrictive philosophy about children's exposure to sexual matters. This misguided nurturance, while well-meaning, may evolve into overpermissiveness. First, the child may be provided with accurate information, but it becomes available at such a level and with such frequency that it exceeds the child's developmental capacity to understand and respond to it. Second, the child may be exposed to nudity or adult sexual behaviors in absence of the recognition that this may stimulate the child. This stimulation could lead to the adoption of similar behaviors of premature experimentation. Some adults believe that a totally open and honest approach to sexuality is in the child's best interest. What is missing in this formulation are pacing and timing considerations. This approach may ultimately become abusive to the child's developing sexuality by overwhelming the child with too much information too soon, overstimulating the child, and failing to model appropriate boundaries for these activities. An example of how a permissive approach can go awry can be found in the S. Family:

> Mr. and Mrs. S. were each raised by parents who provided no information or guidance about sexual matters. Each partner reported experiencing confusion, fear, and anger associated with not having adequate information about sexual development. When they married, Mr. and Mrs. S. agreed that a lack of sexual information during childhood and adolescence is harmful. They decided to provide their children with a more "open" approach to sexuality and adopted a permissive philosophy about sexual information and childhood sexual experimentation. Consistent with this philosophy, Mr. and Mrs. S did not discourage their children from observing sexual activities between themselves. Overall, nudity at home was the norm, children and parents often bathed together, discussions about sexual matters were frequent, and children explored themselves or each other openly. However, neither parent engaged his or her children in sexual activities for personal gratification.
>
> Mr. and Mrs. S. believed their open philosophy about sexuality was beneficial to their children until they began receiving reports

from teachers of possible sexual misconduct by their five-year-old daughter Sara and eight-year-old son Paul. According to her kindergarten teacher, Sara was "preoccupied with sex and masturbated compulsively in the presence of other children." When asked to stop Sara would often reply, "it's only natural, we all do this at home." Several of Paul's female classmates complained to teachers that he would expose himself and offer to "teach" them about sex. When they refused he would become more assertive and attempt to fondle their "private zones." Paul also expressed some sexual interest in his female teacher.

At first Mr. and Mrs. S. dismissed the reports as overreaction by individuals who misinterpreted their children's "healthy openness" about sexuality. However, they began to acknowledge problems when a Child Protective Services investigation revealed that Sara had also attempted to perform fellatio on several young children and Paul had forced a younger boy to remove his clothes and masturbate in front of other children. Professionals investigating this case agreed that Paul and Sara were "highly sexualized" by their parents' well-meaning but inappropriate approach to their children's sexual development. No "traditional" forms of abusive sexual contact between parents and their children were discovered.

The Negative Environment

The all-too-familiar negative approach is heavily laden with misinformation, negative attitudes, and fear tactics. The child is told that sex is bad, evil, abnormal, harmful, a sign of moral weakness, and something to be avoided. Little accurate information is provided, and attempts by the child to obtain information are blocked or punished. The child may be emotionally or physically punished for exploring his or her body. Obviously, this abuses the child's opportunity for evenly paced sexual development. From an early age, for example, the child may associate sexual feelings with shame and aversive consequences. The confusion, guilt, ambivalence, and anxiety that evolve from this environment are true abuses of the child's sexuality that may have long-term ramifications. Rob's case illustrates a negative environment:

Rob's parents were well educated and held professional positions. The family appeared stable, and the three children received above average material benefits. However, Rob's mother "hated sex" and created a negative environment regarding sexual matters. From an early age she told Rob "horror" stories about masturbation and heterosexual contacts of any kind. He was physically punished and verbally abused by his mother whenever she discovered Rob exploring his body. "I wasn't even masturbating, I was just touching and looking at myself." By using fear tactics, his mother also actively discouraged any attempts by Rob to establish relationships with females his own age. "By the time I was a teenager she had me believing that any girl who would go out with me was a slut with every venereal disease in the universe and would become pregnant with a mere touch." While homosexuality was not a focus of his mother's attacks, she also described this form of sexuality in unforgiving terms.

As an adolescent and young adult, Rob never dated. He reported severe anxiety associated with nearly any form of interaction with most females. His plans for heterosexual dating were always aborted because he could never gain enough "courage" to ask for a date. He would occasionally masturbate with fantasies of age appropriate females but would then experience considerable anxiety and guilt associated with this "forbidden" act. He found himself isolated and fearful. Rob eventually drifted into a series of infrequent ego-dystonic homosexual contacts. After his first homosexual experience he became suicidal and required crisis hospitalization. A year later he "slipped" again into a homosexual activity and then the contacts, while still infrequent, began to increase. Rob believed that his primary sexual orientation was heterosexual and his homosexual activities only occurred because "it is easier and less threatening than attempting to date females." However, he felt extremely guilty, ashamed, and depressed following each homosexual encounter. Rob feared he was slowly becoming a "dreaded" homosexual.

The Seductive Environment

The seductive environment provides the child with messages that an adult is interested in the child in sexual ways. While these messages may be verbal or behavioral, overt sexual contact does not usually occur. Rather, the child may be exposed to seductive posing, gestures, or verbal messages. The adult may emphasize the sexual attractiveness of the child, for example, by providing the child with the suggestion that the adult would enjoy sexual activity with the child. The adult may expose his or her body to the child in an "inadvertent" or teasing manner which may have underlying sexual purposes.

Information about sexual matters in this environment may be presented in ways which titillate rather than inform. Mixed messages abound, hinting at the desirability of sexual contact between the seductive adult and the child but which continue to condemn such behavior superficially. These mixed messages, accidental exposure or touching, and the labile nature of the sexual feelings in the environment generally serve as significant disruptions to the possibility of normal sexual development. Consider George's mother:

George was raised in a family that was dominated and controlled by a very critical and demanding mother. She would express extremely high expectations of George and would become verbally abusive when he was unable to reach her goals. George remembers receiving no praise for any achievement and began both to fear and resent his mother's demanding and punitive approach to parenting. His mother was also very seductive and gave frequent messages that he could only be "sexual" around her but probably would not be able to establish a "successful" sexual relationship elsewhere. Throughout George's childhood and adolescence his mother would often arrange to be seen in the nude. Once detected she would act surprised and cover herself or run away. George felt that she also was more physical with him than was necessary. Physical contacts included holding, kissing and caressing but no genital contact. When he was approaching puberty his mother showed an inappropriate interest in George's development. He describes being visually "inspected" more often than was necessary to insure that he was physically healthy. As a child George found his mother's approach to him confusing, frightening, demeaning, controlling, but at times titillating.

During pubescence, George began having sexual fantasies, most of which were "pretty bizarre" and often included his mother. He began to develop a strong interest in pornographic materials and used the pornography for masturbatory purposes. He also began to peep about this time. By the time George became a young adult, his interest in pornography and his voyeuristic behaviors were well established and compulsive. Overall, George found sexual activity with consenting females much less satisfying than masturbatory activity utilizing pornographic material and/or fantasies stimulated by these materials. He also found it difficult to engage in sexual activities without his partner wearing "sexy" apparel and arousing him through a "show" of some kind.

While most of George's voyeuristic behavior involved "safe" activities such as visiting porn-stores with peep shows, and bars with nude dancing, or watching neighbors from the privacy of his home, George eventually began to engage in riskier ventures such as stalking and street peeping.

The Overtly Sexual Environment

This environment presents overtly sexualized contact between adult and child. Included here would be activities such as attempted or successful vaginal or anal intercourse, cunnilingus, anilingus, fellatio, genital fondling, digital penetration, clothed or unclothed touching of genitals, lingering sexualized kissing or hugging, simulated intercourse, intentional genital exposure, and directed exposure to adult sexual activity. Also included here would be the provision of sexual information for the purposes of sexual contact or sexual exploitation. For example, exposure to pornographic materials or misuse of educational materials should be considered overt sexual responses. As is obvious, most of the activities found in legal definitions of child sexual abuse are found in this environment. But it must also be remembered that, in this environment, covert sexual activities are not confined to the adult-child partnership. The adult may encourage inappropriate sexual contact among children without making direct sexual contact himself or herself. A sibling or peer may engage a child in any of these activities against the child's will or in the name of normal sexual experimentation with the cooperation of the adult(s) in this environment. Consider these experiences by John and Dan:

> *John.* John referred himself for psychotherapy because he was having problems "getting along with coworkers." He reported being on the verge of losing his third job in as many years. He described being anxious around coworkers in general, but very anxious when relating to females in any setting. He also described explosive angry responses when pressed by a female supervisor for more productivity on the job. John recognized the inappropriateness of his behavior but seemed unable to understand it or control his responses. Initial evaluation, including sexual history procedures, revealed no unusual sexual experiences. Overall, John's childhood environment appeared fairly typical for an upper middle-class family.
>
> After nearly six months in therapy, John began a session with a statement-question: "I don't suppose this has anything to do with anything, but I wonder if having sex before you are supposed to can

help or hurt your sexual relations?" Exploration of this topic revealed a previously unreported severe erectile dysfunction and extensive childhood molestation experiences. With difficulty over the next few sessions, John described how he was "taught" to have sex by a woman in her thirties when he was about nine years old. The sexual "curriculum" consisted of mutual masturbation, fellatio, cunnilingus, and intercourse. The woman babysat and cleaned his parents' house over most weekends and she "taught" him nearly every weekend for about four years.

John never disclosed this as a child because, "I was confused. I didn't like what she was doing to me—especially when I had to eat her cunt—it was awful. But how many guys get a chance to fuck before they are a teenager? Sometimes I liked the touching but overall I think I was scared to death that someone would catch us and I would be in big trouble. As a teenager I was nervous around girls and had trouble dating. One night I told my date to impress her and she thought I was a pervert. You are the only other person who knows. I didn't tell you before because it's difficult to talk about and I was afraid you would think I was a pervert, too."

Dan. Dan presented a history of promiscuous homosexual behavior since about age 14 years. While he always regretted his activities Dan found it nearly impossible to resist the urges to frequent parks, restrooms, and other places used for quick homosexual contacts. He often would engage in three to six homosexual contacts nearly every day. Dan seldom achieved orgasm through these contacts and often felt like "a sex machine for others."

Although Dan's primary sexual orientation was homosexual, he dated females and eventually married. He reported that he enjoyed the intimacy of his marital relationship and even found pleasure with the sexual activity with his wife. However, his urges to visit "glory holes" and continue his homosexual contacts with strangers remained strong and barely controlled.

Educational history was unremarkable. Dan was a good student although not always motivated to do his best. His peer relationships were good and, in fact, he was popular and active in extracurricular activities.

Dan was the only child born to his biological parents who divorced when he was about seven or eight years old. His mother received custody and Dan saw little of his father after the divorce. He doesn't remember much about his father but described his mother in favorable terms. He could not recall any form of abuse by either parent.

When Dan was about 11 years old a male boarder came into his room and began to make sexual advances. When Dan refused his requests the man "simply took my clothes off and fucked me. He was a large muscular man and I was no match for him. It was terrible. It hurt and he tore me up." Dan reported being terrified at the time and too afraid to tell anybody. The man subsequently established a "personal" relationship with Dan and "while it still hurt a lot I let him do what he wanted." Dan reported having mixed feelings when the man moved about eight months later. "I was relieved that I didn't have to experience the pain and blood anymore but I missed his friendship."

For the next few years Dan felt ashamed of the sexual relationship but wondered what it would be like to have a relationship like that again. At about age 13 or 14 years Dan was in a public restroom and was propositioned by an adult male. He allowed the man to perform fellatio but found the experience less than satisfying. Shortly after this experience Dan began having promiscuous homosexual experiences, none of which seemed satisfying.

The utility of the Abuse of Sexuality model for the clinician is straightforward. The clinician must assess the developmental environment in which the child or adult progressed before being capable of understanding any of the manifestations of that experience. The presentation may be an adult male who is perpetrating sexual violence against males or females, an adult with neurotic anxieties and depressions, or a child with virtually any dysfunctional behavior. But, the origin is likely to be the destruction resulting from the demands of growing up in one of the unstable environments in the model.

The foundation of the model is that there are multiple points of potential abuse in the adult's responses to a child's developing sexuality. To date, however, clinical and legal thinking regarding sexually abusive environments between adults and children has focused upon a single point along the environmental continuum, the overtly sexual environment. This represents a shallowness in clinical thinking toward all children and most particularly toward male children—a group less likely to be directly sexually assaulted than females but perhaps more likely to be exposed to the other destruction implied by this array of aberrant environments.

It is understandable that overt sexual activity between adults and children has become the focus of clinical study whether the victim is male or female. The obvious inappropriateness of such activities hardly tests the behavioral sophistication of the clinician. While we must certainly continue our efforts to understand and eventually eliminate these activities, we must expand our intellectual curiosity toward the more subtle abuses in this area. Today, adults who provide negative, seductive, or evasive environments are virtually never confronted for the abuses which they impart to children. The psychological damage still exists in those children as they, as adult survivors of such environments, challenge clinicians to define the origins of their mysterious pain. This is an adult manifestation of inappropriate sexual interaction between adults and children as certainly as any other, and one which could have been prevented.

In addition to expanding clinical assessment of sexually abusive environments, there is a call here to look beyond the traditional in viewing male sexual development. Direct sexual assault of male children does occur. That is the first point that must be accepted. The second point that must be accepted is that it is just as difficult to develop sexually as a male in our world as it is to develop as a female. In fact, the differential sexual socialization experienced by male and female children may make it more difficult for the male. The male's road is more difficult to travel as a result of the reduced degree of protectiveness toward him, the greater expectation of competency at an earlier age, and the expectation that he will have less to fear along the way. This unrealistic social environment, perhaps as much as the underprotective adult-child environments in the Abuse of Sexuality model, sets the stage for intrusive experiences. The social environment of the male child is not yet capable of protecting against these abuses, and as a result it has become the clinician's role to pick up the pieces. We are only just now reaching the level of awareness necessary to play that role effectively.

Sexual Abuse Yesterday and Today: The Legacy of Too Little Too Late

Clinicians no longer require Sgroi's 1978 challenge to admit to the presence of child sexual abuse; at least with respect to female children. Some greater skepticism may exist regarding the frequency of victimization in male children. Yet, virtually no experienced clinician can deny that the consequences of these confusing and aberrant interactions are manifested clinically on a daily basis in the lives of children and adult survivors of both genders. The difficulty facing the clinician is that of a currently incomplete literature base. The literature must move closer to the pragmatic information critical to the clinician. The Abuse of Sexuality model is an attempt to merge this literature base with clinical manifestations of the problem—in both male and female victims.

The sexual abuse literature today is questioned even by some of its principal contributers. The problem revolves around traditionally vexing research design issues. Definitions remain vague, sampling is questionable, and selection of research targets (e.g., perpetrators vs. victims) remains a limiting factor. Experts (see Finkelhor, 1986) have explored these limitations in depth. A brief historical overview of these concerns is a sensible starting point for the clinician.

Definitional Shortcomings

The major "question" associated with the child sexual abuse literature rests with the definition itself. Since those working with physical child abuse have struggled for three decades for a manageable definition, it would be naive to believe that this issue would be less troubling for child sexual abuse students. From the perspective of the Abuse of Sexuality model, sexual abuse or misuse is defined by the perpetrator's or victim's self-perception. If an environment was experienced as oppressive it must be accepted clinically as such. Those working in the legal areas of child sexual abuse probably do not have the "luxury" of accepting self-report as an "operational definition," but the clinician must if a relationship is to be built with the patient.

The absence of a uniformly accepted operational definition remains an unsolved issue (Finkelhor, 1986). Child advocates fear that the full scope of the problem may never be known as a result (Tierney & Corwin, 1983). There are several points of concern in an effort to reach a common ground. First, there are disagreements as to whether non-contact offenses (e.g., solicitation or exhibitionism) should be considered abusive. The Abuse of Sexuality model would suggest inclusion. This is vital to situations involving male children, as "conventional wisdom" has some tendency to view many noncontact situations considered to be abusive to females (e.g., exhibitionism by an adult male) as less disruptive to the male child (Schultz, 1980). This "wisdom" remains to be tested. The typical approach in the literature has been to include both contact and noncontact events as "sexual assaults." Finkelhor (1983) finds this position defensible from a research perspective in that both forms are criminal acts and psychological consequences are assumed. Any application of the Abuse of Sexuality model would demand that both be included.

A second consideration in reading the existing literature involves the specification of the actions described by the research. Russell (1984) has noted the common use of the terms sexual abuse, sexual victimization, sexual exploitation, sexual assault, sexual misuse, child rape, child molestation, or sexual mistreatment in the literature. In many cases these uses are parallel but without regard for behavioral description. The clinician must seek specificity in any research to be applied. The absence of such specificity reduces the clinician's ability to place the information within one of the environments in the Abuse of Sexuality model.

A third concern in the interpretation of the research is perpetrator specification. Finkelhor (1986) warns of the common assumption that the perpetrator in sexual abuse is an adult. Work with the juvenile sex offender has brought the definition of perpetrator into sharper focus. The juvenile perpetrator is capable of acts which hold the same negative consequences for the child as those predicted by the adult-child interaction. There is no age level exclusivity to these destructive consequences.

Sibling perpetration has also been understudied. Sibling sexual exploration has been viewed as a somewhat benign event that is normalized across American families. Once euphemistically termed "sex play" these events are now understood to hold the potential to be experienced as an abusive event. The changing composition of the "typical" family with its greater prevalence of single parents, blended sibling groups, and nonbiological children presents a less protective family environment than has been assumed in the past (Bolton, 1983). Increasing evidence of intra-familial assaults by juvenile offenders are beginning to remove the "benign" cloak of sibling sexual contact. There is speculation that at some point the age differences between intrafamilial participants reaches a level which predicts a coercive and abusive event (Finkelhor, 1986). The fact is that the location of a sexual interaction (e.g., intra-familial vs. extrafamilial) is not a discriminator of its coercive nature (Russell, 1984).

Another point of warning in reading the child sexual abuse literature rests with concerns over sampling strategies. Much of this literature will be found reliant upon non-representative and poorly defined research populations that are most often examined in retrospect. Much of this body of literature rests upon the tenuous memorial reports of adult survivors found within clinical settings. This is not a firm foundation. Even if conducted with representative respondents this work would be open to criticism about selective recall and distortion. As it exists, the absence of control/comparison groups and reliance upon clinical and college student samples brings questions of integrity and generalizability (Finkelhor, 1986; Tierney & Corwin, 1983). Fortunately, these concerns are slowly being recognized and addressed.

A final concern in the clinician's responsibility for absorbing the child sexual abuse literature rests with the core elements of the definitions used. These elements typically include the upper age limits of the children studied, the age discrepancy between victim and perpetrator, behavioral specification, classification of the act as to seriousness, location, and degree of coerciveness. Consider these in light of the following information.

Defining child sexual abuse demands defining the boundaries of childhood. Many states currently define the age of legal consent as 18 years of age. This age criterion has been adopted by the National Center on Child Abuse and Neglect (NCCAN) as the upper limit of childhood as well. Yet, research exists that defines the upper age limits for study as 15 (A. Burnam, 1985), 16 (Fromuth, 1983), or 17 (Lewis, 1985; Seidner & Calhoun, 1984; Wyatt, 1985). Differential age limits may be set for differing forms of abuse. For example, Russell (1983) selected 17 as the upper limit for incestuous abuse and earlier ages for other varieties of abuse. Because clinicians typically work within legal parameters, 18 will be the upper age limit for the child described in this work. But in reading other works and in using the Abuse of Sexuality model, the clinician is encouraged to recall that the seriousness of the act, as well as its probable impact may vary across age groups.

Some definitions of child sexual abuse incorporate perpetrator-victim age differences. Kinsey and his colleagues (1953) viewed perpetrators as those at least 15 years old, for example. Both the Kinsey group (1953) and Finkelhor (1984b) see age discrepancy between tim and perpetrator of at least five years as important. Others (Fromuth, 1983) have used this five-year differential up to a victim age of 12 and a 10-year differential for older victims. The point is that these differences may sometimes vary. Clinically, no hard and fast rule is likely to have uniform application. Discounting victimization because a five-year age difference does not exist may result in improper clinical planning and inappropriate intervention.

In specifying the sexual behaviors within the definition used, the contact versus noncontact issue is revisited. Sgroi and her colleagues (Sgroi, Blick, & Porter, 1982) describe a continuum of behaviors from noncontact abuses (e.g., nudity, disrobing, genital exposure, and observation of the child) to those which require obvious contact (e.g., penetration). Another strategy is that used by Russell to define behaviors on a "least serious" (e.g., attempted touching) to "very serious" (e.g., forced intercourse) scale of abuses. Still other patterns define the act as more or less abusive depending upon the age of the child victim. The point here is that the clinician must be aware of the range of behaviors being described in the research being considered. The lack of uniformity in the literature can be compensated for clinically through the Abuse of Sexuality model's focus upon environments rather than acts exclusively. But, the clinician is cautioned against generalizing from research studies that are actually referring to differing behaviors toward children of differing ages. When these definitional vagaries are viewed in terms of the additional differences introduced by whether the act occurred inside the family or outside the family, and when the consideration to the degree of coercion is provided, it becomes clear that the literature describing "child sexual abuse" is really a study of a range of behaviors and situations. Fortunately, there appear to be some reasonably predictable themes in this literature.

First, the upper age limit for considering a victim to be a child is never lower than the approximate onset of pubesence, and most researchers accept 18 years of age as the cutoff. Second, the age discrepancy of five years difference between perpetrator and victim seems to be gaining in popularity. But, this does mask sexual abuse between peers and must be accepted with caution, particularly if the contact is forced or unwanted (Finkelhor, 1986). Third, most definitions recognize at least the majority of overt forms of sexual behavior. Fourth, power, authority, force, exploitation, and coercion appear implicitly or explicitly in nearly all definitions.

The establishment of scientific fact demands validation that the same behavior is investigated in each research work. For the clinician's use, however, it is only necessary that the characteristics of the acts and sample described by the individual work be known. Given this information, the clinician may make an informed decision as to where the information may be placed in the Abuse of Sexuality model as well as how it applies to the case at hand. Other clinical information, from social history to psychological testing, modifies the use of research knowledge in the case to determine diagnosis, treatment goals, and appropriateness of the intervention. It is this model that allows the clinician to determine the degree of abuse of sexuality that has occurred. Using this strategy, the clinician is able to build a program of treatment for an individual or family even in those situations in which the more restrictive legal or research definitions of child sexual abuse make it difficult to determine whether or not a specific abusive event has occurred. Given these warnings regarding interpretation of research information, a short historical review will be offered.

The Knowledge Base: An Historical Review

General Incidence and Prevalence Rates

Recent reviews of adult's sexualized approaches to children found that such events were known to early psychological clinicians but greeted with skepticism and suppression (Masson, 1984). Finkelhor describes mention of child molestation in the professional literature as early as 1929 (Hamilton, 1929). Two decades later, the Indianapolis sexual behavior research team led by Alfred Kinsey lent authority to the earlier reports by describing such aberrant behavior in their groundbreaking work of the late 1940s and early 1950s for males (Kinsey, Pomeroy, & Martin, 1948) and for females (Kinsey, Pomeroy, Martin, & Gebhard, 1953).

Today's child sexual abuse researchers informally date the "modern" era of child sexual abuse research from the estimates of S. K. Weinberg (1955) and DeFrancis (1969). The 1970s, reflecting the growth in mandatory child abuse reporting in America, brought a newly "official" flavor to child sexual abuse numbers. "Officially reported" cases began to reach unexpectedly high rates. As a result of the "too high" as well as the "too low" concerns surrounding "official" reports (Bourne & Newberger, 1979), the U.S. government funded the National Center on Child Abuse and Neglect's study of "known" and "unknown" cases of child maltreatment of all types. In addition, broader surveys of college student population (Finkelhor, 1979) and attempts at surveying representative populations (Russell, 1984) began to add to the understanding of the magnitude (if not the etiology) of the problem. By the 1980s the consumers of child sexual abuse literature had a variety of incidence and prevalence rates to support their arguments.

Some of these incidence and prevalence findings are as follows:

1. 9 cases of child sexual abuse per million population (S. K. Weinberg, 1955)
2. 65% of American women reported nonaccidental sexual contact (including exhibitionist events) during childhood (J. Landis, 1956)
   14% of all of California's child maltreatment cases were sexual in nature (Helfer & Kempe, 1968)
3. 40 cases of child sexual abuse per million population (DeFrancis, 1969)
4. 25% of American women reported nonaccidental sexual contact (including exhibitionist events) during childhood (Gagnon, 1965)
   500,000 female children from ages 4 to 13 were being sexually abused, or 20-25% of middle-class children and 33-40% of lower-class children (Gagnon, 1965)
5. 20 million Americans were projected to have been involved in incestuous situations at some point in their lives (Herman & Hirschman, 1977)
6. The "official" position that between 60,000 and 100,000 American children were being sexually abused on an annual basis (National Center on Child Abuse and Neglect, 1981)
   336,000 cases of child sexual abuse per year

From this variation, it became clear that an "officially sanctioned" estimate of the incidence and/or prevalence of this problem was needed. One of the major nongovernmental sources of child maltreatment rates at this time was the American Humane Association's Children's Division (since renamed the American Association for Protecting Children, Inc.). This clearinghouse, gathering information from 31 states and 3 American territories, found that sexual abuse cases had increased from 1,975 in 1976 to 4,327 in

1977, and to 22,918 in 1982 (Finkelhor, 1984). Of this final number, about 16% were male victims (L. G. Schultz, 1980).

A similar, though more extensive, governmental study was also being conducted at this time. The National Center on Child Abuse and Neglect (NCCAN, 1981) had undertaken a far-reaching survey of child abuse cases in the community. This work was to include those cases "known" to child protective services, to ancillary service providers in the community, and to persons in the community who were not service providers. This study was designed to combat the sense that officially reported child maltreatment cases were only the "tip of the iceberg." Using a sample of 26 U.S. counties, this survey estimated:

1. .7 per 1000 for sexual abuse
2. 1.0 per 1000 for emotional neglect
3. 1.7 per 1000 for physical neglect
4. 2.2 per 1000 for emotional abuse
5. 2.9 per 1000 for educational neglect
6. 3.4 cases per 1000 for physical assault

Translating this incidence figure to actual number of cases would describe 44,700 cases of sexual abuse for the year beginning May 1, 1979 (Russell, 1984; Finkelhor, 1986).

A tandem movement to surveys of "official" reports was the search for general population estimates uninfluenced by clinical syndromes and/or official reporting bias. Such studies reported the following estimates:

1. College student samples
   19.2% of the women and 8.6% of the male college students were self-reported victims of sexually abusive situations as children (Finkelhor, 1979)
   8% of the women and 5% of male college students were self-reported victims of sexually abusive situations (Fritz, Stoll, & Wagner, 1981)
   22% of female students were self-reported victims (Fromuth, 1983)

2. Random sample of women in San Francisco area
   38% of the women reported at least one experience of incestuous or extrafamilial sexual abuse before reaching age 18 (Russell, 1984). Clinicians should be alert to the breadth of the definition

used for sexual abuse in this study because it reaches beyond those events typically given attention in the clinical setting.

3. Random sample of Texas driver's license holders
   A self-reported sexual abuse rate of 3% for males and 12% for females (Kercher & McShane, 1984)

4. Sample of parents
   6% of the males and 15% of the females had experienced sexual abuse at the hands of someone at least 5 years older than they by age 16 (Finkelhor, 1984).

The difficulty occurring from these diverse results rests with the necessity of providing a synthesis which results in some reliable estimate. The fact is that prevalence rates for child sexual abuse remain extremely variable. This is clearly a problem which begs for additional clarification.

Finkelhor (1979) has concluded that the incidence of adults physically molesting girls has been about the same for the past 30 years. Tierney and Corwin (1983) cite Henderson (1972) as well as Burgess, Groth, Holmstrom, and Sgroi (1978) in offering a triad of conclusions. First, the rate of child sexual victimization is much higher than once believed. Next, a significant portion of child sexual abuse occurs within the family with fathers, stepfathers, and mother's male companions comprising the largest categories of perpetrators. Finally, there is a lack of consensus regarding the influence of social factors, psychological traits, and situational factors in the etiology of such events. Finkelhor (1986) seems to have drawn the most supportable conclusion in the following remark: "The reality is that there is not yet a consensus among social scientists about the national scope of sexual abuse" (p. 16).

The information on the prevalence and incidence of male sexual victimization appears to be even more confusing as will be evidenced in the chapter to follow.

2

Male Child Sexual Abuse

Prevalence and Perpetrators

Male children are at clear risk from sexual victimization, misuse, and abuse of developing sexuality. Gender differences often assumed to protect against this risk do not. An argument may be made that the lesser protectiveness extended against potential sexual victimization of male children may contribute to this risk. Yet, recognition, reporting, prevention efforts, and treatment of child sexual abuse all hold a clear female focus (Swift, 1980). There are several possible reasons for why this is the reality.

First, there is disagreement over how serious the consequences of various forms of child victimization may be (Giovannoni & Bercerra, 1979). We tend to be more protective of female than male children. Consequently, the victimization of female children, particularly their sexual victimization, may raise greater concern than a similar situation involving a male (Groth, 1979). Also, male sexual experience of any type plays to the masculine stereotypes.

Second, since males are socialized to be "strong" and to "take care of themselves," male victims may be more reluctant to report their own victimization (Finklehor & Baron, 1986). Finkelhor (1986) extends this hypothesis by suggesting that male victims have "more to lose" in reporting. Victimization not only violates the male ethic of self-reliance, it raises the stigma of homosexuality. These stereotypes and socialization messages serve to keep professionals and parents from identifying the warning signs of victimization when they are present (Finkelhor, 1986). An example of this tendency can be seen in the findings of J. Landis (1956) in which only 26.8% of the parents of an identified sample of sexual abuse victims had prepared the male children for this danger while 44.1% of the parents of female victims had discussed this possibility with their daughters. Today's parents, with a greater awareness of the problem, might present different numbers. But the fact that male child sexual abuse victims have more difficulty seeking out help and protection remains a reality (Brandt & Tisza, 1977).

Finally, the problem does remain a more evident risk for female children. Finkelhor (1986) has reviewed the incidence and prevalence figures for the sexual victimization of both male and female children. His conclusion from studies with a defensible methodology was that female children are at greater risk than male children. His review finds a risk ratio ranging from more than 4.0 female victims for each male victim to 2.5 female victims for each male victim in community based studies. Studies of college students present a risk ratio of 1.5 female victims for each male victim. Finkelhor does acknowledge the writers whose speculative estimates find male and female risk to be equal, but dismisses their findings to poor methodology. He finds those studies which predict the most dire male risk to be built upon a single study (Tobias & Gordon, 1977) which demonstrated some serious methodological shortcomings (Finkelhor, 1986). This does not indicate that Finkelhor's review minimized the risk of sexual victimization facing male children.

Finkelhor describes the greater attention, study, and analysis focused upon female child sexual abuse victims as "unfortunate." This attention is unfortunate in the sense that it contributes to the mistaken impression held by the public that male children are only rarely sexually victimized. In addition, it has contributed to the abbreviation of the knowledge base regarding male children who have been sexually abused, especially as compared to knowledge held about female victims (Finkelhor, 1986, p. 63). The clinician must not fall victim to those same mistaken impressions. Male children are, and have been, at great risk for sexual victimization.

The number of male children being reported as victims of sexual assault has risen in recent years (Finkelhor, 1984; Nielsen, 1983). Nielsen has noted that male victims comprise 25-35% of the caseloads of clinicians working in the sexual abuse area. According to Nielsen, these known cases represent about 1 in 12 of the 46,000 to 92,000 male children she estimates to be sexually assaulted in the United States yearly. Although the origins of Nielsen's estimate are somewhat elusive, the knowledge of male sexual victimization risk is not new.

An early study in the area (Bender & Blau, 1937) suggested that male risk for sexual victimization was equal to that of females, given the use of common definitions for the event. Again, male versus female exposure to male nudity was called into question. Although the Bender and Blau study has been criticized for its small sample size, its concerns have been repeated recently. Swift (1980), for example, has called for the inclusion of exhibitionism as a victimizing experience for young males in order to increase the recognition of the parallel risks for sexual victimization being faced by both male and female children. Perhaps it was best said in the "classic" DeFrancis (1969) study, "Boy victims are numerous . . ." (p. 1).

Survey research results regarding male child sexual victimization are mixed. In his initial survey of 796 college students, Finkelhor (1979) found that 9% of the males surveyed reported sexual victimization (within the scope of that survey's definition) during childhood. A more recent survey of Boston parents found that 15% of the women and 6% of the men had been sexually victimized. Male children constituted 39% of the children who told their parents about real or attempted abuse. The adjusted percentage for male adults who reported victimization as children (adjusted for male-female composition) was 26%. Finally, a 1980 survey of driver's license holders in Texas reported a 3% rate for male sexual victimization. Clinical studies provide additional support for the presence of risk.

A review of clinical studies by DeJong and colleagues (DeJong, Emmett, & Hervada, 1982) reported male sexual abuse rates somewhere between 11% and 17% of the populations studied. The DeJong et al. work found a rate in its own study population of slightly less than 14%. This rate is very close to the percentage of males within all sexual abuse cases (15%) reported by the American Humane Association (AHA, 1978). And a review of studies undertaken by Showers and colleagues matched the 15% rate reported by AHA (Farber, Showers, Johnson, Joseph, & Oshins, 1984; Showers, Farber, Joseph, Oshins, & Johnson, 1983).

In other studies, Ellerstein and Canavan (1980) found an 11% prevalence for male sexual victimization in their chart review of the emergency room records of a Buffalo, New York Hospital. Pierce and Pierce (1984) found clear differences between a sample of 25 male victims and 180 female victims. Etiology aside, the risk to children of both sexes remained clear. Beyond those studies which make a direct effort to examine the risk of male victimization, there are those which make an indirect but significant statement as well.

Perpetrator studies, particularly research on incarcerated male sex offenders, have provided strong suggestions that males are sexually victimized at rates exceeding those generally understood or expected (Prentky, 1984). A. Nicholas Groth has described male children as targets of sexual victimization in at least one third of the offenses committed by male adults (Groth, Hobson, & Gary, 1982). Groth's 1979 study of convicted male sex offenders found that 28% selected male victims exclusively and another 21% selected the gender of the victim based upon convenience only. A similar study in the Netherlands (Bernard, 1975) indicated that incarcerated male sex offenders reported that they would select a male victim, if more convenient than a female victim.

There are wise cautions to adopt in accepting studies of incarcerated populations. First, there are differences between persons sufficiently deviant to be incarcerated and the full range of non-incarcerated offenders (Russell, 1984). Second, sex offenders with a relatively exclusive sexual interest in children (as opposed to those involved with both children and adults) are not only those most likely to commit enough offenses to be apprehended and incarcerated; they are also those offenders who may show the greatest preference for male children (Lanyon, 1985). The only supportable conclusion from these studies is that which has been repeatedly presented here: Male children are at risk from sexual victimization. And, since a 1985 study of the prevalence of child sexual abuse in Great Britain found that 8% of the males surveyed had been sexual abuse victims (Baker, 1985), this is a risk which is not only deep into the United States but wide (international) in its scope.

Male and Female Child Sexual Victimization: Similarities and Differences

Differences in reporting likelihood and patterns in male sexual victimization, when compared to female victimization, may lead to the presentation of mixed and erroneous information about such events. In one sense, the reluctance to report frequently found in the male victim creates a "self-victimization" in which others minimize the impact the event may have recorded upon the child. The male victim, when faced with an inescapable need to disclose the event, may overtly minimize the impact himself. Fearing allegations of homosexuality or working from male socialization messages demanding "macho," this young male reports, "I'm fine." This feeds social needs to see such victimization as somehow less traumatic to the male than it might be for the female child (Russell, 1984). The consequence is that sources of help turn away at the precise moment they are most needed. Bravado is not the only obstacle to accurate information.

Like the earlier conclusions about female child sexual victimization, current conclusions regarding male child sexual victimization are being overwhelmingly drawn from "reported" cases. The vagaries of reporting may well lead some writers to adopt premature conclusions. As Groth, Hobson, and Gary (1982) point out, "dependable information in regard to sexual molestation of male children is very limited and much more research needs to be directed toward this issue" (p. 144). Consider the information available on age at victimization as an example. Russell (1984) has described males as being older at the time of their reporting than females. Finkelhor (1984) and DeJong et al. (1982) describe the fact that male victims are so young that their relative youth is a "striking characteristic." Ellerstein and Canavan (1980) present a third position by reporting no differences between males and females with respect to the age at which the case comes to light. Obviously, there is some confusion.

Finkelhor (1984), by the way, attributes some of these relative reporting differences to the individual data collection sources. For officially reported samples, his presumption is that females will be proportionately older. This is a result of the fact that the age being reported is actually the age at the time of investigation and substantiation. If the behavior has been ongoing in a secretive way for some time, the actual age at first victimization would have been much younger. Male victims, being assaulted outside the home more often and not having families who withhold the information, may have the information about their victimization come to the surface more quickly. It is also his speculation that older males will be more likely to withhold disclosure as a result of a greater awareness of the "costs" of reporting previously mentioned. As can be seen in Table 2.1 there is ample room to clarify all aspects of what is known about child sexual victimization.

Table 2.1 Variance in Reported Characteristics of Male Child Sexual Victimization Cases

Age at Assault

1. 3.3 years—16.4 Years/Mean = 9.4 years
   (Ellerstein & Canavan, 1980)

2. 6 months—16.9 Years/Mean = 8.7
   50% Between 5–9 Years
   (DeJong et al., 1982)

3. Throughout Childhood
   (Finkelhor, 1980)

4. Older Than Female Victims
   (Russell, 1984)

5. Young Victims; 38% under 6 years of age
   (American Humane Association, 1978)

Location of Assault

1. (Young Victim) Own Home
   (Older Victim) 50% in Public Place
   (DeJong et al., 1982)

2. 64% "In Place of Public Access"
   (Ellerstein & Canavan, 1980)

3. Out-of-Doors
   (Farber et al., 1984)

Victim-Assailant Relationship

1. Acquaintance and/or Relative
   2/3rds of Assailants Known to the Child
   (DeJong et al., 1982)

2. 44% Known to Child
   (Ellerstein & Canavan, 1980)

3. Outside the Family
   (Finkelhor, 1986)

4. Father or Step-Father but Not Commonly Reported
   (Finkelhor, 1986)

5. Male Age-Mate
   (Adams-Tucker, 1982)

6. Family Member or Male Known to the Victim
   (Showers et al., 1983)

Patterns of Assault

1. Multiple Victims, Same Sex, and Other Sex
   (Finkelhor, 1984a)

2. Multiple Victims, Same Sex, and Other Sex
   (Burgess, Groth, & McCausland, 1981)

continued

Table 2.1 Continued

Violence and Coercion

1. Violence and Coercion Increases with Victim Age
   Violence and Coercion Increased with Decreasing
      Victim Familiarity
         (DeJong et al., 1982)
2. Frequent Coercion
         (Showers et al., 1983)

General Risk Factors

1. Prior Maltreatment
   Pre-Existing Neurobiological Disorders
   Mental Retardation
   Learning Disabilities
   Seizure Disorders
         (DeJong et al., 1982)
2. Impoverished Family
   Single Parent Family
   Prior Maltreatment
   Poor Paternal Role Model
         (Finkelhor, 1980; 1984a)
3. Differential Preparation for Possibility of Assault
         (Swift, 1980)

From Table 2.1 it is obvious that there is little perfect agreement regarding the development and events surrounding the male sexual abuse situation. It does appear that males may be more at risk outside the home than females; although, even in this, some of the younger males were victimized at home. The range of perpetrators is a wide one, but there is some suggestion that the incestuous pattern commonly found in female children may be less than norm in male children. Of vital interest is the frequency with which males are sexually assaulted in the presence of other victims. This may occur in a "sex ring" situation (Burgess, 1984) or it may simply be in the course of being with siblings or playmates. There is a pervasive possibility that more than a single child was affected in many cases involving male child sexual assault. Finally, as the male victim gets older it does appear that coercion does play a more frequent role.

Prior maltreatment, possibly indicating a less-than-protective family, seems to be a factor in the high-risk equation. As has been the case with physical child maltreatment (Friedrich & Borishin,

1976) difficulties in the child may also help to contribute to the victimization. And families who must struggle with poverty, single parenthood, and an incompetent or absent family member (paternal) may provide greater exposure to risk for the child. These are risks which are known both in the male and female child sexual victimization experience. Such commonalities have led some writers to speculate that the features of the child sexual abuse circumstance which lead to the selection of either a male or female victim rest not within the event itself but within the perpetrators (Farber et al., 1984; Showers et al., 1983)—a group which requires intense study.

The Perpetrator in the Sexual Abuse of Children

The most widely held view of the perpetrator of child sexual abuse is

1. He is likely to be a male, although that has been brought into question of late.
2. He is post-pubertal, although perhaps only just so, as the current increase in recognition of younger and adolescent offenders suggests.
3. The contact is sexual despite the fact that it may not appear so in some cases.

Beyond these reasonably probable characteristics, information regarding perpetrators is so imprecise and absent in uniform definition that it is difficult to compare studies.

Etiological Quandaries

Historically, beliefs regarding sex offenders have held some loosely accepted commonalities. First, there has been a bias that sex offenders are intra-psychically unique from other troubled individuals. Second, the in-home perpetrator was seen as different from the out-of-home molester. Thirdly, criminal and sexual elements of the assault, particularly in-home assault, were ignored in the belief that the perpetrator was merely demonstrating the sexual expression of such nonsexual needs as intimacy. Current writers (Conte, 1984;

Lanyon, 1985) suggest that it is time to put these polarities and assumptions in the past.

Lanyon (1985) suggested that our endless search for psychopathology in the perpetrator is the pivot upon which our definitional and treatment failures rest. He has viewed the "traditional" view of such sexual deviance to hold two fundamental assumptions. First, there has been an assumption that all sexually deviant behaviors are etiologically similar. Second, their assumption has been that a character disorder is at the heart of this etiology. Together, these assumptions led to a search for a single theory of deviant behavior which would find its roots in difficulties in psychosexual development. Such theories grew into treatment strategies that required a total restructuring of the individual's character and, not surprisingly, were not very successful (Lanyon, 1985). At least, such theoretical assumptions and treatment approaches have not helped clinicians to get a great deal closer to resolution of the problem in the large number of cases. Recent research calls many of the basic theoretical and clinical assumptions about this population into question.

There is growing recognition today that the individual sex offender may have a large number of victims. This is especially true in the case of the offender in the child sexual abuse situation (Abel, Becker, Murphy, & Flanagan, 1981). In the perpetrator strategy known as the "Sex Initiation Ring" (Burgess, Groth, & McCausland, 1981), for example, perpetrators have been known to hold records of 1,000 or more children who have been victims of their pedophilic careers. And, there is every reason to believe that the father who perpetrates in the home can, and in some cases does, perpetrate on the streets—perpetrations that involve children of both genders. Recognition of these facts leads the clinician to the point that no amount of denial, distortion, or minimization can alter the fact that sexual abuse of children of either sex is, at its core, a sexual act (Conte, 1985). It is time that some new clinical approaches begin to encompass the research knowledge now becoming available.

The facts, while harsh, seem relatively straightforward. First, inadequate personality is not a theory which is adequate to describe causation in child molestation (Conte, 1984). In fact, Lanyon's review (1985) of empirical work on the personality of the sex offender discovered that perpetrators have not been found to be remarkably different from other troubled individuals, with the exception of the perpetration of the sexual assault itself and in demonstrating some difficulty in establishing satisfactory emotional and sexual relationships with opposite sex peers. Second, a search for differential physiological arousal patterns in sex offenders has produced ambivalent results (Langevin, 1983). Third, descriptive efforts which attempt to capture etiological differences in sex offender types have not succeeded in arriving at precise points of departure between offender types which can then be translated into therapeutic approaches. In fact, flying in the face of psychopathological models of the origin of sexual offenses are the behavioral models which presume no psychopathological underpinnings, but which seem to be offering some hope at this time (Abel, Blanchard, & Becker, 1978; Lanyon, 1985). The tower of typologies which has been constructed since the clinical recognition of this problem began in earnest will be a difficult monument to topple, however. Table 2.2 describes some of the distances that researchers and clinicians have traveled in attempting to confine child sex offenders to a discernable variety of "types."

The Father Offender

While cases of homosexual incest have been described in the clinical literature (e.g., Awad, 1976; Bender, 1954; Raybin, 1969; Rhinehart, 1961), the rate of father-son sexual victimization is not clearly known. One study (Orr & Prietto, 1979) reports that 12 of the 14 male sexual abuse victims in their study were victimized by fathers, but the more commonly assumed risk is from public or nonfamilial assault. On the other hand, identities of perpetrator and victim may be clouded, but the risk for homosexual rape and its negative psychological consequences is very real. In fact, Bell and Weinberg (1978, 1981) while studying homosexuality itself, encountered the fact that 2.5% of the heterosexual men they surveyed had experienced a "prepubertal" sexual experience with a male and this same type of event had occurred with 4.9% of the males who later adopted a homosexual orientation. The relationship between such early homosexual rape and its consequences continues as a topic of research attention (Kaufman, DiVasto, Jackson, Voorhees, & Christy, 1980). The ultimate finding may be similar to the speculative one of Kempe and Kempe (1984) that "incest between father and son is not rare" (p. 73).

Table 2.2 Sex Offender's Typologies

Author(s)	Descriptor	Etiology
Karpman (1954)	Preference Offenders	Stable Erotic Attraction to Children
	Surrogate Offenders	Use of the Child as a Surrogate for Adult Partner
Mohr (1962)	Multiple Perversion	The Polymorphous Perverse Nature of Man
Gebhard & Gagnon (1964)	Mental Defective Sociosexually Underdeveloped	A Fixating Sexual Experience in Childhood
	Alcohol Involved Offender	Alcohol/Substance Abuse
Cohen, Seghorn, and Calmas (1969)	Fixated Offender	Passive Dependency/ Social Immaturity
	Regressed Offender	Life Stress. Inadequate Masculinity. Poor Marital Adjustment. Confrontive Sexual Experiences in Adolescence
Swanson (1971)	Fixated Offender	Poor Social, Educational, and Employment Adaptation
	Situational Offender	Response to Life Stresses
	Brain Damaged Offender	Impairment in Intelligence, Perception and/or Judgment
	Inadequate Sociopathic Offender	Lack of Regard for Others, Possibly Compounded by Alcohol Dependency or Misuse
McCaghy (1971)	Offender Working With Children	Seeking Legitimate Contact through Occupational or Volunteer Roles
	Career Molester	Sexual Fixation upon Children. Incestuous Molester. Marital Instability

continued

Table 2.2 Continued

Author(s)	Descriptor	Etiology
	Spontaneous Molester	Response to Life Stress
	Aged Molester	Dementia
Summit & Kryso (1978)	Incidental Offender	Erotic Interest or Dependency
	Ideological Offender	Belief in the Benefit to the Child
	Psychotic Offender	Confusion in Reality Testing
	Rustic Environment	Isolation
	Endogamous Incest Offender	Distorted Family Relationships
	Misogynous Incest Offender	Fear or Hatred of Women
	Imperious Incest Offender	Household Emperors
	Pedophilic Incest	Erotic Fascination with Children
	Child Rapist	Masculinity vs. Power Confusion
	Perverse Incest Offender	Exploring That Which Is Most Forbidden
Groth & Birnbaum (1978)	Preference	Fixated on Attraction to Children Through Psychosexual Experiences in Development
	Situational	Sexual Expression of Extrasexual Needs Brought About by Current Circumstances
Justice & Justice (1979)	Symbiotic Offender	Dependency
	Introverted Offender	Family Fusion. Shutting out the World
	Teacher/Offender	In-home Sex Education
	Protector/Offender	Providing a "Safe" Introduction to Sexuality

Table 2.2 Continued

Author(s)	Descriptor	Etiology
	Alcoholic Offender	Alcohol/Substance Abuse
	Psychopathic Personality/Offender	Character Disorder
Howells (1981)	Preference Offender	Primary Sexual Orientation to Children. Unplanned and Compulsive Assaults (Usually of Males). Not Precipitated by Stress. Do Not Understand Society's Concerns
	Situational Offender	Normal Heterosexual Development and Orientation. Social Skill Deficits. Significant Life Stresses
Seghorn (1981)	Fixated Offender	Both Fixated (Persistent) and Regressed
	Regressed Offender	(Sporadic) Had Perpetrators Who Were (a) Seeking Sexual Gratification, and (b) Seeking Relief of Aggression within Their Classification
Groth, Hobson, & Gary (1982)	Fixated (Classic) Offender	Primary Orientation to Children from Adolescence. Compulsive/ Obsessional. Unresolved Psychopathology
	Regressed Offender	Conflict in Adult Roles. Impulsive Responses to Adult Stress. Alcohol Use

continued

Table 2.2 Continued

Author(s)	Descriptor	Etiology
	Child Molester	Builds Relationship with Child. Slow and Patient Seduction
	Child Rapist	Aggressive Act Against Child in Which There Is No Personal Investment
Bauman, Kaspar, & Alford (1983)	Aggressive Offender	Dominance Need Incestously Directed
	Passive Offender	Poor Self-image. Shallowness. Awkwardness. Socially Inept
Conte (1984)	Cross-Over Offender	Sexually Motivated in Multiple Paraphilias/ Offenses Involving Both Children and Adults
Burgess (1984)	Group Offender	
	Solo Ring Offender	Operating Alone with a Small Group of Children
	Transition Ring Offender	Using to Exchange or Sell Pornography of Children
	Syndicated Ring Offender	Organization Used to Recruit Children. Produce Pornography, Direct Sexual Services, and Develop Customer Network

The Female Offender

Although the clinical literature contains case histories of mother-son incest (e.g., Lukianowicz, 1983; Marvasti, 1986; Masters, 1970; Shengold, 1980; Wahl, 1960), aunt-nephew incest (Lukianowicz, 1983), and male sexual molestation by females (Sarrell & Masters, 1982), there is presently no arguing that male perpetrators far exceed female perpetrators in sexually victimizing events with children. DeFrancis found only 3% of his perpetrators to have been female (1969). S. K. Weinberg (1955) examined 200 cases of sexual victimization in the home and found only 2 of the cases to involve mother-son dyads. The American Humane Association and National Center on Child Abuse and Neglect (NCCAN, 1981) found female perpetration to be rare and not usually involving a male victim. Finally, in many of the cases that do involve a female perpetrator, the event is often found to be a cooperative event between a male and female adult both involved in some coercive relationship with a child of either gender (Russell, 1984).

However, not all are in agreement as to the rarity of female perpetration. Psychologists Blair and Rita Justice (1979) suggest that the low reported rates for such an event may be traced to mothers engaging in secretive sexual activity which is passed off as childcare (e.g., fondling, exposure, caressing in a sexualized manner, and coercive relationships which promise a sexual reward). Groth (1979) concurs with the Justices' view and indicates that the small number of known mother-son cases is the result of the fact that (a) women may "mask" sexually inappropriate contact through the guise of bathing and dressing the victim, (b) the child may be much more reluctant to report when the perpetrator is a parent, and (c) male children may simply be more reluctant to disclose overall.

While female perpetration may be "there," no one is exactly certain "where" and "to what degree." However, the interest in studying female sexual offenders has increased markedly in the past five years (e.g., Brown, Hull, & Panesis, 1984; Clark & Grier, 1987; Mathews, 1987; O'Connor, 1987; Wolfe, 1985). Some of these recent studies suggest that the number of females involved in the sexual victimization of males may be greater than previously believed. For example, when Knopp and Lackey (1987) surveyed 44 programs providing evaluation and treatment services to female sexual abusers, they found that 51% of the victims were male in cases involving "hands-on offenses" such as child molestation and rape. Additional support for a higher level of female perpetration can be found in Johnson and Shrier's retrospective study of male sexual abuse victims (1987). They found that among adolescent males who described childhood sexual victimization experiences, 60% had been molested by females. This percentage was reported to be considerably higher than those found by Finkelhor (1984), Bell & Weinberg (1981), and Gebhard, Gagnon, Pomeroy, & Christenson (1965).

As more information about the female sexual abuser is gathered, our understanding of the female's role in the Abuse of Sexuality model will increase. Some preliminary typologies are already emerging from clinical work with these females. For example, Mathews (1987) suggests the following descriptions of females who self-initiate sexual offenses against male children:

1. *Exploration/Exploitation.* Abusers are typically 16 years old or younger. They are frequently described as having few social skills, anxious, active and average to excellent students. Sexual acceptance concerns are usually present. Victims are usually male (nonsibling) children under the age of 6 years. The abusive event may occur only once and usually happens during babysitting.

2. *Personality Disordered/Severe Abuse History.* Abusers are usually adolescents or adults. They are often described as self-destructive, depressed, and verbally and physically aggressive, and show very poor overall emotional, social and academic adjustment. Severe sexual and physical abuse, usually by a male family member, is the norm. Their victims may be male but are more often female children between the ages of 0-10 years with whom they have a relationship, including their own children. The abuse often seems to be a reenactment of their own victimization.

3. *Developmentally Arrested or Regressed.* Abusers are married, divorced or single adults. They are usually seen as socially isolated or not self-sufficient. About 50% of these women have sexual abuse histories. They also seem similar to "fixated" and "regressed" pedophiles. Victims tend to be related or nonrelated males between 11 and 16 years of age with whom they have a self-initiated "love affair."

Sociologist Diana Russell attributes this increased interest in female sexual abuse perpetration to two somewhat related phenomena. First, the sudden increase in awareness of cases generally has raised the absolute number of reported cases of both male and female perpetration markedly. Consequently, the number of female perpetrated incidents, although small, has grown. Second, many people assumed that females "never" perpetrated such acts, and so any evidence to the contrary has a more marked impact than that of a more commonly recognized male assault (Russell, 1984). Both Russell (1984) and Finkelhor (1984a, 1986) have taken a particular interest in this topic and have undertaken reviews which allow them to sustain their belief that pedophilia in particular and child sexual abuse in general is a male-dominated deviancy. Referring to the "Male Monopoly" Finkelhor (1986) cites his own work and that with his colleague Hotaling (Finkelhor & Hotaling, 1983, 1984) in which reviews of the National Study on the Incidence and Severity of Child Maltreatment and other "officially reported" data sets reveal that 90% of offenders in cases of this nature appear to be men. And, even in those few cases where female perpetration does occur, it is in consort with a male perpetrator or voyeur (Finkelhor, 1986). This 1986 conclusion is both in agreement and at odds with conclusions from his 1984 review of the American Humane Association (AHA) data.

In Finkelhor's review of the AHA data he notes that a female was listed in 41% of the cases where males were victimized and 31% of the cases where females were victimized. He does, however, point out that while females were somehow involved, it was actually the males doing the molestation. For cases in which the female was the lone perpetrator, he reports that 14% of the victims were males and 6% were females. From this he concludes that both male and female victims are primarily abused by males (1984a).

In Russell's 1984 work, a chapter co-authored by Finkelhor returned to some of the earliest incidence/prevalence studies to examine the male/female perpetrator issue. Beginning with the early DeFrancis study (1969) which reported a 3% female perpetrator rate, this chapter also examined the National Incidence Study (NCCAN, 1981), the American Humane Association Study (1978), and some of the male sexual victimization studies cited elsewhere in this work in its examination of the "Gender Gap" in child sexual abuse perpetration. Terming the National Incidence study "misleading" in its reporting (p. 217), these authors cited the Finkelhor and Hotaling (1983) report previously discussed. And, they faulted the American Humane Association study for "making it impossible to distinguish between perpetrators who committed abuse and those who simply allowed it"—a critical point in the female perpetration picture (p. 219). The only conclusion with which they were comfortable from these perspectives upon "official" cases was that the notion that female perpetrators usually direct their attention toward male victims is in error. That conclusion is based on the fact that while 14% of the female perpetration was against males, as opposed to 6% being directed toward female victims, there are so many more female victims than male victims that the "absolute" impact is much greater upon females (p. 219).

Self-report studies present a slightly different picture in the Russell and Finkelhor review. From a heterogeneous set of studies examining college students, homosexual men and women, the general population, sex offenders, and attendees at a Parents United conference, these authors continued to offer only that "sexual abuse of children by older women represents a distinct minority of child sexual abuse cases" (p. 221). For a study which reported, among college students, that males reported that 60% of their childhood sexual experiences were with older females (Fritz, Stoll, & Wagner, 1981), Finkelhor and Russell concluded that there must have been an "unusual sample or error in tabulation" (p. 222). A lesbian sample in which 22% described childhood sexual experiences with older women (Bell & Weinberg, 1981) was explained away by differences in sexual orientation. Finally, the incarcerated population (25% reportedly victimized by a female) (Groth, 1983) and the Parents United population (33% victimized by females) were placed aside due to an inability to generalize to the wider population from these unique groups (p. 223). These issues reflect the difficulties inherent in synthesizing the current research findings into a meaningful whole.

According to Russell and Finkelhor (1984) several sociocultural elements feed directly into the male dominance in child sexual abuse perpetration. On the female side of the sexual socialization issue, women are taught to prefer older, larger, and more powerful partners. Women also learn much earlier to distinguish between sexual and non-sexual forms of affection, and do not generally act as initiators of the first sexual encounter with a partner. Males, on the other hand, are taught to be aggressive and to overcome resistance, as it is thought to be artificial (i.e., "she doesn't really mean no"). Men seem to be more promiscuous (according to these authors), can be aroused more easily and by exclusively sexual stimuli which are divorced from the relationship context. Finally, sexual success (i.e., conquest) is a larger part of the male self-identity (Russell & Finkelhor, 1984). Ultimately, as will be seen in other portions of this work, these same socialization factors play a part in male sexual victimization as well. And, it is important for the purposes of this work to recognize that, no matter how differing rates are explained, the fact remains that females do, indeed, victimize males in some cases.

The Juvenile Offender

Between 195,000 and 450,000 juveniles commit sexual assaults involving force each year (Ageton, 1983). Abel, Mittelman, and Becker (1985) have recently reported that 57% of a large (411) sample of perpetrators of sexual assault experienced the onset of their deviant sexual pattern prior to age 19. Longo (1982) evaluated 17 adolescent sex offenders and discovered that 76% had assaulted others prior to their own twelfth birthday. And, in a recent work Becker, Kaplan, Cunningham-Rathner, and Kavoussi (1986) found, in a sample of 22 adolescent males charged or convicted with sex crimes in the family, that 63.6% had a prior sex crime arrest and 9.1% had two or more arrests. The question must be asked, "where did they come from?"

In Finkelhor's 1979 study of 796 college students, a full one third of the women reporting prior victimization indicated that the molester was a male youth between the ages of 10 and 19. Yet many, if not most, of these crimes have tended to go unreported. In part, this reluctance to make an assault known can be tied to a reluctance to report an offense by a young offender who is a family member (Groth & Loredo, 1981). In part, this previously underrecognized problem speaks to a cultural view of adolescent male sexuality.

The Kempe Center on Child Abuse and Neglect's Gail Ryan has established a national network of programs dealing with adolescent sex offenders. In this center's review of such offenders, the conclusion was that there has not been adequate "accountability" for offenders of this description. Rape of older women is treated with a "boys will be boys" approach, child molestation is passed off as "experimentation," and many sexual offenses are placed under the diagnostic label of "adolescent adjustment reactions." The net result of all this watering down is a set of adolescent sex offenders who get no treatment during the time when treatment might well be most effective. Surveys suggesting that adolescent sexual assault is simple "sex play," "experimentation," or the result of "normal adolescent aggressiveness" provide a dangerous view that such circumstances are minor infractions (Chatz, 1972; Reiss, 1969; Roberts, Abrams, & Finch, 1973). They may be difficult to categorize along the lines drawn for adult offenders (as poor as those are), but to do nothing is to ignore the possible manifestation of pedophilic or deviant sexual behaviors that may persist into and through adulthood (Costell,

1980). At the very least there should be some concern with the typical adolescent's influence over siblings, or perhaps with babysitting responsibilities.

The Sibling Offender

There is some suggestion, although the exact rates of occurrence remain elusive, that some adolescents who are uncertain about their sexual approach to peers may elect to begin with a more positive referral group (i.e., siblings). In other cases, in which no sibling is available, a nonfamilial child may be selected as a safer mechanism of sexual introduction than a peer. This choice seems to hinge not so much upon self-esteem, as might be expected, as it does upon circumstance and the adolescent's prior experience level. And, there are certainly sibling offenders who are simply demonstrating an aggressive assault.

A. H. Green (1984) reviewed the work undertaken with offenders who had aggressively assaulted their siblings. In general the behavior seemed to be attributable to an intensification of sibling rivalries. This intensification seemed to follow more from outside forces than from something internal to the child. That is, there is some evidence that parental neglect of an individual sibling may increase the likelihood that an aggressive attack may be directed toward another sibling. The quality of the care afforded them in the family may be so variant from that given the siblings that they find themselves unable to control aggressive impulses (A. H. Green, 1984). If this older sibling was an older child at the time of birth of the younger, and the new child had long been considered intrusive, it appears that the sibling bond of protectiveness is substantially weakened.

The reconstruction of the American family brings this issue more clearly into focus than it was in the past. Sibling incest is no longer seen as that benign child behavior that allows some measured transition into sexual knowledge. Rather, with the increasing number of blended families, stepsiblings of differing ages, and foster children, and the absence of a biological bond, the issue of intrafamilial sexual contact between brothers and sisters takes on new meaning (Kempe & Kempe, 1984). If coercion is involved, and, if the perpetrator is substantially older (e.g., five years) than the victim, this should be treated as any sexual assault. Rest assured that it does occur, as the 15% of females and 10% of males in Finkelhor's college student sample were able to verify (Finkelhor, 1980).

The Pedophile

Despite the number of terms and nosological concepts that have been offered to describe the child sexual offender, the greatest source of misunderstanding in the area flows from a single term: pedophilia. This term is used in nearly every official recording of a child sexual abuse situation, used by expert witnesses in courtrooms on a daily basis, and as a point of judgment in determining the suitability of treatment for the offender. Yet it rarely, if ever, holds the same meaning for any two users.

In commonplace usage, most people consider the term *pedophile* to refer to the enduring nature of the individual's sexual attraction to children. For example, the *Diagnostic and Statistical Manual of Mental Disorders* (DSM-III) (American Psychiatric Association, 1980) qualifies the use of the term when there is an indication that children are the "repeatedly preferred or exclusive method of achieving sexual excitement" (p. 271). Lanyon (1986) calls this criterion the "preference versus situational" discriminator. As such, the perpetrator would always select a child over an adult for sexual relations. Although this is probably the most widely understood discriminator in electing to use this dangerously underdefined term, there are wide variations on this theme. For example, the revised edition of the *Diagnostic and Statistical Manual of Mental Disorders* (DSM-III-R) (American Psychiatric Association, 1987) offers a modified definition of pedophilia which now includes two types: "Some people with Pedophilia are sexually attractive only to children (exclusive type), whereas others are sometimes attracted to adults (nonexclusive type)" (p. 284). Another example of variation can be found in Freund, Heasman, Racansky, and Glancy's (1984) differentiation between pedophilia and pedohebephilia. Pedophilia, in this structure, is a sustained preference for the body shape of children (under age 11). Pedohebephilia, as used here, refers to the approximately equal attraction to not only those children under 11 but pubescent children as well. Other variations include the age of the perpetrator as well. Quinsey (1977) saw the problem as one defined by a male who had sexual contact with a child of 13 years of age or younger when the male was at least 16 years of age or older and at least five years older than the child. Kempe and Kempe (1984) echo the concern with the perpetrator's age, as they posit greater damage if the perpetrator is at least four years older than the child victim.

Both Maas (1986) and Lanyon (1986) have reviewed points of discrimination between pedophilic and nonpedophilic labeling. Perhaps the broadest is represented by Sandfort (1979) who believes that pedophilic feelings can be experienced by many individuals to some extent, but only when these feelings are "very strong" or "exclusive ways" are they an indicator of pedophilia (Maas, 1986). Although almost exclusively subjective and nearly impossible to determine, this is not an uncommon basis for inexperienced clinicians to use in classifying child molestation perpetrators into various types for the purpose of assessment and treatment. Even more dangerous in some cases than the subjective and all-over-the-map approaches are those that make absolute determination based upon situational variables.

One traditional point of departure in the clinical setting has been the in-home versus out-of-home perpetrator. In general practice the assumption has been that the in-home perpetrator is at reduced risk for actual presentation as a pedophile than the out-of-home offender. The "catch-all" terms that are often thrown about are the *fixated* versus *regressed* offender. These are terms which have long been attached to sexual abuse perpetrators, although their popularization came about through A. Nicholas Groth and his study of incarcerated offenders (Groth, Hobson, & Gary, 1982). The fixated is generally thought to be the more intractable of the two with a greater likelihood of being a pedophile in generally understood terms. So popular have these terms become that expert witnesses are often asked by the legal professionals in a court setting whether or not the perpetrator in question is fixated or not? Lanyon (1986), in his recent review of the research literature in this area, has made it clear that this traditional split classification system based upon nothing more than an incestuous or non-incestuous presentation is spurious. His conclusion is that, except for the fact that the incest situation predicts complex family dynamics for the clinician to work with, this distinction is not useful in understanding the offender. In fact, recent research suggests that there is little difference in the sexual preference pattern of the two offenders (Abel et al., 1981).

The gender preference of the perpetrator is sometimes wrongfully considered as a criterion for pedophilic labeling. The implication is when viewing both homosexual and heterosexual child molesters that the homosexual molesters may be more impervious to treatment. This assumption may flow from early work with child sex offenses in which the pederast was described as the primary offender. Overall, the pederast was seen to be an adult male who enjoyed both giving sexual pleasure to and receiving it from a male child. Typically, these male children were recruited from the ranks of adolescent male prostitutes who worked the streets. The pederast may have been a male who was using the boy as a substitute for unavailable women, a panderer or pimp who wished to exploit the boy, a promiscuous adult male who made contact with every boy he could, a "careful" pederast who did not relate to young males exclusively, or a "responsible" pederast who knew of his proclivities but avoided them at all costs (Rossman, 1980). Costell (1980) describes similar characteristics in hebephilic offenders (preferring adolescent girls) and ephebophilic offenders (preferring adolescent boys). And, he sees their activities as being "parallel" to those of the pedophile. In reality, most molesters of boys indicate that they do not have adult homosexual preferences. And, some international studies have indicated that molesters will interact with a child of either gender if it is possible. What is sought is the "childness," not the maleness or femaleness of the child (Finkelhor, 1984b). It seems likely, then, that gender itself says little or nothing about the presence of actual pedophilia, or its absence.

There is also a prevailing sense that the pedophile is operating from a character or behavior disorder of some type. Evidence of this, according to some writers (Bell & Hall, 1971) may be found in the presence of schizoid or passive traits as well as in the excessive dread of adult sexuality. The Bell and Hall work assumed that the depression and self-doubt that characterizes the tension-ridden pedophile would be displaced in a sexual act. Through this act, childhood experiences may be relived and resolved largely through the facility of dominating others—a domination that was unavailable in their family of origin.

To some degree, the need to dominate explains other antisocial acts undertaken by pedophiles (Cohen, Seghorn, & Calmas, 1969; Groth & Burgess, 1979; Virkunnen, 1976). Some writers (McCreary, 1975a) have suggested that the severity of the personality disturbance in the pedophile is directly related to the number of offenses he will commit. Yet, aggressiveness is not a constant in the pedophile's operating style, again throwing this entire theory base into question (Henn, Herjanic, & Vanderpearl, 1976).

Whether or not "true" pedophilia occurs in females is not immediately clear. As far back as 1886, Krafft-Ebing (1950) [1886] posited the presence of female pedophilia by citing two cases reported by Magnan. More contemporary review of these cases has concluded that the women's reports were more delusional than concrete. Yet, there remain many writers and researchers who continue to proffer the belief that women frequently engage in sexually abusive behaviors toward children under the guise of caretaking (Groth, 1979) or in the course of "expected" female roles with children (Justice & Justice, 1979; Plummer, 1981).

The pedophile and the abuse of sexuality. Family history is often the backdrop against which the clinician predicts the relatively enduring nature of a child-oriented sexual preference. Unfortunately, there is only a very modest body of knowledge to support the use of this variable in this way. And, the two most significant works were conducted more than two decades ago. In 1964, Mohr, Turner, and Jerry examined a group of pedophiles in an effort to uncover any unique relationship characteristics between these males and their own parents. While the homosexual pedophiles in the group reported distant fathers who did not appear to care about them, the heterosexual pedophile group did not evidence parent-child problems to any great degree. During that same year Gebhard and Gagnon (1964) compared a nonsex crime, a convicted sex crime (not child sexual abuse), and a convicted child sexual assault group as to their self-reported rearing patterns. In that the offender groups were all drawn from disrupted home settings, the researchers concluded that such disruption was a characteristic common to all deviant groups. However, the validity of these works is often questioned due to the heavy reliance upon self-report data.

Recently, Gaffney, Laurie, and Berlin (1984) conducted a well controlled examination of the presence of sexual deviancy in first degree relatives of hospitalized pedophiliacs and other hospitalized paraphiliacs who were not pedophiliacs. For the paraphiliacs generally, sexual deviancy of some nature was found in 18.5% of their families. In the case of the nonpedophiliac paraphiliacs, the families' sexual deviancy was also most commonly nonpedophilac in nature. For the pedophiliacs, the sexual deviancy which appeared in the families was, indeed, pedophilia. Although difficult to generalize from, these results suggest a possible intra-familial pattern. It will be some time before controlled studies allow for an examination of the genetics versus behavior issues presented by preliminary works such as this one.

One recurrent question regarding the family history of the pedophile is that of sexual history. While some fixating sexual experience has long been posited as an element of the sexual deviant's life, there has been much written lately about the child sexual abuser's specific experience of having been a sexual abuse victim himself in childhood (Finkelhor, 1984a). To some degree, the actual prevalence of sexual assault among children would suggest that some pedophiles had been victims. Remember that Mrazek's (1980) review of such victimization suggests that 10-15% of all children and adolescents experience some form of sexual assault. About three quarters of those who do the assaulting choose exclusively female victims, about one quarter choose male victims, and the balance select victims of both sexes (Groth & Birnbaum, 1978; Langevin, 1983). However, the current suggestion is that the consequences of this assault, especially among males, may be the generation of an adult offender, an adult attempting to master his own victimization experience (Finkelhor, 1984a; Russell, 1984).

A recent review by Finkelhor (1986) provides conditional support to this notion by indicating that there is an "unusual" frequency of such histories among convicted child molesters, and that it is a "consistent" finding of the research. However, the "exact proportion" is difficult to determine (pp. 103–104). In arriving at this tentative conclusion, Finkelhor reviewed the work of Gebhard and colleagues (1965) who found that 10% of a female-object molester group had experienced sexual contact with an adult female, and 18% had experienced such contact with an adult male. The male-object offenders revealed a 33% victimization rate. Those offenders who had perpetrated incestuous assaults showed a rate much closer to the controls than the child molester group. Other works on incarcerated populations continue to support the male childhood victimization thesis among this group (Groth & Burgess, 1979; Langevin, Handy, Hook, Day, & Russon, 1985). The key question here, of course, is the relative generalizability offered to the wider population by a group of incarcerated offenders (Russell, 1984). And there is the question, also put forth by Russell (1984), as to why male children respond to sexual victimization in this way while female child sexual abuse victims (a much larger group) do not? They could, of course, grow up to be mothers of victims (Goodwin, McCarthy, & DiVasto, 1981) although this theory requires more empirical support before reaching viability.

Others have found the pedophile's motivational structure to be less sexual and more a reaction to other needs which went unmet in childhood. The psychoanalytic literature, for example, relies upon the offender's non-sexual need to master some victimization experienced during growing up. Or, there may be an affectional reward in the act which compensates for a perceived absence of intimacy in his world. The difference seems to be the pedophile's inability to cope with the difference between his own childhood and that which he idealizes in his view of others' developmental years. The idealization of childhood seems to be a consistent presence in the operating style of the pedophile. This idealization influences both the offender's object choice (children) and the fear and anxiety associated with sexual approaches to healthy adults (Lanyon, 1986).

Overall, however, it seems safe to conclude that the major elements of the Abuse of Sexuality model (sexual information, sexual experiences and sexuality) are all significant points of confusion in the family life of the developing pedophile. Morgan (1985), for example, found that pedophiles acquire neither adequate nor accurate sexual information during the developmental years. In place of normal transitions toward normal sexuality there is a series of repetitively traumatic experiences. In fact, even "normal" sexual experiences (e.g., masturbation) may evoke traumatic responses from members of the pedophile's family (Adams-Tucker, 1982; DeJong, et al., 1982; Oliver, 1967).

The pedophile and psychiatric/psychological evaluations. A number of researchers have attempted to classify the pedophile through psychometric instrumentation. In reviewing these efforts, Lanyon (1986) has found no consistent findings, with the exception of the usual feminine identification of the pedophile and the shy, passive, and unassertive stance that he often takes in comparison to the stance of the average male (Langevin, 1983). When the population focus shifts to the incestuous male, the trend in behavior also shifts toward domineering and controlling styles (Lanyon, 1986).

McCreary (1975b) was among the first to administer the MMPI to a group of these individuals. In this study, 33 persons convicted of child molestation were placed in two distinct groups dependent upon the presence or absence of previous sexual offenses. The result of this two-group examination provided a relationship between the severity of the personality disturbance (as measured by MMPI scoring) and the greater number of prior arrests per offender. Chronic offenders were seen as more impulsive and unconventional (Pd), more bizarre, confused, and alienated (Sc), and they had more authority conflicts and psychosomatic complaints (Hs and Hy) than the child molesters with no prior arrests. As indicated by the Lanyon (1986) review, no differences were found in measures of masculinity (Mf) or social introversion (Si). Whether the members of either group were married or not seemed also to generate some difference. It seemed that the child molesters who had not been previously arrested were likely to have had stable marriages. The researcher (McCreary) concluded from this finding that the existence of a stable marriage was indicative of a higher degree of social competency and maturity in the offenders without a prior arrest. However, this remains nothing more than a speculative conclusion.

In an interesting effort to compensate for the large number of studies which rely upon incarcerated pedophiles, Wilson and Gosselin (1983) attempted to examine personalities in a sample of pedophiles who were "at large" in the community. That is, these individuals had not been brought to the attention of either the mental health or the law enforcement community. A sample of 77 pedophiles, all members of the self-help group called the "Pedophile Information Exchange (PIE)" were given the Eysenck Personality Questionaire and a specifically designed instrument entitled the Pedophile Questionnaire which dealt with social background, sexual behavior, and feelings about being a member of this group. The Eysenck results found the pedophiles to be higher on scales describing psychoticism, introversion, and neuroticism than age-matched controls. The pattern was one that is familiar to those who work with sex offenders and sexual deviates generally, as transvestites, transsexuals, and masochists also tend to demonstrate this submissive personality and sexual style (Wilson & Gosselin, 1980). After considering the full range of data presented by their study, Wilson and Gosselin (1983) concluded that the ability to achieve social dominance over the child may well be a key to understanding the pedophile's sexual object selection. That is, if the male's sexual socialization demands some degree of social dominance in order to generate adequate arousal and performance, and pedophilic males are not particularly successful in this sort of competition, the choice of a child may provide at least partial sexual comfort. Dominance and submission are characteristics which pedophiles both admire and feel to be important characteristics in people (Howells, 1981). A final note must be offered here that while most studies of pedophilic males do indicate the presence of at least some degree of social difficulty, the fact that the majority of the molesters studied have been apprehended may also offer up speculation that those who are more socially skillful may go undetected. There are both sexual factors in pedophilic relations (Money, 1977) and emotional factors (Howells, 1981; O'Carroll, 1980). And, there can be pedophilic relationships without sexual contact as well as sexual contacts only in the absence of a relationship (Sandfort, 1984). As has remained true from the beginning, there are no single factor theories adequate to explain this phenomenon in and of itself. Some recent work with physiological response patterns does present some promise, however.

The pedophile and physiological responsiveness. The measurement of sexual arousal patterns and magnitudes has been used in the pedophilic group both to assist in identification and classification and to get at the effect of treatment (Mavissakalian, Blanchard, Abel, & Barlow, 1975). In most cases the measurement device is the penile plethysmograph which measures penile tumescence after exposure to a variety of stimulus modalities which include pictures, fantasies, written or spoken descriptions of deviant behavior, or pornographic materials of any other type. At this point, the one best method has not yet been determined.

Physiochemical studies have been essentially nonconclusive in the recent work although some suggestion has come about recently that there are biochemical differences in pedophiles. Rada, Laws, and Kellner (1976) found normal levels of testosterone in a pedophile group. However, Gaffney and Berlin (1984) have studied the hypothalamic-pituitary axis in pedophilic and normal men and found some suggestion of abnormality in those exhibiting pedophilic behavior. This suggests some possible endocrinological differences between pedophilic males and normal males, but the methodological concerns attached to this work are far too broad to begin to posit that male-female differences in pedophilic dominance are related to fundamental biological differences.

With convincing evidence in absence in these studies, the recommendation to view the victim and perpetrator through environmental variables gains strength. At this time clinical hypothesis building must rely upon information based upon a predominance of female victims. Very shortly, information regarding differential consequences by gender may be available. The following reviews what is known.

3

Whatever Happened to Baby John?

The Aftermath

The Consequences of Child Sexual Abuse

There is a general agreement across the recent literature on child sexual abuse that the consequences of the experience can be both significant and enduring. For the clinician who sees those who grow up in these abusive environments, there is no question of damage. Among researchers, there are those who would seek to minimize predicted effects.

In the 1950s Raskovsky and Raskovsky (1950) suggested that sexual contact between an adult and child fostered psychosocial adjustment in the child. Beliefs such as these are taken to extremes by such organizations as the North American Man-Boy Love Association (NAMBLA) and the Renee Guyone Society. Organizations such as these live by slogans such as "sex before eight [years of age] or it's too late." They claim to represent a network of thousands of parents uniformly eager to involve their children in "gentle and loving sex" with adults. To complicate matters, some groups encourage both homosexual and heterosexual contact. Although these groups appear extreme in their beliefs, the appearance of a recent proposal in Holland which would lower the age of sexual consent from 16 to 12 years of age (Freeman-Longo, 1986) suggests that the presence and possible acceptance of adult-child sexual contact is widespread.

Finkelhor (1986) has referred to researchers who consider the negative effects of child sexual abuse to have been exaggerated as "minimization" theorists. Feminists writers are more strident and find these researchers to be members of a "pro-incest" group (Herman, 1981). In spite of these protests, those who advocate for less attention to the consequences are both vocal and familiar. An early Kinsey report, for example, noted:

> It is difficult to understand why a child, except for its cultural conditioning, should be disturbed at having its genitalia touched or disturbed at seeing the genitalia of other persons, or disturbed at even more specific sexual contacts. (Kinsey, et al., 1953; cited in Russell, 1984, p. 245)

More recently, noted child maltreatment specialists C. Henry Kempe and Ruth Kempe (1984) provided the following prognostic insights to the child involved in an out-of-home molestation:

> A single molestation by a stranger, particularly a non-intrusive, non-violent one, as an encounter with an exhibitionist, may cause only transitory harm to normal children living with secure, reassuring parents. (p. 188)

However, the Kempes did go on to caution that "the event still needs to be talked out and explained at an age-appropriate level, and all questions must be answered."

Others in the field agree that child sexual abuse can produce emotional and behavioral problems, but disagree over the nature and severity. A variety of variables such as the age and sex of the child, the type of sexual activities, and the identity of the perpetrator have been posited as elements of differential effects. The clinician must remember in reading all of this that this is a body of literature easily criticized for its autobiographical accounts, single case studies, methodological flaws, and lack of definitional agreement. On balance, however, it would have to be concluded that the majority of the work in this area predicts that growing up in an environment which abuses the child's sexuality will be likely to result in some form of childhood, adolescent, and/or adult emotional problems. Table 3.1 provides a perspective on the range of problems that have been identified in the victim.

While a comprehensive review of these studies has been usefully undertaken in other works (Finkelhor, 1986; Kempe & Kempe,

Table 3.1 Sexual, Emotional, and Behavioral Problems Reportedly Related to the Experience of Sexual Victimization as a Child

SEXUAL PROBLEMS
1. Sexual Experimentation (Pomeroy, Behar, & Stewart, 1981; Rosenfeld, 1976)
2. Homosexuality (Rascovsky & Rascovsky, 1950)
3. Sexual Dysfunction (Tsai & Wagner, 1979; Glasner, 1981; Blumberg, 1979)
4. Sexual Stigmatization (Finkelhor, 1984)
5. Compulsive Participation in or Avoidance of Sexual Activity (Finkelhor, 1984)
6. Confusion over Sexual and Nonsexual Behaviors (Finkelhor, 1984)
7. Compulsive Masturbation (Brandt & Tisza, 1977)
8. Precocious Sexual Behavior (Brandt & Tisza, 1977; Brown & Holder, 1980; Glasner, 1981)
9. Unmeant Affectional Needs (Browne & Finkelhor, 1979)
10. Association of Sexuality with Aggression (Kempe & Kempe, 1984)
11. Adolescent Pregnancy (Herman, 1981; Kempe & Kempe, 1984; Romanik & Goodwin, 1982)
12. Seductive Behavior (Kempe & Kempe, 1984)
13. Prostitution (Silbert & Pines, 1981)
14. Problems in Marital Sexuality (Blumberg, 1979)
15. Sexually Transmitted Diseases (Sgroi, 1978)

EMOTIONAL PROBLEMS
1. Hopelessness (Kempe & Kempe, 1984)
2. Anxiety (Kempe & Kempe, 1984; Brandt & Tisza, 1977)
3. Personality and Character Disorders (Pomeroy, Behar, & Stewart, 1981; Blumberg, 1979)
4. Guilt and Shame (Tsai & Wagner, 1979; Brown & Holder, 1980; DeFrancis, 1969; Byrne & Valdiserri, 1982)
5. Depression (Tsai & Wagner, 1979; Kempe & Kempe, 1984; Lister, 1982; Janas, 1983)
6. Poor Self-image (Tsai & Wagner, 1979; DeFrancis, 1969; Kempe & Kempe, 1984; Janas, 1983)
7. Emotional Instability (Mrazek, 1980; Brown & Holder, 1980)
8. Inhibitions and Fears of Tenderness (Goodwin, McCarthy, & DiVasto, 1981)
9. Anger Toward and Distrust of Parents (Tsai & Wagner, 1979; Kempe & Kempe, 1984)
10. Feelings of Betrayal (Finkelhor & Browne, 1986)
11. Distrust of Males (in Female Victims) (Tsai & Wagner, 1979)
12. Loneliness (Kempe & Kempe, 1984)
13. Hostility (Janas, 1983)
14. Poor Sense of Identity (Kempe & Kempe, 1984)

continued

Table 3.1 Continued

BEHAVIOR PROBLEMS
1. Runaway Behavior (Brown & Holder, 1980)
2. Poor Social Skills and Unsatisfying Social Relationships (Janas, 1983)
3. Self-destructiveness (Anderson & Shafer, 1979; Kempe & Kempe, 1984)
4. Suicide (Anderson & Shafer, 1979)
5. Delinquency (Koch, 1980; Kempe & Kempe, 1984)
6. Impulsiveness (Kempe & Kempe, 1984)
7. Alcohol and Drug Abuse (Kempe & Kempe, 1984)
8. Hyperactivity (Brandt & Tisza, 1977; Kempe & Kempe, 1984)
9. Compulsivity (Brandt & Tisza, 1977)
10. Fantasy and Withdrawal (Kempe & Kempe, 1984)
11. Continued Victimization (Goodwin, McCarthy, & DiVasto, 1981)
12. Perpetration of Abuse as a Parent (Goodwin, McCarthy, & DiVasto, 1981)

COMMON CHILDHOOD DISTURBANCES
1. Sleeping Problems (Brandt & Tisza, 1977; Browne & Finkelhor, 1986)
2. Fears and Phobias (Brandt & Tisza, 1977; Brown & Holder, 1980; DeFrancis, 1969; Kempe & Kempe, 1984)
3. Learning Problems (Brandt & Tisza, 1977; Browne & Finkelhor, 1986; Brown & Holder, 1980)
4. Enuresis/Ecopresis (Brandt & Tisza, 1977)
5. Nightmares (Brandt & Tisza, 1977; Brown & Holder, 1980)
6. School Problems (Browne & Finkelhor, 1986; Kempe & Kempe, 1984)
7. Psychosomatic Disturbances (Brown & Holder, 1980; Kempe & Kempe, 1984)

1984; Russell, 1984) an historical summary may be of use to the clinician using this work. Conte (1985) dates scientific inquiry into causes and consequences of child sexual abuse from 1937. The foundational study, although "inadequate by current scientific standards" (p. 115), was undertaken by Bender and Blau (1937). The Bender and Blau effort relied upon anecdotal reports and concluded that many victims experienced few lasting ill effects from the experience. These early authors were followed by several others offering essential agreement with their "minimal effects" position (Bender & Grugett, 1952; Lukianowicz, 1983; Schultz, 1975; Sloane & Karpinski, 1942).

From those studies which posit effects, Conte notes that some victims are less affected than others. There appear to be contradictions regarding who is affected and who is not. His conclusion is that effects may appear within physical, behavioral, psychological and interpersonal realms of the victim's life. However, the identification of the variables in the experience which account for direction, intensity or area of manifestation is currently out of reach. Conte also pointed to an issue in the literature that is vital to the clinician's understanding of its "political" nature.

Conte (1985) suggests that the sexual abuse information may be used "politically" to legitimize sexual abuse of children. He notes that "there often appears to be an unspoken assumption that if sexual abuse turns out not to produce significant long-term trauma, that there is nothing wrong with it" (p. 117). It is the fear of acceptance of these positions by the public which encourages some professionals to offer such sweeping statements as "children never lie" or "all children are harmed by sexual contact." These statements, scientifically vulnerable due to their "every situation" assumption, are made to protect defenseless children. The clinician knows that the effect of violence of any type must, by definition, be negative in some way. But reaching beyond the data can open the clinician's position to refutation.

From the knowledge base at this time, it seems most wise for the clinician to adapt some of Conte's recent work on assessment, treatment planning or testimony. A recent review by Conte and Schuerman (1987a) noted that ". . . some children are profoundly traumatized by sexual abuse, some exhibit milder or transient problems, and some appear not to have been affected by the abuse" (p. 201).

The review also offered a differential view of risk for males and females, noting that duration, time elapsed since the event, and the closeness of the relationship between victim and perpetrator all influence the impact upon the male victim. For females, the closeness of the perpetrator remains important, but frequency and severity of the act also tend to influence the outcomes.

In a review which parallels Conte's, Browne and Finkelhor (1986) concluded that there is little or no question that sexual victimization brings authentic change to a child's life. These changes may occur within a two-year period following the event (initial effects) or persist for years, even into adulthood (long-term effects). Early effects appear to be anxiety, depression, anger, and inappropriate sexual behavior. Longer term effects are described by adult females with a history of childhood sexual victimization as depression, self-destructive behavior, anxiety, distrust, isolation, sexual maladjustment, substance abuse, and poor self-esteem. The overall view is one which leans heavily toward the possibility of revictimization in almost any functional life area. The outcome of this review was supportive of Finkelhor's earlier work (1984a) in which he concluded that sexual victimization in childhood can be harmful, and in those events where it does not appear to leave a permanent scar, it still remains an unpleasant and negative event.

With respect to clinical presentation, it does not appear that a specific action determines a specific consequence. What seems to lead to psychological harm is that the sexual nature of the act is clearly inappropriate. In addition, the relationship with the perpetrator is exploitative, parents may not have been sufficiently protective, the family cannot be trusted, and relationships are confusing and not what they were promised to be by the world at large (Justice & Justice, 1979; Summit & Kryso, 1978). It is not surprising that victims see themselves as being isolated from others who present a public view of having these life variables appropriately in place.

The Impact upon the Male Victim

Clinically based literature provides the sense that male victims of child sexual abuse may have a more difficult time with the event than female victims do. Kempe and Kempe (1984) raise this concern in the following manner:

> Boys do worse than girls as victims of sexual abuse. Both mother-son and father-son incest leave a boy with such severe emotional insult that emotional growth is often blocked. Some of the boys tend to be severely restricted and may be unable to handle stress without becoming psychotic, while others may have symptoms but never be recognized as incest victims. Incest, then, can be ruinous for the male, while it can be overcome with, or sometimes without help by many girls. (p. 190)

However, the clinician must approach the consequences issue as he or she does all other clinical presentations, one patient at a time. Given the tenuous nature of our current knowledge base it is impossible to empirically substantiate any perspective. The position taken

Table 3.2 Impact of Sexual Abuse on Males: Emotional Distress

Author(s)	Sample (N)	% Male	Source	Findings
Adams-Tucker 1982	28	21.5	Clinical Records	Diagnosis related to age at event: 2-6 year olds, marked anxiety; 6-7 year olds, depressive neurosis, behavior disorders, psychosis; 7-10 year olds, anxiety, withdrawal, depression; 10+ years, depression, withdrawal, self-destructive behavior.
Conte & Schuerman 1987a 1987b	369	23	Symptom Impact Checklist/ Child Behavior Profile/ Clinical Assessment Form	Most children reveal negative effects; poor self-esteem, aggressiveness, withdrawal, acting-out, anxious efforts to please.
De Francis 1969	250	13	Court Record	27% emotionally stable; 52% mildly to moderately disturbed; 17% severely disturbed. Guilt and poor self-image most frequent descriptors.

continued

by this work is that the abuse of any child's sexual development poses significant risk to that child, irrespective of gender.

The Browne and Finkelhor review (1986) referenced earlier found that victim studies tend to exclude males, include a relatively small number of males, or fail to report differential results by gender. Of the studies they reviewed which included both male and female victims, males comprised 28% of the total sample group. Additional studies with males included as part or all of the sample have since been published. A brief overview of studies which include male victims of sexual abuse would seem helpful to the clinician. This review is organized here by apparent outcome.

Table 3.2 Continued

Author(s)	Sample (N)	% Male	Source	Findings
Hunter, Kilstrom, & Loda 1985	31 (Known Sexually Abused) 50 (Masked Sexually Abused)	11	Medical Evaluation	Masked group showed more physical than behavioral symptoms. Problems more likely in early adolescent group in which sex abuse was intrafamilial and of earlier age at onset. Male victims more likely to present masked presentation than females.
Tufts New England Medical Center 1984; and Gomes-Schwartz, Horowitz, & Sauzier 1985	156	22	Louisville Behavior Checklist	Clinically significant pathology in 40% of 7-13 year olds; 17% of 4-6 year olds. 36% of adolescent show fear of additional harm. Depression and sexual dysfunction predicted in adulthood if unresolved.
Woods & Dean 1984	86	100	Nonclinical Adult Male Sex Abuse Survivors	Initial fear, shock and surprise. Later fear, confusion, anger, or resentment. 25% heightened curiosity about sexuality.

Emotional Distress

Despite the heterogeneous nature of sampling and research strategy in the studies reviewed in Table 3.2, it seems defensible to suggest that male victims experience emotional distress as a result of sexually abusive experiences. Suggestions are also present here that the effects of this experience are carried forward in some cases to and through adulthood. In a literature review of the current perspectives of the sexual abuse of boys, Nielsen (1983) concluded that two thirds of male victims of childhood sexual abuse experienced some form of emotional difficulties. Guilt, depression, low self-esteem, sleep disturbances, and behavior problems were the most common effects described. She also proposed that depression and sexual dysfunction may occur in adulthood if the trauma was not resolved. A comprehensive view would find a mixture of self-directed (internal) symptoms (i.e., low self-esteem, withdrawal, guilt and depression) and other-directed (external) symptoms (i.e., acting out, efforts to please, resentment and aggression). As these data influence the Abuse of Sexuality model, it must be noted that ongoing sexual dysfunction has been hypothesized unless clinical intervention takes place prior to adulthood. Four other findings from these studies hold clinical application as well.

In one of the earlier works, Adams-Tucker (1982) concluded that very young child sexual abuse victims seemed to receive less severe diagnoses than children victimized in pre-teen and adolescent years. This finding occurred despite the greater severity and more enduring nature of the victimization. Adolescents were found to present with more compelling emotional problems even with events that were relatively recent or descriptively less severe. Being female, lack of a supportive adult, molestation by a father, molestation by more than one relative, and being genitally molested were all correlated with receiving a more severe diagnosis. Of particular interest to this work, male victims who had been forced to perform fellatio received less severe diagnoses than female victims who had been genitally molested.

A second clinical finding in these studies was that the emotional distress generated by sexually abusive events was genuine here. However, the overt distress symptoms appeared to be somewhat less dramatic than those which occur in psychiatrically-referred emotionally-disturbed children who were not sexual abuse victims. The level of clinically significant psychopathology also seems to vary by the age of the child at the initial event. Overall, school age children appear more inclined to manifest significant psychopathology than preschoolers or adolescents.

The third noteworthy synthesis of these study findings indicates that the single most important variable in reducing the trauma associated with the sexually abusive event for both sexes was the availability of a support system for the child. Simply put, victims from families which demonstrate significant problems and pathology do worse than those who have supportive relationships with nonoffending adults and siblings. Other variables of influence include the victim's perception of his or her role in the event, relationship with the perpetrator, and innate coping mechanisms of the individual child.

A final special note should be made of the Woods and Dean (1984) study of a nonclinical sample of adult males who had been sexually victimized as children. In this work the perpetrator's gender seemed to reveal some differential effects. Here, males abused by females reacted with about the same amount and type of distress as those abused by males. Yet, while 52% of the males homosexually assaulted continue to perceive the experience as negative, only 30% of the heterosexually assaulted males persist in this negative perception. In fact, 50% of those heterosexually assaulted see the experience as positive in retrospect. Only 16% of the homosexually abused males share this positive perception.

When asked what effect the sexually abusive experience had upon present functioning, a majority of homosexually assaulted males report a negative (53%) or neutral (37%) effect. In contrast, 38% of the heterosexually assaulted males describe a positive effect and 38% a neutral effect. Both groups did report some long-term effects of this victimization. In addition to the sexuality issues serving as consequences of the experience, these male victims also report "victim issues" such as feelings of responsibility, guilt, feeling damaged, feelings of betrayal, and alienation. Also present are "relationship issues" such as insecurity, distrust, authority conflict and maturational difficulties. These emotional issues are well known in mixed-gender samples of sexual abuse victims, as are the behaviors which are generated as a result.

Behavior Problems

Studies of behavioral manifestations of sexual abuse in male victims summarized in Table 3.3 have tended to utilize psychometrically sound instrumentation such as the Child Behavior Checklist (CBCL) (Achenbach & Edelbrock, 1983a) to lend credence to their findings. However, clinical case studies also link behavioral problems with the abuse of sexuality. For example, Chasnoff, Burns, Schnoll, Burns, Chisum, and Kyle-Spore (1986) reported behavioral problems including physically aggressive responses toward other children by two of three children (ages 2 to 3 years) who had been molested as infants by their mothers. In general, behavior problems seem to follow in severity the severity of the

Table 3.3 Impact of Sexual Abuse on Males: Behavior Problems

Author(s)	Sample (N)	% Male	Source	Findings
Friedrich, Urquiza, & Beilke 1986	85	28	Child Behavior Checklist	Severe behavioral problems related to severity of abuse, relationship with perpetrator, duration, frequency, and number of perpetrators.
Friedrich, Beilke, & Urquiza 1987	235	38	Child Behavior Checklist	Sexually abused children show greater behavior problems than nonabused children. Equal depression and anxiety to clinical but non-abused group. Less hyperactivity and aggression than clinical sample.
Friedrich, Beilke, & Urquiza 1988	64	100	Child Behavior Checklist	Sexually abused and oppositional males revealed parallel behavioral picture. Conduct-disordered males show more aggression and externalizing problems as well as lower social competence. Sexual abuse victims more sexualized overall.
Kohan, Pothier, & Norbeck 1987	1432	75	Hospitalized Sex Abuse Victims and Other Hospitalized Children	Hospitalized prepubertal sexual abuse victims are more sexually overt and more difficult behavior management problems.

abuse, relationship with perpetrator, duration and frequency of the abuse and the number of perpetrators. These findings show a near perfect "fit" with previous findings regarding mixed-gender samples of sexual abuse victims. For some "lucky" victims, the general behavior problems tend to subside with time. However, sexual problems seem more entrenched and persistent—a pattern supportive of the enduring impact of abuse of sexuality. There are other paral-

Table 3.4 Impact of Sexual Abuse on Males: Sexual Problems

Author(s)	Sample (N)	% Male	Source	Findings
Finkelhor 1979	796	33	College Students	Dissatisfaction with adult sexual experiences
Freidrich, Beilke, & Urquiza 1987	235	38	Child	More sexualized overall victimization of other male children
1988	64	100	Behavior Checklist	
Woods & Dean 1984	86	100	Nonclinical Adult Male Sex Abuse Survivors	Sexual dysfunctions, sexual preoccupation, dissatisfaction, infidelity, possible sexual attraction to children

lels in male and female victimization with the differences found in the greater tendency of males to demonstrate more aggressive, anti-social and undercontrolled externalizing behaviors. Female victims seem to internalize more and demonstrate more fearful, inhibited, depressed and overcontrolled internalized effects. The greatest clinical concern originating in this group of studies is the significantly greater sexualization of the behavior of the male child sexual abuse victim.

Sexual Problems

Clinical concern exists that the consequences of sexual victimization of the male child will center about inappropriate sexual behaviors as adults. Studies summarized in Table 3.4 seem to support this concern. The abuses of the male child's developing sexuality may not only fixate the child at inappropriate levels, but its resultant twists and turns may contribute to frankly deviant outcomes. For example, although colored by the family disruption which may have followed disclosure of the sexual abuse, the sexually abused male children in the recent Friedrich, Beilke, and Urquiza (1987, 1988) work exhibited excess masturbatory activity, were overly interested in their mother's body and clothing, and were drawn to sexually explicit materials. Victimization of other male children was also discovered. Information such as this is moving many clinicians to speculate upon some cyclical nature to the sexual victimization of male children and later perpetration as adults in the worst cases, and general concern about normalized sexual development in nearly every case.

Studies of victims who appear to have developed sexuality patterns that occur within normalized boundaries still reveal challenges to normality. For example, Finkelhor (1979) found that college students sexually abused as children had generally lower self-esteem in all areas. Among those males who had prior victimization there was a greater likelihood of reported dissatisfaction with adult sexual experiences overall.

When the Woods and Dean (1984) nonclinical adult male victim group was asked what effect the victimization had on their sexual attitudes, almost half (45%) reported no effect. Of the balance, 22% said it was a positive impact and one third (33%) reported a negative impact upon their sexuality overall. Among those who had been heterosexually assaulted, the majority reported a positive (54%) or neutral (33%) effect with only 13% finding a negative impact upon sexual attitudes. When asked about impacts upon direct sexual function, a majority of the homosexually assaulted males reported a neutral (50%) or negative (31%) effect, with 19% seeing the event as having been positive. A majority of the heterosexually assaulted males reported either a neutral (50%) or positive (37%) effect on their sexual functioning, while 13% reported a negative effect. Of those reporting negative effects, sexual dysfunctions, preoccupation with sex, sexual dissatisfaction and infidelity were common themes. In addition, nearly half (49%) of the respondents reported being sexually attracted to female adolescents either "sometimes" (35%), "often" (10%), "very often" (2%), or "always" (2%). Sexual attraction to male adolescents and/or young children of either gender was reported by 16% of the sample. Sixteen percent reported having sexual fantasies involving children, 20% agreed that "parents should show their kids sexual practices," and 14% expressed the belief that it is "healthy" for parents and children to engage in sexual activity.

From these studies it can be seen that differential circumstances in the sexually abusive event may have differing consequences. The worst case scenario, of course, is that of replicating the event against another helpless victim.

Cyclical Victimization

No perfect correlation exists between previous victimization and future perpetration; suggestions do exist that there is some relationship (Haynes, 1985). The link between childhood sexual victimization and subsequent aggressive sexual behavior by adolescent or adult sex offenders is posited by the literature (Groth, 1979). It has also been proposed that children of parents who were child sexual abuse victims may be at some increased risk for sexual victimization and abuse of sexuality. These hypotheses find predominant support in theories which suggest that victimized children become victimizers in an attempt to master the trauma of their own experiences and take on the power that the adult victimizers held over them (deYoung, 1982; Russell, 1984). The studies which examine this as yet unproved notion are overwhelmingly based within samples of incarcerated sex offenders and built upon a tenuous structure of unverifiable self-report; as can be seen in Table 3.5, closer examination of the studies seems a mandate.

Longo and Groth (1983) have noted prolonged histories of inappropriate sexual behavior in the lives of incarcerated sex offenders. In a manner that parallels developmentally appropriate patterns of sexuality, much of this behavior is initiated in adolescence and escalates through young adulthood. It is from this group, hypothesized here to have experienced an abuse of sexuality, that adolescent sex offenders and highly sexualized preadolescents are developed.

Fehrenbach, Smith, Monastersky, and Deisher (1986) have described the adolescent sex offender as a multiple perpetrator. There is no "typical" adolescent offender pattern. Rather, these young males may perpetrate offenses that range widely. According to these authors, the most frequent offense is that of indecent liberties in which sexual touching, which falls short of penetration, occurs. This relatively common circumstance is followed in frequency by rape, and "hands-off" offenses such as exhibitionism, peeping, stealing female undergarments, and obscene phone calls and letters. Not to be forgotten is the relative frequency of "date" or "acquaintance" assaults (Ageton, 1983) within this group. Sixty-three percent of offenses studied here were rapes or indecent liberties committed by male adolescents with children less than three years younger than the offender himself. Descriptively, only 11% of these offenders had a history of sexual abuse with an additional 7% reporting a com-

Table 3.5 Impact of Sexual Abuse on Males: Cyclical Victimization

Author(s)	Source	Findings
Becker, Kaplan, Cunningham-Rathner, & Kavoussi 1986	Adolescent Incest Offenders	23% reported previous sexual victimization.
Fehrenbach, Smith, Monastersky, & Deisher 1986	Adolescent Sex Offenders	19% reported previous sexual victimization.
Friedrich & Luecke (1988)	Sexually Aggressive Children Ages 4 to 11 Years	80% had a history of severe sexual abuse. Sexual offenses by these children often paralleled their own abuse. Parents more pathological than control groups.
Gaffney, Laurie, & Berlin 1984	Hospitalized Paraphiliacs and Families	18.5% of the paraphiliac's famlies evidenced additional sexual deviants; true of only 3% of the general psychiatric control group.
		Among pedophiles the predominant intrafamilial paraphilia was pedophilia; not true of other paraphiliacs.

continued

bined history of sexual and physical abuse. Another 16% of these youngsters reported exclusively physical victimization although the authors caution against the validity of these self-reports.

Among the critical elements of the Fehrenbach et al. work is the separate history of offenses of male adolescents with sexual victimization in their own past. These youngsters tended to engage in hands-on rather than the seemingly more benign hands-off acts. The physically abused group revealed a similar pattern for rape but a somewhat higher rate for indecent liberties and hands-off activities. Other factors such as social isolation and chronic adjustment or developmental problems correlated with these perpetration patterns as well. There seems to be room for clinical alertness in situations involving previously victimized male children. Staying open

Table 3.5 Continued

Author(s)	Source	Findings
Gomes-Schwarz 1984	Adolescent Sex Offenders	38% reported previous sexual abuse (confirmed) with another 17% probable.
Groth & Burgess 1984	Incarcerated Adult Male Sex Offenders	32% reported sexual victimization as children.
Groth & Freeman-Longo (see Groth, 1979)	Convicted Adult Male Sex Offenders	80% reported sexual victimization as children.
Longo 1982	Adolescent Sex Offenders	47% reported sexual victimization as children.
Petrovich & Templer 1984	Adult Rapist	59% reported being molested by a female as a child. Authors uncertain if heterosexual molestation predisposes to becoming a rapist.
Serrill 1974	Incarcerated Male Sex Offenders	75% reported sexual victimization as children.

to the possibilities is not equal to an assumption that deviant sexual behavior will follow every abuse of the male child's sexuality.

From the works reviewed to this point it would seem wise for the clinician to accept Finkelhor's (1984a) caveat that it is not the majority of sexually victimized children who go on to become perpetrators or parents of victims. However, among hospitalized paraphiliacs and incarcerated sex offenders sexual victimization is a common historical feature by self-report (Groth & Burgess, 1979; Langevin, 1983; Seghorn & Boucher, 1980). There appears to be some greater risk of perpetration by males who have been sexually victimized. But indications are that those who go forward into later perpetration are somehow different from those who do not (Russell, 1984). Unfortunately, clinically identifiable and verifiable variables which discriminate between these two groups remain elusive to this point.

Research exists which describes differences in the abuse of sexuality environments common to the developmental years of the differing types of perpetrators. Groth and Burgess (1979) have found that the child molester's early sexual experience was characterized by forcible sexual assault, with the rapist's experience that of being pressured into sexual activity by a known adult. These are findings which remain unreplicated to date. More pressing clinically than defining the specific environment of origin for each sexually deviant act is reaching Sgroi's position of having clinicians uniformly accept the fact that deviant sexuality may indeed occur, and at an early age.

Sexually aggressive behavior in young children is a clear presence in the clinical literature (Arroyo, Eth, & Pynoos, 1984; Fortenberry & Hill, 1986; Pomeroy, Behar, & Steward, 1981; Yates, 1982). There are young children who use some form of directed force in order to engage in sexual activities with other children, adolescents, parents and other adults. Friedrich and Luecke (1988) evaluated 22 of these children ages 4 to 11. Since 81% of these children were male the study bears directly upon the question in this work. Six of the twenty-two were found not to have been sexually aggressive and became a comparison group. An additional group of boys (5 to 13 years of age) who had been sexually abused and had also completed a treatment program for behavior problems became an additional comparison group. The combination of these comparison groups and the solid psychometric instrumentation applied (e.g., TAT, Roberts Apperception Test for Children, and MMPIs for the parents) make this a more clinically valid work than some of its predecessors.

Friedrich and Luecke (1988) found that 13 of the 16 sexually aggressive children had a history of severe sexual abuse which involved aggression, genital contact, fellatio and sodomy. The type of sexual offense perpetrated by these young males often paralleled their own experience. Diagnostically, the behavior disorders identified followed the overall aggression in the behaviors (e.g., conduct and oppositional disorders). Socialization patterns were attenuated as well with poor object relations and defective empathy for others being commonplace. Functional issues were present in the poor educational performance histories present. Not surprisingly, indicators of sexual preoccupation were present in most of the instruments.

These results might have been predicted from the earlier clinical literature. Added to this, however, was the additional discovery of a high level of parental pathology and history of parent-child problems predating the sexual abuse. The parents of the sexually aggressive children were clearly more pathological than in either of the two groups. The authors of the study reinforce the importance of the aggressive and undersocialized psychopathology of these sexually aggressive children. But they also counsel the clinician to be alert to premorbid family issues which center about inconsistent and primitive parenting, lack of parental empathy, and covert reinforcement of the child's aggressive behavior. These are the abuses of sexual development which not only predict conduct problems and oppositional behavior but also serve to "channel" the "emerging aggressiveness" into a sexualized manifestation (Friedrich & Luecke, in press, p. 24).

A summary view would find these studies to regenerate the longstanding issues of the cyclical nature of child victimization. It seems wise for the clinician to be informed by these apparent consistencies in early victimization and later perpetration. But, the evidence is far from conclusive. Clinical prediction remains a risk. In a strong review of the literature on this matter, Kaufman and Zigler (1987) suggest that unqualified acceptance of the belief that abused children of any type are likely to become abusive parents is unfounded. Their review collapses the overall intergenerational transmission rate to about 30%. While this rate is six times the base rate reported for general population studies (Parke & Collmer, 1975), two thirds of parents with abusive backgrounds seem to care for their children adequately. The Kaufman and Zigler work offers that mediating factors such as emotionally supportive experiences with nonoffending parents and others seem to be critical to stopping the potential replications of abuse in adulthood. It is hoped that a supportive relationship with a clinician will serve a parallel and equally successful purpose.

Sexual Orientation Conflicts

Some increased likelihood of a homosexual adult sexual orientation has been described for the developmental path of the male child sexual abuse victim. This concern follows from the prevalence of homosexual assaults of male versus female child victims. The simple fact is that most child sexual assaults involve male perpetrators. When that assault involves an adult male and a male child, two broadly accepted social standards are violated: victimization of a child and evidence of a homosexual act. Homosexuality itself is not clinically aberrant in all cases but it does remain questionable in the minds of the general public. For the male child victim, it is often the breaking of these social rules which defines his reaction to what has happened.

Some clinical studies point toward some relationship between the sexual victimization of a male child and the child's later homosexuality (Brunold, 1964; Finch, 1967; Finkelhor, 1984). No similar association has been drawn in studies involving female victims. Finkelhor reports that young males sexually abused by older males are about four times as likely to engage in homosexual activity as adults as are nonvictimized males. He speculates that the victim may label himself homosexual as a result of his apparent attractiveness to the male perpetrator of the assault. If the child experienced some physical pleasure during the assault the likelihood of this self-labeling seems increased. Results from those infrequently occurring cases involving a female perpetrator find later sexual aggression to be common. But, homosexuality is not necessarily a more frequent component of the earlier victim's pattern (Brandt & Tisza, 1977; Scacco, 1982).

In a relatively recent review of the homosexuality question, Johnson and Shrier (1985) found a homosexual identification seven times greater and bisexual identification six times greater for victimized males than for comparison groups of non-sexually assaulted males. Sixty-five percent of those victimized males reported the sexual assault as having had a significant effect upon these decisions and later sexual dysfunction.

With slightly less imposing findings, Woods and Dean (1984) report 12% of a nonclinical population of males with a history of sexual abuse reporting any sexual experiences with males during the previous year. Of those reporting homosexual activity, 31% had been sexually abused by a nonfamily male and 20% by a male family member. Only 5% report the perpetrator as a nonfamily female and only 2% as a female family member. One in ten of the respondents reported a "frequent" attraction to adult males, 1% found themselves to be "sometimes" attracted, and 12% had feelings of attraction but "very seldomly." Bell and Weinberg (1981) echo the caution of the Woods and Dean study in their finding that only 5%

of homosexual males in their study report a history of childhood sexual experiences with adults.

A clinical overview of this data would seem to support the commonly accepted clinical sense that the roads to a homosexual orientation are many. It may be that a history of childhood sexual assault is one of those roads in some cases. But, information to date does not hold sufficient clarity to identify which cases will resolve themselves in that manner.

Prostitution

Until recently, prostitution was considered by the general public as primarily an adult female "occupation." Males were seen as "Johns." While the terms *sexploitation, kiddieporn, solo sex rings, transition sex rings,* and *syndicated sex rings* (Burgess, 1984), still are not household words, the general public gained a greater awareness of children's involvement in various forms of prostitution as these activities received increased media attention.

However, the young male's role in these activities is still a source of confusion. For example, Janus, Scanlon, and Price (1984) propose that prostitution among boys may occur at about the same frequency as among girls, even though studies of delinquent males did not find a widespread occurrence (Finkelhor, 1984a). But there is agreement that prostitution is a form of sexual victimization, and for some male children, involvement in these activities can be seen as a continuation of earlier victimization. For example, in a study of 28 young male prostitutes, Janus, Scanlon, and Price (1984) found 39% had been involved in incestual relationships prior to their involvement in prostitution. Of this group, 55% had sexual relationships with a father or foster father, 36% with siblings, 27% with cousins, and 18% with uncles. A high incidence of negative sexual experiences prior to becoming a prostitute was also found: 86% reported a coercive sexual experience (forced to comply with sexual demands of another), 79% reported that their first sexual experience was coercive, and 33% reported multiple negative experiences prior to hustling. In these cases, the early sexual victimization may have predisposed these children to continue their victimization through prostitution. It is important to note, however, that these children also reported additional family problems such as physical abuse, neglect, parental discord and alcohol abuse.

Burgess, Hartman, McCousland, and Powers (1984) studied 66 children involved in sex rings. While the number of male children was not revealed, all of the case studies presented were male. Three main categories of reactions by these children following disclosure were described: reexperiencing the traumatic event, diminished responsiveness to the environment, and development of symptoms not present prior to disclosure. Reactions by these children two years after disclosure indicated that some were able to "integrate" the event into their lives as a traumatic event, but one that no longer created problems for them. In other words, they were able to "overcome" the problems created by the event. Another group appeared to employ an "avoidance" of the event strategy and seemed to function well until they had to face dealing with the event again, which would produce anxiety, fear, and other difficulties. A third group showed recurrent symptoms indicating a continuation of the trauma. The final grouping was classified as having "identified with the exploiter." These children were sympathetic with the exploiter, believed that the world was harmful and they were justified in their inappropriate sexual and other antisocial behavior. Many of these children turned to exploiting others or continued their victimization through prostitution.

From case studies it appears that childhood sexual abuse may lead some children into other forms of sexual exploitation, such as prostitution. However, male prostitution is a relatively new area of study. Too little is known at this point to provide an understanding of why prostitution becomes part of some and not other children's responses to earlier victimization experiences. A review of the child victim's pattern of coping with traumatic experiences, such as the abuse of sexuality, could be helpful to the clinician in this regard.

Coping Patterns

What has been described in this chapter may be loosely construed clinically as patterns of coping or accommodation to the experience of being sexually victimized as a male child. Necessarily, this chapter has focused more upon potential dysfunction than the functional adaptations often seen in these cases. An orientation to "wellness" rather than pathology in clinical work with sexual abuse survivors is a welcome change in the rather grim clinical landscape that has followed the discovery of the breadth of this problem in the lives of children. The path to accommodation is arduous, but many children are successful in putting the negative elements of the sexually abusive experience in a manageable position in their adult lives. Summit (1983) has described the points at which this accommodation process can become dysfunctional. A review of this process will help the clinician understand the points at which the struggling victim may present himself. Helping the male victim through these stages will serve to reduce the likelihood that one of the deviant outcomes described as possible by earlier portions of this chapter will become reality.

Summit (1983) has described the process through which the child sexual abuse victim "accommodates" to the sexually abusive experience. In this process the child is first confronted with the need to deal with the response of adults and other authority figures at the point of disclosure. Disbelief and rejection are commonplace—perhaps more so in the case of the male victim. The result is fear and confusion about whether to report and how much to say, as well as concern about the adult's feelings toward the victim. In the male, especially, self-blame at not being more self-protective enjoins the ordinary helplessness and hopelessness that follow the event. Guilt and rage are common clinical presentations (Summit, 1983).

The festering anger and betrayal in the child victim seems to sponsor ongoing miscommunication throughout the child victim's environment. A specific example is the sudden loss of power and control: two foundation elements of male socialization (see Chapter 1) now missing from the developmental path. Behaviors which range from withdrawal to active aggression result, depending upon the child's propensity to accept the loss or recapture his earlier sense of control over his world.

Summit (1983) suggests that aggression and antisocial behavior are the model choices of the male sexual abuse victim. Not being as tolerant of his helplessness as the female child, the male may rationalize that this dysfunctional sexual relationship is actually positive. The danger is not only that he will accept this relationship, but keep the power of it alive in his own adulthood through a series of similar relationships with young males, himself. This is the type of dysfunctional adjustment that clinicians must redirect.

It must be remembered that children do adapt to even the most malevolent forms of victimization. This often appears to occur shortly after the event is disclosed and protection is introduced. The appearance of this apparent "adjustment" is often so welcome to the anxious family and clinician that one or both will reduce or terminate clinical intervention too quickly. The child appears to be surviving in the immediate environment. The question of how he will survive over time has not been answered at this point, however.

The "silent" reaction of the child victim or that of the "too resilient" adjustor is dangerous. It should arouse the suspicion of the clinician, particularly that clinician working with the male victim. Whether the child is defending through denial, repression, or outright lies to the clinician, the anger which grows out of the victimization experience is not so easily accommodated. Left unresolved, this anger may be directed toward self or others. It is a common precursor to psychopathology or behavioral dysfunction, as the several aberrant paths described by this chapter point out (Burgess & Holmstrom, 1979). Many life areas will find competent functioning. But, in many cases, at least some dysfunctional behavioral choices may be traced back to the victimization experience (MacFarlane & Korbin, 1983).

One useful way of viewing the potential for dysfunctional accommodation to the sexually victimizing experience is offered by Finkelhor and Browne (1986). According to these authors the sexually victimizing experience alters the child's cognitive and emotional orientation to the world. These changes, in turn, influence not only self esteem but general affective capacities. These effects are posited without consideration of the gender of the victim (p. 180). The four major areas of affective vulnerability are thought to be traumatic sexualization, betrayal, powerlessness, and stigmatization.

Traumatic sexualization is described as a shaping of a child's sexual feelings and attitudes in a manner inappropriate for the child developmentally, and interpersonally dysfunctional. Some examples would be overall confusion about sexual matters, preoccupation with sex, aversion to sex, sexual dysfunctions, love-object confusion, and sexual identity confusion.

Betrayal occurs when children recognize that they are being harmed by trusted individuals on whom they are also dependent. When this dynamic occurs, as in the case of sexual abuse by a family member, a child or adult survivor of childhood sexual abuse may respond with depression, anger, lack of trust in intimate relationships, overdependence, and antisocial behavior, as examples.

Powerlessness is also defined as *disempowerment* and refers to a consistent contravening of a child's sense of efficacy, will, and desires when a "child's territory and body space are repeatedly invaded against the child's will" (Finkelhor & Browne, 1986, p. 183). Fear and anxiety, impairment in coping skills, and dysfunctional needs to control or dominate others are given as examples of effects of this dynamic.

Stigmatization is described as the negative connotations associated with the child's sexual abuse experiences and the subsequent incorporation of these negative ideas into the child's self-concept. Feelings of guilt and shame, lowered self-esteem, self-mutilation, and suicide thoughts and attempts are given as examples of the impact of stigmatization.

While this traumagenic model was developed from an analysis of the literature on child sexual abuse dominated by accounts of female victimization, a few examples of how the model applies to males are presented by Finkelhor and Browne. For example, traumatic sexualization may produce concerns about a homosexual identity in a young male molested by an adult male. An example of a possible response by sexually abused males to the traumatic dynamic of powerlessness is aggressive and delinquent behavior, including reenacting their own abuse. Our review of the sexual abuse literature associated with male victimization and our clinical experience suggest Finkelhor and Browne's traumagenic model is excellent and can be very useful in examining males' responses to childhood sexual victimization.

To illustrate this point, we propose that most sexually abused males experience most of the trauma described by the four dynamics, and their reactions can be quite similar to those displayed by female victims. For example, males who have been betrayed often develop angry feelings and may express this anger in antisocial behavior and other forms of delinquency. Interpersonal relationship problems, sexual dysfunctions, and overall confusion about sexual matters are not uncommon complaints of males who were molested as children. Self-destructiveness ranging from "suicidal gestures and self-mutilation to reckless use of drug combinations and multiple 'accidents'" can be found in males molested by fathers (Dixon, Arnold, & Calestro, 1978).

Overall, it appears that the male victim may feel a greater sense of shame than the female does as a result of the additional trauma of having his masculinity undermined. He has been placed in a nonmasculine passive role. He has violated one and possibly two social taboos. He is made to feel himself to be a "sissy" when compared to companions and peers (Russell, 1984).

While we are proposing that males may experience trauma similar to that experienced by females, it should be noted that males may not admit their distress as readily to themselves or others as do female victims. As Kaufman, DiVasto, Jackson, Voorhees, and Christy (1980) state: "Boys are taught from an early age to remain stoic in the face of discomfort" (p. 223).

As can be seen by a review of the empirical and clinical literature, many males who experience abuse of sexuality also experience some form of negative effects. However, each male may have a different response to the sexually abusive event, depending upon the circumstances. In fact, some males exhibit few, if any, negative consequences of a sexually abusive event even when the abuse is considered by most as very serious such as repeated forced penetration, while other males may exhibit severe emotional problems following a seemingly less serious sexual event such as a one-time fondling experience. Some clinicians become so perplexed by these cases that they may "insist" that their patients are not "in touch" with either the sex abuse or the negative consequences. After all, how can someone endure forcible rape at age 10 years and *not* show serious emotional problems? And how can just one occurrence of homosexual fondling at age 9 years produce pedophilia?

While there is agreement that such cases occur, little agreement exists regarding *why* they occur. Part of the problem seems to be a focus on the *event* as the major contributing factor. The pervasive philosophy proposes that negative consequences will indeed follow sexual abuse, and the more serious the abuse the more damage we should expect. For example, Eisenberg, Owens, and Dewey (1987) found that health professionals believed that intercourse would result in greater and longer lasting harm to the child than would fondling. This attitude is much too narrow to be useful to the clinician and can lead to serious misconceptions about the effects of sexually abusive situations. This approach also assumes that we can accurately rate an abusive event a priori even when factors other than the event itself are also significant in determining the impact. Individual differences appear to be the norm rather than the exception and, at the very least, the male victim's subjective responses to the abusive situation must be considered as important as the abuse itself.

Thus, for the male victim of the abuse of sexuality, the impact could range from nominal to quite damaging depending upon a number of environmental and personal variables. The task for the clinician is twofold: accurately assess the nature of the abuse and its relative importance to the presenting problems and develop an effective treatment program accordingly.

4

Building a New Life

The Paths to Recovery

For many children, the experience of sexual victimization produces negative sequelae persisting into adulthood. Yet Ryan, Lane, Davis, and Isaac (1987) note:

> ... there is little recognition of the impact upon the male victim, and few services attempt to identify and aid him in coping with and resolving the feelings of anger, powerlessness, and lack of control which victimization may produce. In the United States, society expects that males will protect and defend themselves. (p. 386)

Ryan et al. also suggest that males usually do not seek help or protection and tend to "internalize" the guilt associated with their victimization experiences. However, as seen in the previous chapter, males are exempt neither from sexual exploitation nor its negative consequences.

There is no question that the need for treatment programs designed for male victims of sexual abuse is great. Resources are not keeping pace. In our recent informal survey of programs providing services to victims of child sexual abuse in the U.S., less than 5% described programs specifically designed for the male victim of any age and fewer still for the male adult survivor of childhood sexual abuse. The exceptions were programs designed for male sex offenders, many of whom report histories of childhood sexual victimization. Also discovered in this survey was a small network of dedicated practitioners who share information associated with male victim treatment issues through personal correspondence.

Many of the network members are preparing publications in the area. Perhaps this informal network will eventually develop into a resource for clinicians struggling to find effective techniques to use in the treatment of male abuse of sexuality victims.

Although few techniques have been developed specifically for males, therapists (e.g., Bear & Dimock, 1988; Lew, 1988) have identified various stages or steps involved in the successful treatment of male sexual abuse victims. In this chapter we will discuss these stages or steps along with a general approach used to assist the male victim with each stage. In the next chapter we propose additional treatment strategies specific to certain dysfunctions within a multidimensional framework.

Structuring the Therapy

Victim or Survivor?

Throughout most of the clinical and research literature, persons who have childhood sexual abuse experiences are referred to as *victims*. While this designation may be technically accurate, victim is an unfortunate term, especially for adult males. As discussed previously, males often eschew the victim role.

Some clinicians prefer to use the term *survivor*, while others use *adults molested as children*. Our experience has shown that males respond fairly well to the term survivor because it has the "feeling" of strength rather than weakness. However, the use of victim appears acceptable when describing the abusive experiences or the person currently experiencing the abuse. In this regard, children are often referred to as victims, but when the abuse stops or when they begin to "cope" with the abuse, male children become survivors. The point for the clinician is to use terminology that assists the male "victim" in viewing himself in a more positive manner. For now, survivor appears to have some utility.

Diagnosis

Male victims and survivors of the abuse of sexuality experience a wide range of emotional and behavioral problems. The symptomatology often satisfies diagnostic criteria described in the *Diagnostic and Statistical Manual of Mental Disorders* (DSM-III-R) published by the American Psychiatric Association (1987). For example, abuse survivors may present with mood disorders, anxiety disorders, sleep disorders, and/or sexual disorders. Alcoholism and other substance abuse problems are also common.

While many diagnoses are possible, some authors suggest that the array of symptoms most often presented by abuse victims appear to parallel closely those contained within the DSM-III-R diagnostic category, Post-traumatic Stress Disorder (PTSD) (Blake-White & Kline, 1984; Courtois, 1986; Donaldson & Gardner, 1985; Eth & Pynoos, 1985; Frederick, 1986; Goodwin, 1984; Lindberg & Distad, 1985). Symptoms characteristic of PTSD include reexperiencing the traumatic event, persistent avoidance of reminders of the trauma, psychic numbing, and increased arousal (sleep disturbances, hypervigilance, exaggerated startle response, nightmares). Associated features include depression, anxiety, impulsive behavior, emotional liability, and physiological symptoms.

Other authors suggest that PTSD does not accurately reflect the problems experienced by abuse victims and survivors. For example, Finkelhor (1988) indicates that PTSD does not adequately account for the vast array of symptoms; PTSD only accurately accounts for the symptoms of some abuse victims—in others the PTSD symptoms may be altogether absent; and no strong theoretical formulation is provided by PTSD explaining how sexual abuse produces the symptoms. As an alternative to PTSD, Finkelhor offers his Traumagenic Dynamics Model of Child Sexual Abuse (Finkelhor and Browne, 1985) discussed elsewhere in this volume.

Still others recommend a separate diagnosis to include symptoms specific to sexual abuse rather than attempting to fit sexual abuse symptoms into other diagnostic categories. For example, Briere (1985) and Briere and Runtz (1988) suggest Post Sexual Abuse Trauma (PSAT) to describe the long-term effects of childhood sexual abuse. PSAT incorporates the essence of Summit's child sexual abuse accommodation syndrome (1983). More specifically, PSAT "refers to those experiences and behaviors that were initially adaptive responses, accurate perceptions, or conditioned reactions to abuse during childhood, but that elaborated and generalized over time to become 'symptoms' and/or contextually inappropriate components of the victim's adult personality" (Briere & Runtz, 1988, pp. 92-93).

It is our position that arriving at a specific diagnosis or even multiple diagnoses is less important than arriving at a thorough understanding of each survivor's emotional and behavioral dysfunctions and the connections between the abuse and the dysfunction. The label is unimportant, but the formulation of a treatment plan based upon an accurate evaluation of the effects of the abuse of sexuality is crucial. The present accepted psychiatric nomenclature is of little assistance in this regard.

The Therapist

Personal victimization experience. While therapist characteristics are important to the success of treating any mental health problem, these characteristics appear even more critical in the treatment of the abuse of sexuality. Some argue that a therapist must also be a survivor in order to treat sexual abuse victims effectively. The major premise for this argument is that you must first experience what the victim experienced before you can really understand the problems. While few would argue that experiencing something may be the best way to develop knowledge about it, there are many paths to knowledge; direct personal experience is but one of several. It is our position that the *process* of obtaining accurate information about the nature of child sexual abuse, the problems it creates for males, and effective treatment strategies is less important than the end product—the knowledge itself. In other words, a therapist need not be a survivor of the abuse of sexuality in order to be an effective therapist.

Having been a victim of the abuse of sexuality does not, in itself, prepare a clinician to be an effective therapist in cases of sexual abuse. While a survivor/therapist may possess, through personal experience, considerable knowledge about sexual victimization, he/she may not have come to grips with his/her personal victimization issues sufficiently to be an objective and effective therapist. Providing therapy for other survivors is not the place to resolve one's own personal victimization issues.

Gender. While some suggest that males are more comfortable with a therapist whose gender is opposite that of his abuser, this approach may be too simplistic. For some victims, the gender of the therapist may be an important variable. But for many others, the gender of the therapist is less important than the therapist's knowledge, experience, and skill level. It is important not to assume, for example, that a male abused by another male will be unable to establish a therapeutic relationship with another male. It is more important to explore the survivor's feelings about the therapist's gender and other variables before deciding on the appropriateness of a male or female therapist.

Theoretical orientation. Theoretical orientation becomes less of an issue as the therapist gains knowledge about and experience with victims of the abuse of sexuality. No one theoretical approach can capture the diverse problems often presented by an abuse victim. However, theoretical approaches which posit a more passive, analytical role for the therapist tend to be too unresponsive to the therapeutic needs most often presented by male victims. An active therapist utilizing a mix of theoretical concepts and approaches stands a much better chance of providing an efficient and effective treatment plan regardless of the age of the victim or survivor.

The Therapeutic Setting

The key to providing an appropriate therapeutic environment for male victims and survivors is to assume nothing and continuously evaluate the patient's comfort level with the therapeutic setting. For example, some males become uncomfortable in a room with couches rather than chairs. Closed doors may increase anxiety in some males but may be requested by others. Proximity of therapist to patient can be important to males with personal space issues. For others, being near an "escape route" such as an unlocked door can be comforting. While these variables may seem trivial to the inexperienced, these factors are often important concerns for males who struggle with trust and personal safety issues.

Of particular importance in establishing a safe environment is recognizing that many male victims find even normally appropriate physical contact unpleasant and anxiety provoking. While a handshake may seem innocuous enough, some males may view this socially accepted greeting as an unwanted intrusion into their "safety zone." While pats and hugs may seem comforting to most non-victims of sexual abuse, victims often view such acts as reminders of the sexual abuse or precursors to an unwanted sexual contact. For example, one adolescent male survivor finally had to terminate therapy with a female therapist who insisted on extended hugging and patting episodes at the beginning and end of each session. He explained, "While she was a good therapist in other ways, I dreaded going to see her because I knew we had to hug before the session. And I would often sit through the session dreading the hug at the end. Even when I finally told her how uncomfortable I was she insisted that the hugging would be therapeutic for me because it would help me get over my fear of women. It didn't, and I just couldn't go see her anymore."

Any sexual contact with a patient is strictly prohibited. Establishing a sexual relationship within a therapeutic environment is harmful to all patients. It can be particularly destructive for patients who have an abuse of sexuality childhood history. The therapist must provide a safe environment and address the issues of sexuality in a therapeutic manner. To do otherwise is exploiting a victim's vulnerability.

Individual or Group Therapy

While some therapists would argue that group therapy is the best approach for survivors, others express equally strong feelings about using an individual therapy approach. Individual therapy can provide the opportunity to focus. This is an advantage over group work because the patient's issues can be addressed specifically and intensely rather than having to share therapeutic time with the issues of others. However, group therapy with other survivors allows patients to share feelings and experiences as well as providing mutual understanding and support. This can be helpful in a number of ways, including that of ending feelings of isolation and learning that recovery is possible. The group also provides a "safe" place to be because the survivor's story is believed and his feelings understood and accepted.

Our position is that both approaches have merit and a combination of the two can enhance the therapeutic effect depending upon the individual needs of the survivor. For example, before being "ready" to participate in a group, a male survivor may need extensive therapy to reduce his anxiety associated with interacting with males. To place him in a group too early may only serve to reinforce his fears. On the other hand, group therapy at the outset may be helpful in reassuring a survivor that his story is believable and his feelings real. Buoyed with this reassurance, survivors often are then more prepared to discuss their victimization individually with a therapist. Acceptability must be determined on an individual basis.

On a national level, self-help organizations such as Parents United and Parents Anonymous (PA) not only offer groups for abusing parents but for sexually abused children. While Daughters and Sons United (DSU), an adjunct to Parents United, offers various groups for either or both genders depending on the age of the child, the majority of DSU are female victims of incest (Giarretto, 1982). In addition to providing age-appropriate group activities with a focus on victimization issues, DSU also provides a number of community liaison and support services for sexually abused children.

While PA was the first nationally organized self-help program for abusing parents, its primary focus was on physical and emotional abuse rather than sexual abuse. However, in 1982, PA began a children's treatment project which offered self-help programs for abused children and their parents. In the first year of operation 19% of the children served were sexually abused (Baker & Morris, 1984). Although programs varied from state to state, most programs included direct therapeutic services such as counseling, play therapy, and group therapy. Child care services and advocacy activities were also important aspects of most programs. Approximately 40% of the children served by the programs on a national basis were males.

The Path to Recovery for Adult Males

Once males decide to enter therapy for the abuse of sexuality, they often want to speed up the recovery process by unrealistic proportions. An unwary therapist might "buy into" an accelerated therapeutic process because he/she genuinely believes the survivor can achieve recovery within the time specified. A therapist may also have an inflated sense of therapeutic prowess and believe he/she can provide a rapid solution to years of emotional distress. Survivor and therapist must both learn patience. The path to recovery is seldom well paved. Rather, it is more akin to a seldom traveled wilderness trail. One can hardly speed along such a route without great risk of missing an important component of the recovery process.

While it is important for the therapist to allow the survivor to develop a reasonable pace toward recovery, it is equally important to teach the survivor realistic expectations. In some incest cases it may take as long to recover as the abuse itself. Even some one or two incidents of sexual abuse episodes may produce long-term therapeutic needs. But, the therapist must also be responsive to which survivors may be ready for the next step and provide the encouragement necessary to make it. The therapist must always be mindful that most males eschew the victim role and become impatient with lingering problems, demanding return to problems once thought of as resolved. It is important, therefore, for therapists to provide encouragement to survivors that recovery is possible but at the same time present a realistic appraisal of the recovery process. To do less ill-prepares males for the long adjustment process.

There appear to be several steps or stages in the recovery process. While they are presented in logical sequence, few male survivors follow the sequence exactly. Therapists should expect each survivor's path to recovery to be somewhat different. Some steps may be brief. Other steps may require repeated visits. All steps are considered important to the recovery process and should be addressed with each survivor.

Breaking the Silence

During a training session for newly hired child protective services caseworkers, one of the authors was illustrating the possible long-term effects of childhood sexual abuse by presenting a case involving a male victim who did not enter therapy until he was an adult. By that time a pattern of various dysfunctions was in place. During the discussion of the case, one of the caseworkers exclaimed, "Well, why did he wait so long? Why didn't he just tell somebody about the abuse when it was happening?" Another joined in with, "Even if he was afraid to tell at the time, why wait ten or fifteen years to tell or seek help?" These workers had little appreciation for the power embodied in secrecy and how difficult it is for victims to disclose their sexual abuse, especially for males who are expected never to be victims.

In cases of long-term incest, secrecy allows the sexual abuse to continue. One word from the child and the perpetrator not only loses a sexual partner but may also suffer other losses such as a family, job and freedom. Since so much is at stake for the perpetrator, he/she will use whatever means necessary in order to establish a pact of secrecy with the child. Common to all the techniques is inaugurating some form of real or illusionary power over the child. Some examples are:

1. Threats to harm the child.
2. Threats that the child will be taken away from the family.
3. Threats that the relationship with the perpetrator, an important person in the child's life notwithstanding the sexual abuse, will be lost.
4. Threats of violence against other loved ones such as a parent, sibling, or pet.
5. Isolation from others.
6. Convincing the child that no one will believe his story and he will be punished for lying.
7. Bribery (providing favors, money, material goods for sex and secrecy).
8. Developing a "special" relationship with the child.

The importance of secrecy is clear. The misuses of power in developing the secrecy are also clear. While the damage to the child is real and enduring, the victim seldom recognizes the damage created by maintaining the secrecy until he is an adult. Even then most survivors remain reluctant to reveal the secret lest the power of the perpetrator be unleashed again.

While all of the above applies to both male and female victims, male victims also experience additional disempowerment. The male child is expected to be strong and handle adversity without "crying about it." To break the secret would be to "tattle" and show a sign of weakness, a form of "crying." In addition, males who are abused by males fear being seen as a homosexual. Males who are abused by females may not discuss the trauma because they often redefine or realign feelings about sexual abuse from females to fit the cultural stereotype.

The road to recovery begins with breaking the silence. The therapist must encourage and assist survivors in disclosing. A therapist is a good place to start. First disclosure in a group setting is also an excellent idea. However, a trusted individual outside of the professional ranks can also be a place to begin. The point is, the male victim must first break the silence before a focused treatment for the abuse of sexuality can begin.

Once a survivor breaks the silence, a flood of emotions may follow. More often than not there will be relief, anger, sadness, anxiety, and betrayal. The patient may experience bouts of depression and fear. Periods of confusion are common. Episodes of angry and aggressive outbursts may also occur. The feeling of relief may be short-lived as it quickly becomes overpowered by other, more negative emotions. However, relief along with hope gradually returns as the survivor begins to recognize two important aspects:

1. Breaking the silence did not produce all of the dreaded events he had been led to believe would occur.
2. He is now truly on the road to recovery.

Accepting the Experience

While "breaking the silence" may seem synonymous with accepting the sexual abuse experience, these events are actually separate aspects of the recovery process. Males may eventually break the silence by telling someone about their childhood abuse of sexuality experiences, but they often continue to use denial strategies with themselves. They may acknowledge that a sexual event occurred but are reluctant to actually accept the experience as abusive. This is a frequent method used by males to protect themselves from having to deal with strong feelings as well as being forced to see themselves as a victim.

To assist male survivors through this step, therapists must guide males into breaking the imaginary bond between weakness and victimization. It is helpful to explain the power differential between the adult abuser and the child victim. Males do not become victims because they are not manly but because they are children without the knowledge, experience, and power that adults possess. When adults misuse their knowledge, experience, and power it often becomes an abusive event for the child. A male adult survivor usually sees the event through a male adult's eyes and evaluates himself accordingly. Assisting him in ignoring gender expectations and seeing the event through a *child's* eyes will bring him closer to accepting the experience as real and abusive.

Separating the Abuse from the Abused

Once the male victim has broken the silence *and* accepted the experience as abusive, he is ready for the next step: assigning the responsibility for the abuse to the abuser and not to himself. Many victims of the abuse of sexuality have learned to believe that they are somehow responsible for what happened to them. Males are particularly susceptible to this type of erroneous thinking because of another belief: They should have been able to protect themselves. Correctly assigning the responsibility for the abuse to the abuser is a crucial step in the recovery process.

The therapist can guide the male survivor toward this goal by again using the adult-child power differential model. An emphasis should be placed on the concept that no child should be abused in any way, and it is *always* the more knowledgeable, experienced and powerful adult who has the responsibility for the safety and well-being of children. If an adult chooses to abuse a child, that decision is the abuser's responsibility not the child's, regardless of the child's characteristics. It is *always* the abuser's problem, not the child's, which creates the abuse.

No Thanks for the Memories

Dealing with the abuse of sexuality means having to recall painful childhood memories. Many male adult survivors of abuse of sexuality have worked diligently to forget those experiences. As they attempt to lock painful experiences away, other childhood memories may be also locked away. For some males it is as though they had no childhood experiences at all.

For male victims, the road to recovery includes unlocking childhood experiences. For some males, especially male victims of incest, once a few memories are allowed to surface others burst on the scene. Before long he may be overwhelmed with a flood of emotionally traumatic memories. It is important for the therapist to prepare the victim or survivor for the potential barrage of unpleasantness. Informing him in advance that many painful memories may emerge as he works toward recovery is the preferred approach.

While dealing with memories of childhood experiences is a necessary part of treating male victims, it is unnecessary to press for total recall. Pursuing specific details about abusive experiences can be counterproductive if an individual is not yet ready to cope with those details. Many males have spent a lifetime developing strategies to defend themselves from those painful childhood abusive experiences and are ill-prepared to deal with them in ways other than denying, distancing and forgetting. Often therapists believe that recovery is not possible without total recall and a painful examination of all details associated with the sexual abuse. This is a misconception. Recovery is possible without total recall of abusive experiences. Pressing for total recall may actually impede progress in some cases.

Real Men Don't Have Feelings

Male children are taught the "dos and don'ts" of manhood. Most of the "dos" include such "positive" attributes as being strong, fearless, assertive, independent, clever, successful, and powerful. The "don'ts" include such "negative" attributes as being weak, fearful, nonassertive, and dependent, and having/showing feelings. While some feelings, like anger followed by assertive or aggressive behavior, may be acceptable for males, most other feelings are viewed with disdain and signify weakness. Males, therefore, are usually taught that they must gain control over unmanly feelings and the expression thereof in order to be accepted as a "real man." Males quickly learn that feelings are the enemy and must be conquered lest they will conquer you.

While this irrational belief system creates conflicts for nonvictimized young males, it creates additional problems for the young male victim of the abuse of sexuality. Strong "nonmasculine" feelings are triggered by the abuse and are usually so strong that extraordinary efforts must be employed in order to keep them in check. The victim must remember not to be afraid, not to cry, not to hurt, and not to feel weak when everything that's happening to him actually makes him feel that way. Many eventually learn to be stoic as their male role dictates, but at a tremendous emotional cost.

As the male child becomes older he may become more successful at controlling his feelings through denial strategies. However, for some males, the feelings remain out of control or become channeled into a severely constricted mode of expression through aggressive acts. By the time the male victim becomes an adult, his method of "coping" with feelings is fully operational and, sadly, usually quite dysfunctional.

Establishing a less dysfunctional approach to one's feelings is a difficult step for most male survivors and may require considerable time and effort. Some males may have their feelings so rigidly over-controlled that they "feel" numb. When the process of therapy or some other emotion breaks the controls, these males may suddenly feel overwhelmed by a flood of feelings. This can be a rather frightening experience for someone who has not actually allowed himself to feel anything since childhood. Others have been overwhelmed with feelings for years and have engaged in a losing battle for control. Still others have all the "unmanly" feelings under "control" but are extremely angry individuals who often act out their angry feelings in inappropriate ways.

Regardless of the method employed by a male victim to cope with feelings, in order to recover he must learn the following about feelings:

1. The cultural belief that real men don't have feelings prevents the normal and healthy ability of all humans, regardless of gender, to experience all sorts of emotions.
2. Having a feeling does not mean you have to act on it.
3. Having a feeling or even lots of feelings does not necessarily mean you are losing control.
4. Share your feelings by talking to someone about how you actually *feel* about something.
5. Learning appropriate expressions of feelings is possible, such as when to laugh, when to cry, and how to confront.
6. Acknowledge that feelings are as real for you as they are for the other guy.
7. Your very strong feelings are most likely connected to your childhood abuse experiences and less likely connected to present experiences. In this regard the male victim must learn to recognize **why** he is so angry, for example, before he can resolve the issues creating the anger. Other feelings such as guilt, fear, depression, and anxiety may also be more strongly connected to the childhood abuse than to present events and must be dealt with accordingly.
8. Feelings can be a normal, natural, and often wonderful part of life.

Mourning Lost Childhood

Most children are allowed and encouraged to engage in activities normally associated with the various childhood developmental stages. Victims of child abuse lose their right to many of these important childhood experiences. While few individuals experience "ideal" childhoods, most people have childhoods with a reasonable amount of those elements deemed necessary for fostering a sense of well-being in a child. Abused children are cheated. They are robbed of nurturing childhood experiences. Their sense of well-being is stripped from them.

While all forms of childhood abuse pervert the "normal" childhood experience, the abuse of sexuality may be one of the most damaging. It is through "normal" childhood physiological and psychological experiences and growth that we learn of ourselves as people with the potential for adult sexual experiences. General sociocultural sanctions against most "normal" childhood sexual thoughts and activities create serious enough barriers to the development of a "healthy" sexual identity without introducing specific abusive events into childhood. The introduction of these events causes the child to lose the opportunity to develop his/her sexuality through the usual childhood experiences. Children are whisked prematurely out of childhood and suddenly thrust into the world of adult sexuality. Few children are prepared for normal childhood sexual experiences much less adult sexual experiences. Once a child is sexualized, the opportunity to learn of sexuality in the "normal" childhood way is lost. Other childhood losses occur as well. Some of the most important losses besides childhood sexuality are trust, security, self-esteem, personal boundaries, healthy social interactions, love, intimacy, control, self-confidence, and childhood playfulness.

Many adults with abuse of sexuality experiences feel the sense of loss and embark on a never-ending search for their lost childhood. It is too late. Childhood experiences occur in childhood. Once lost, they are lost forever. This is a sad reality, but one that victims of child sexual abuse must understand. It is best to mourn the loss and proceed with the recovery process.

For most male survivors, mourning the loss may seem like giving up all hope of finding love, happiness, nurturing and protection, but the opposite is actually the case. By not mourning the lost childhood, the adult will continue to seek those unobtainable experiences rather than seek other experiences which are within reach. The goal here is assisting the male victim to recognize that he cannot return to childhood and recover that which was lost. But he can recover from the loss. He can experience happiness. He can learn to nurture and be nurtured. And he can develop appropriate protective boundaries.

This mourning process is both similar to and different from grieving for other significant losses. It is similar in that the male experiences strong feelings of sadness and despair over the loss itself as well as having no choice but to accept the reality. It is different in that the male also begins to recognize that *he* was not responsible for the lost childhood but someone else actually *stole* his childhood from him. Many males react with strong feelings of anger and threats of acting out against the abuser as the mourning process proceeds. When this occurs the feelings should be acknowledged, and appropriate expressions of them should be discussed and resolved.

Self-Image

Most males who feel damaged by the abuse of sexuality develop a negative self-image. While the "damaged goods" concept is not unique to male victims of childhood sexual abuse, males subjected to incest and/or same-sex molestations seem especially vulnerable to feelings of worthlessness. A major contributing factor is the male victim's belief that he *should have been* able to protect himself. Some male survivors develop such difficult self-images that it is next to impossible to convince them that they have any value at all. Others may admit to a few strengths but otherwise see themselves as generally worthless.

Survival strategies based upon a negative self-appraisal range from complete resignation to a compulsive quest for perfection. Capable male survivors may not attempt to achieve anything worthwhile because they are convinced that they are not capable or worthy of any achievement. Other male survivors cannot stop achieving because they believe that each of their accomplishments is flawed in some way.

Most male survivors reinforce negative self-images with an internal dialogue involving a high frequency of negative evaluative statements. Most survivors tell themselves that they are weak, stupid, incompetent, ugly, unlovable, and sexually unattractive. External indications that their self-appraisals are inaccurate are often received with strong skepticism or rejected completely. Direct attempts by others to correct the male survivor's erroneous perception of himself, therefore, usually meet with little or no success. However, most male survivors are capable of developing a more positive self-image.

The male survivor must be guided toward an understanding of why he has developed a negative self-image and away from his erroneous belief that he actually has no value. Replacing faulty perceptions with accurate information is the key to this process. The faulty perception is that the abuse actually transformed a *worthwhile* person into a *worthless* person. The truth is that while abuse does produce negative effects in the child, the person's worth remains intact.

In many ways the erroneous belief system is both result and perpetuation of the abuse; but now the abuse is self-administered. Like the abuse, the faulty belief system keeps the survivor weak, powerless, and unable to assess his worth accurately. Understanding this process allows the survivor to recognize that the power base actually remained with him even though it had been temporarily breached by the abusive experiences. With repairs he can regain enough power to disband another abuse in his life—his faulty belief system about himself.

Once the male survivor begins to show an understanding of the process of developing a negative self-image as a result of sexually abusive experiences, he can begin decreasing the frequency of negative evaluative statements about himself. This process begins by establishing a heightened awareness of the negative thoughts and a concentrated effort to force the thoughts out of consciousness. While this is a difficult task, most males report successes. In addition, many report a secondary gain of feeling a growing sense of power and control. At some point in the process, negative thoughts should be replaced with positive self-evaluations. Some male survivors can begin this phase early in the overall process, while others need considerable practice in just reducing the frequency of negative thoughts before introducing positive thoughts about themselves.

The next step is to guide the male survivor in altering the behavioral indices of his negative self-image. For example, males with a low frequency of "worthwhile" activities can be encouraged to increase this frequency. Males with a quest for perfection can be encouraged to accept imperfection. These slow changes in behavior will bring positive changes in the survivor's life and clearly demonstrate that what is flawed is his belief system about himself and not himself. He does have the power to correct his beliefs.

Discarding a negative self-image and replacing it with a much more favorable one is a difficult task for most persons. It is especially difficult for survivors of the abuse of sexuality. Throughout the process, the male survivor will require reeducation, cognitive restructuring, thought stopping, encouragement, and patience. The successful completion of the other steps toward recovery also facilitates the development of a positive self-image.

Relationships, Then and Now

When a child is subjected to the abuse of sexuality he is exposed to a perverted example of how people interact with each other. He may learn that personal boundaries mean nothing to others. He may learn that trust only brings pain. He may learn that love is contingent on providing sex. He *does not* learn normal social skills. Instead, he develops strategies which allow him to endure or deal with the abusive experiences. By using these strategies he becomes a survivor rather than just a victim.

While the survival strategies work during childhood, they take their toll during adulthood. This is especially true in the area of prosocial behavior. Few survivors possess an understanding of or the normal skills for healthy interpersonal relationships. Relationships are formed upon unmet childhood needs, misconception about interpersonal relationships, and other strategies developed for survival. When the survivor learns that what seemed to work for a child/victim no longer has much utility for an adult, he is left without resources. Thus, interpersonal relationships tend to be unsatisfying and dysfunctional. Some examples are:

1. *The Rock.* Some survivors are so well insulated that they appear unmoved by anybody. They may have relationships but they seldom form an emotional bond with anyone. Trust is the main issue, as The Rock seldom trusts anybody.

2. *Come close, but not too close.* While some male survivors yearn for the love found in close relationships, they can tolerate only moderate amounts of intimacy before becoming too fearful to continue. The issue here is typically trust. That is, can he really trust this individual not to abuse him? Uncertain, the male survivor will only

allow himself to be somewhat vulnerable; then he will typically engage his protective strategy of not letting people get too close.

3. *Clinging vine.* Some survivors are so desperate for love, affection, and protection that they form extremely dependent relationships with others. They typically expect the most significant person in their lives to provide for all their needs. These unrealistic expectations cannot of course be met, and this type of survivor frequently feels rejected and fearful in relationships.

4. *Sexualized.* For some survivors intimacy and sexual behavior have become so fused that they tend to sexualize all relationships. As children, most of these survivors received what they perceived as intimacy through sexual behavior. They seldom had the opportunity to learn that a close interpersonal relationship was possible without some form of sexual activity. As adults, they introduce sexual behavior into the relationship early on and often develop a compulsive need for sexual contact.

5. *Power and control.* One of the best ways of getting what you want in a relationship is to be powerful and control the other person. Most sexually abused males learn this lesson well as a child victim and then play it out in their relationships as an adult. Sometimes the power is used at moderate levels, but at times it may reach abusive proportions. In this regard, male survivors may be emotionally and/or physically abusive in relationships. Sexually abusing a partner may also become part of the scenario.

6. *Deserving-undeserving.* Some adult male survivors' self-concepts have been so shattered that they believe that they deserved to be abused as a child. They often believe they were to blame for the abuse and deserved no better. As adults they continue to have negative self-concepts and feel incapable and undeserving of healthy relationships. These survivors typically avoid attempting a relationship with a desirable person and often find themselves interacting with undesirable or unsavory characters who will most likely give the survivor what he believes he "deserves," more abuse.

For male survivors to learn how to establish healthy relationships they first must learn how their childhood survival strategies prevent them from doing so. Revealing the connection between the survival strategies and the abuse of sexuality is an important component of this process. Since most of the child victim survival strategies are based upon misinformation and abusive experiences, the adult survivor must also be guided toward a better understanding and an accurate perception of prosocial behavior. Most survivors remain frightened and confused. By starting slowly and working toward relationships one step at a time, most survivors can learn that other, more healthy relationships exist and are within their reach.

As the survivor begins work on interpersonal relationship skills, he should be advised that his current relationships may be impacted in a "negative" way. That is, current relationships based upon old survival strategies may no longer be viable once different and more adaptable skills are learned. This is not to say that all survivors will rid themselves of significant interpersonal relationships as they improve. It does mean that they now have the option of selecting relationships based upon something other than the results of being abused as children.

While a number of therapeutic techniques can be used in this process (e.g., cognitive restructuring, assertiveness training, relaxation, desensitization), the following steps are recommended for most survivors:

1. Recognize the connections between the abuse of sexuality and the misconceptions about yourself and interpersonal relationships.
2. Recognize that most of what worked for a child victim no longer works for an adult survivor.
3. Break misconceptions about relationships and learn accurate information.
4. Learn new survival techniques which incorporate normal social skills.
5. Develop a social support system to help you learn these skills.
6. Allow yourself to explore all reasonable options for relationships.
7. Prepare significant others for possible changes in your interpersonal relationships.
8. Learn to trust someone.
9. Learn to trust yourself.
10. Learn to be vulnerable.
11. Explore your feelings at each step.
12. Be patient.

Confusion About Sexuality

For most males, abuse of sexuality experiences misdirect the otherwise natural development of their sexuality. This creates confusion about sexuality beyond that which would normally be expected. Sometimes the misinformation is so severe that the victim or survivor becomes dysfunctional regarding sexual feelings and behavior. Sexual responses often become confused with anger, power, and even love. Self-esteem, shame, and trust also become so intertwined with sexuality that many male survivors can neither identify their "real" feelings nor understand their sexual responses. This is manifested in a variety of interpersonal and sexual problems. Some may abstain totally from sexual contact. Others become promiscuous. Some may develop inappropriate sexual responses to children and/or nonconsenting adults. All sorts of clinical sexual dysfunctions are reported by male survivors.

The most frequently occurring problem with males victimized by a male is confusion associated with sexual orientation. Our society allows little latitude about same-sex sexual behavior. The message to males is: If you engage in homosexual behaviors, your sexual orientation is suspect. If you enjoyed the experience, you must certainly be homosexual. While some progress is being made in changing society's attitudes towards homosexuality, the prevailing view remains negative. This negative attitude provides little useful information about sexuality in general. It does provide negative misinformation about homosexuality, especially male homosexuality. It is not surprising that male children with abuse of sexuality experiences with adult males develop considerable anxiety and confusion about their gender and sexual orientation.

This confusion may be manifested in homophobic responses such as fears of all men, fears of gay men, and fears of becoming homosexual. These fears are played out in a variety of ways ranging from total avoidance of all male physical contact to overt aggressive acts towards homosexuals. Some males feel compelled to prove their manhood and embark on a never-ending quest to do so. Some male survivors find reassurance that they are not gay by engaging in activities normally associated with masculinity and rejecting activities and ideas even remotely associated with femininity or homosexuality. For example, one male survivor with severe homophobic responses admitted that he had to prove constantly that he was a man because he feared that he would become "queer" like the man who molested him as a child. His fears were heightened because he had experienced some pleasure during the sexual abuse.

Another frequently occurring problem in male survivors is the interaction of sexual responses and intruding thoughts and other feelings. Some males describe being simultaneously drawn to and repelled by sexual activities. They typically do not understand their responses and become increasingly frustrated. As one heterosexual male survivor explained,

> I enjoy meeting women and getting to know them. In the past I have been able to share at least part of myself with women fairly openly until the relationship becomes more intimate. Then I get confused. I want to have sex and even enjoy the act, but for some reason it always scares the hell out of me. Not only that, the more I care for the person the more frightened I become. After a while I find myself becoming destructive in the relationship. Even though I don't want to lose the relationship, I can't seem to stop myself. I don't understand what's going on but I am tired of ruining every relationship once the relationship becomes intimate and sexual.

Whatever form the issue about sexuality takes, most male survivors seem overwhelmed by their feelings and responses. Often they can only acknowledge that "something is wrong" with their sexual feelings and appear unable to identify the problems. While most male survivors may correctly identify their abuse of sexuality as the cause of their confusion, few understand the dynamics of the misdirection of their sexuality created by the abusive experiences. The goal for the therapist, therefore, is to assist in the development of the male survivor's sexuality. Of course, it is easier to effect these "corrections" if implemented soon after the abuse than much later when the misdirection has led the male survivor significantly "off-course." For example, a young male victim may express fears of becoming a homosexual shortly following the abusive experiences, but he may have yet to develop the various dysfunctional homophobic responses often displayed by older male survivors. In addition, the interaction of other feelings with sexual responses may not yet be as strong in younger male victims as that expressed by older survivors.

No one can predict exactly how any male survivor's sexuality would have developed had he not experienced the abuse of sexuality. It is not possible to redirect a male survivor toward a specific outcome based upon a presumed developmental propensity. For example, we cannot assume that a gay male survivor would not have become gay had he not been molested by a male. Many paths to homosexuality exist, and a therapist should not automatically assume that the abusive experiences misdirected the male survivor toward homosexuality. In this case, it would be a serious error to effect a correction by attempting to redirect a gay survivor's sexuality toward heterosexuality. However, it is important for the therapist to assist the survivor in identifying problem areas and then guide him toward options for sexuality the survivor never recognized before. In this way the survivor can select a direction for his sexuality based upon a clearer understanding of sexuality in general and his own sexuality specifically. This strategy provides a stronger foundation for decision making than misinformation and confusion.

Regardless of the nature of the male survivor's confusion about sexuality, the following approach can be helpful:

1. Explore sexuality issues openly and honestly.
2. Identify dysfunctional responses.
3. Present accurate information about the development of sexuality.
4. Identify and examine connections between the abuse of sexuality and the male survivor's confusion and dysfunctional responses.
5. Assist the survivor in breaking the connections by exploring alternative and less destructive responses.
6. Emphasize that the survivor has many options still available to him.

From Victim to Victimizer?

Many perpetrators of the abuse of sexuality have been sexually abused themselves. While the connection between victimization as a child and perpetration as an older child, adolescent, or adult can sometimes be made, this connection is not clearly understood. One aspect is clear: Not all victims become perpetrators. In fact, the majority of survivors are not offenders, and they tend to be very vocal about being categorized with perpetrators of sexual offenses. This is not to say that the issue of future perpetration should not be addressed in therapy with survivors. In fact, some survivors enter therapy as a result of fears associated with losing control over a sexual attraction to children, even though they have never acted out any of their urges. Others may simply express a concern that their personal victimization experiences may propel them toward inappropriate sexual expressions in the future.

The therapist must be prepared to handle these issues. The first step is to evaluate the probability of the survivor becoming an offender. Again, most survivors will have no history of deviant sexual urges towards children or rape fantasies about adults. For these cases the probability of offending appears rather low and need not become a focus of treatment. However, for those survivors who report deviant urges or fantasies, the probability of offending increases and must become one of the major foci in the overall therapy program. (Specific techniques for evaluating and treating deviant sexual urges toward children are described in Chapters 5 and 6.) Supportive work with reassurance that the probability of offending is low can be offered to survivors who are concerned but show no signs of inappropriate sexual responses to children or others.

Confronting the Abuser

At some point in the recovery process, most male victims or survivors express a desire to confront their abusers. In cases of incest, many therapists encourage confrontation because it is a form of breaking the silence and could provide the victim or survivor with a needed sense of power and control. While confrontation appears a good idea, confronting one's abuser directly can be very risky. Confrontations of any type may not always produce positive results. Poorly planned and executed confrontations can often result in additional trauma for the victim or survivor. When addressing the issue of confrontations, therapists must be mindful that a confrontation may be helpful to some but not absolutely necessary for a successful recovery.

Survivors who have waited years to break the silence may feel, for a number of reasons, that they need to confront their abuser. More often than not these reasons are ill-conceived and, if acted upon, could produce negative consequences for the survivor. Some of the more common inappropriate reasons to confront are:

1. The survivor feels pressure from others such as family members, therapists, and members of a group to confront (they believe confrontation will help in or is necessary for his recovery).
2. The survivor wants to harm the abuser physically.

3. Confrontation is seen as a way the survivor can prove he is a "real" man after all.
4. The survivor believes confrontation will magically transform the abuser into an understanding and caring parental figure.
5. The survivor believes confrontation is the only method to resolve his angry feelings toward the abuser.
6. The survivor believes that confrontation will be the magical cure for all his emotional problems.

Therapist and survivor must address a number of issues carefully before reaching a decision about confronting the perpetrator. First, therapist and survivor must both understand and agree that confrontation is not for the purposes of expressing anger or convincing the perpetrator that his or her actions were harmful. For example, one very angry survivor insisted, "I want to confront the bastard so he will know what he did to me. I want him to understand and feel my pain." Goals such as these are seldom achieved by any means because most perpetrators are neither willing nor able to feel the way survivors want them to feel. And the survivor's anger usually does not diminish following angry exchanges between the survivor and abuser. To allow or encourage a survivor to confront his abuser for those purposes increases the possibilities for failure and increases the probability of his being subjected to additional abusive experiences.

Confrontation must occur from a position of emotional strength and control. In most cases, the survivor should have successfully accomplished most of the steps described in this chapter before confronting his perpetrator. By so doing the survivor has overcome most of the problems associated with the abuse and has learned that he requires nothing from the abuser in order to complete his recovery. The survivor has also gained strength and power far beyond that used by his abuser. Confrontation, therefore, becomes a showcase for this emotional strength, power, and control rather than an expression of angry feelings based upon a need for acknowledgment and an apology.

Once a survivor and his therapist decide that a confrontation is appropriate, consideration must be given to the type of confrontation to be used. While most survivors express a preference for a face-to-face confrontation with their abusers, others seem satisfied and more comfortable using a less direct method. Direct confrontations may not be possible for some survivors due to a number of factors, including the death of the perpetrator. Each method should be examined carefully for logistics and risk factors, and especially for the potential benefits to the survivor. To assist in this process, several methods of confrontation are discussed next.

Direct confrontation. A face-to-face confrontation poses the greatest risk of a potentially harmful outcome for the survivor. This is an encounter with someone who has shown the ability to manipulate and harm another person. For most perpetrators it matters little that their former victims are no longer children; their responses may simply continue to be abusive in some way. Therefore, great care must be taken in order to assure the physical safety and psychological well-being of the survivor during the confrontation. Three areas are of particular importance:

1. Preparing the agenda
2. Selecting the setting
3. Establishing realistic expectations regarding the perpetrator's responses

Preparing the agenda. Survivors must be certain of their goals for confronting and establish an "agenda" accordingly. Goals must be realistic and based upon a position of emotional strength. While it is not a good idea for confrontations to be just a means of expressing anger, it is unlikely that many survivors will not be able to include this as one aspect of their agenda. It must be made clear that angry confrontations resulting in arguments and/or physical altercations seldom prove beneficial to the survivor. While presentations are usually idiosyncratic based upon each survivor's needs and style, some themes emerge more frequently than others. Often survivors open with a factual description of their abuse. They want the perpetrator to hear the truth about the abuse as seen through the victim's eyes, not the perpetrator's. An outpouring of feelings about the abuse and the perpetrator often follows. The survivor may then explain his past unusual or dysfunctional behavior by drawing connections between those events and the abuse. A show of strength is then presented by most survivors which usually includes a statement about their ability to survive the abuse and the success they have had working towards recovery. Most survivors simplify their feelings of emotional strength and self-confidence by ending with a strong affirmation that they will no longer allow themselves to be abused in any way by the perpetrator, or anybody else for that matter.

Once an agenda has been planned, the survivor will need assistance in practicing the actual presentation. Role playing, visual imagery, and rehearsing will be helpful. Best-case and worst-case scenarios should be used in the practice sessions so the survivor will be prepared for whatever may occur. Of particular importance is increasing the survivor's skills in "keeping on track" with his presentation regardless of the perpetrator's responses.

Selecting the setting. The survivor's physical safety is the primary concern in selecting a place for a face-to-face confrontation. Under no circumstances should the survivor meet the abuser alone. While it may not be feasible for another individual to be next to the survivor during the actual confrontation, this person or persons should be nearby and within sight at all times. Persons selected to accompany the survivor should be trusted individuals who are knowledgeable about the perpetrator's abusive relationship with the survivor. They must also be willing and able to act on the survivor's behalf in case the survivor's safety is compromised.

It is never a good idea to meet a perpetrator on his or her own turf. Meeting on the survivor's turf is also a bad idea because the perpetrator's presence in the survivor's living environment may feel like a violation of his "safety zone." Choosing a neutral site is best. The meeting place should be reasonably comfortable for the survivor, with easily accessible escape routes. Each survivor will have his own feelings about what constitutes a safe meeting place, and the setting for the confrontation must be selected according to his criteria and not the perpetrator's.

Establishing realistic expectations regarding the perpetrator's responses. While the survivor may be optimistic about the outcome, he may find that his abuser will react in a different and more negative way from what he expected or desired. Thus, the survivor must prepare himself for a number of undesirable responses from the abuser. At the very least the survivor must be well-prepared to deal with the following likely responses during a confrontation with his abuser:

1. *Denial, denial, and more denial.* Denial may come in just about any form, but it usually ranges from total denial that "anything"

ever happened to acknowledging that "something" might have happened but it must have been somebody else who did it. Survivors must remember that abusers still cling to the cloak of secrecy and they will use whatever methods necessary to maintain the secret. Denial is one of the abuser's most potent weapons against the survivor's attack on the secret. The survivor must also remember that at least two people share the secret, the abuser and the abused. Even though the abuser is denying, the survivor knows the truth. Truth is power.

2. *Admission without remorse.* When confronted, some abusers may admit that the abuse occurred but will neither assume responsibility nor express regret. This stance clearly reflects abusers' unsympathetic and uncaring attitudes about the suffering of others, even the suffering and pain inflicted on children by themselves. The survivor must remember that this type of abuser is an angry, weak, and dysfunctional person who is incapable of empathy. To expect anything remotely resembling a caring feeling is unrealistic.

3. *Admission with accusations.* A favorite ploy by abusers when confronted is to admit that sexual activity occurred but then place the blame on the survivor. This technique is just a manifestation of the rationale used by the abuser to justify his or her acts. For example, if a child is seductive and sexy he must want sex, right? And if he wants sex he must enjoy it, right? And, therefore, the abuser is only providing what the child wanted anyway, right? The survivor must remember that the correct answers to these questions are: wrong! wrong! and wrong! There is never a justification for an adult to engage a child in adult sexual activity.

4. *Admission with perpetuation.* Incredibly, some abusers see the confrontation as an opportunity to convince the survivor that they should resume their sexual relationship. Sometimes the abuser will romanticize the abuse and suggest it can "again" be wonderful for both. Other abusers may resort to threats and attempted rape. At any rate, the abuser is only interested in perpetuating the abuse, and the survivor must be prepared for the possibility of additional victimization.

5. *Admission with manipulation.* While some abusers appear to express regret and remorse when confronted, they often do so to manipulate the survivor into maintaining the secret. Their apology may seem genuine at first, but soon abusers are again suggesting that the survivor should not tell others because there is no reason to disrupt other persons' lives. Or they may ask for forgiveness and then add a request for the survivor to forget about the abuse. The

survivor must be prepared to recognize the manipulation and not fall prey to it. Regardless of the abuser's tactics, the survivor must remain on track and not be swayed from his goals for the confrontation. Anything less may allow the abuser to maintain his or her control over the survivor.

6. *Admission with minimization.* Some abusers will readily admit to the sexual activities but will attempt to minimize the harmful effects. Again, the survivor knows the truth and only he knows how harmful the abuse was to him. The abuser protects himself by believing that the abuse was not really abusive. Regardless of the survivor's confrontation, many abusers will most likely not acknowledge anything other than minimal negative impact.

What happens if the abuser admits to the abuse, acknowledges the harm, and sincerely apologizes? This is a survivor's dream. It rarely happens. When it does, a survivor must remain on track with his recovery plan. It would be a mistake to rush into a "let's let bygones be bygones" alliance with the abuser during or immediately following the confrontation. Pacing and patience are important. The survivor will need time to process the event. He will need help in determining if the perpetrator's response was genuine or another clever manipulation. If found to be genuine, the survivor will need help deciding what *he,* not the abuser, needs from the abuser now. He entered the confrontation with strength and he can continue to use his strength to sort through the various options now available. He must always be mindful that the next step must be in *his* best interest and not the abuser's.

Symbolic confrontation. While some survivors feel the only effective way of confronting their abuser is through a face-to-face encounter, other types of confrontation may serve the same purpose without the risk. For example, within therapy sessions, the survivor and therapist or other group members can role-play a face-to-face confrontation with the perpetrator. This process serves two purposes. First, the survivor's pent-up feelings about his abuse and the abuser may find an expression that is beneficial enough so that the survivor no longer feels a need to confront his perpetrator directly. Second, the role-playing can be used as a rehearsal for direct confrontation. By practicing the face-to-face confrontation, the survivor will be better prepared for the encounter.

Another form of symbolic confrontation is letter writing. Letters can be written to the abuser or other individuals. Some letter writing episodes produce short stories, and even poetry. Whether these documents are ever actually mailed or presented to the perpetrator or others is less important than the process itself. Through writing, the survivor has the opportunity to explore and express his feelings about the abuse, the abuser, and himself as a survivor. These documents also can be helpful in planning an actual face-to-face confrontation or as a guide for the survivor while confronting his abuser directly. Other forms of symbolic confrontations include visits to the place where the abuse occurred and graveside confrontation if the abuser is deceased. By returning to the place where the abuse took place, the survivor can symbolically talk to the abuser, telling him or her how the survivor felt while being victimized. In this way the survivor will be able to say the words in the place where he was too frightened to say them as a child. He can tell his perpetrator about the fear, the pain, the loss of trust, and the anger. He can place the responsibility of the abuse where it belongs, with the abuser.

If the perpetrator dies before any form of confrontation has occurred, the survivor is often left with conflicting feelings. At first, he may feel a sense of relief that his abuser is out of his life forever. He may also feel glad that the abuser finally "got what he deserved." But he may also feel a sense of unfinished business. A need to resolve his feelings about the abuse and the abuser through a confrontation remains. A graveside confrontation may be helpful. A survivor can visit his abuser's grave and symbolically confront him or her. He can talk to his perpetrator in the same way he would if confronting him or her directly. Sometimes, survivors leave their written products at the grave as well.

Legal confrontation. In most places child sexual abuse is a criminal act, and perpetrators can be prosecuted and punished. Some survivors have been successful in gaining restitution through civil lawsuits. But the act of confronting the abuser through some type of legal action carries with it considerable risk for the survivor. Survivors are like most people who trust the system to do what is fair and just. However, the system seldom meets the survivor's full expectations for justice and can be abusive itself. If a survivor is considering some legal action against his perpetrator, he must be prepared to deal with a sometimes costly, often lengthy, frequently abusive, and seldom satisfying outcome. Many of the negative responses that come from abusers when they are confronted directly will occur in a legal action. Not only will the abuser respond in a negative manner, but his or her attorney will also appear abusive. This is not to say that the survivor should never utilize the legal system when appropriate to do so, but the survivor must be prepared for the potentially damaging events to follow.

Confronting others. In some cases of the abuse of sexuality, individuals other than the perpetrator allow the abuse to occur by not responding appropriately to the child's implicit or explicit calls for help. When this occurs, the survivor often harbors deep-seated feelings of anger and resentment toward the nonprotecting or neglectful persons. Some survivors feel they need to confront these individuals as well as their abusers. While these ancillary persons are not perpetrators, their responses to a confrontation are often the same as those of perpetrators. They have a stake in not being held responsible for someone else's inappropriate actions and often respond in a defensive and hostile manner. In fact, the survivor must be prepared for the various denial and minimization responses discussed in this section before deciding to confront others.

Confrontation by others. In some cases, significant persons in the survivor's life may decide to "take matters in their own hands" and confront the perpetrator themselves. This is seldom a good idea unless the survivor is actually prepared for a confrontation himself. While these supportive persons may believe they are helping the survivor, the results of such a confrontation may actually be harmful to the survivor. For example, he may not yet be emotionally strong enough to cope with the almost inevitable denial responses to follow. These responses place him in a vulnerable position for additional trauma. He may not need to confront his abuser in order to recover fully, and an outside confrontation can become an intrusion in the recovery process. Typically, confrontations by others only serve those who are confronting. They seldom provide any benefit for the survivor unless he is ready for a confrontation himself *and* agrees to the confrontation by others.

The Path to Recovery for Male Children

Sexually abused male children also face a recovery process once disclosure of the abuse is made. While the path to recovery may be somewhat different for children from what it is for adults, similarities do exist. The major differences occur as a function of the length of time between the abuse and the beginning of treatment. For adult males, the lengthy interval between the abuse of sexuality and breaking the silence allows for years of maladaptive beliefs and affective responses, and for behavior to become reinforced and integrated into an overall life-style. For younger males, the shorter interval precludes years of reinforcement, but the maladaptive responses and strategies are in place and developing. Without disclosure and intervention, the younger male victim stands a good chance of becoming an adult survivor facing a more difficult path to recovery. Overall, however, impact and treatment issues associated with adults and children with abuse of sexuality histories are quite similar. For example, Porter, Blick, and Sgroi (1982) identify the following impact and treatment issues "likely to affect all children who have been sexually abused, regardless of the identity of the perpetrator" (p. 109):

1. "Damaged Goods" syndrome
2. Guilt
3. Fear
4. Depression
5. Low self-esteem and poor social skills

Also identified by Porter et al. are the following impact and treatment issues "more likely to affect intrafamily child-sexual-abuse victims" (p. 109):

1. Repressed anger and hostility
2. Impaired ability to trust
3. Blurred role boundaries and role confusion
4. Pseudomaturity coupled with failure to accomplish developmental tasks
5. Self-mastery and control

Most of these issues remain problematic for the adult male if left untreated.

While most children find sexual abuse traumatic, not all children respond in the same manner. As a general set of rules, children from stable environments and positive family conditions experience less trauma. Abuses repeated many times over a long period appear more destructive. Feelings of shame and revulsion do appear to be nearly universal. A not so general rule, but one that requires knowing, is that the incest experience during adolescence can be particularly traumatic due to the teenager's heightened awareness of the "wrongness" of the event and the disruption of identity formation and peer group identification tasks (Kempe & Kempe, 1984).

The out-of-home sexual assault is a special case. This is almost always totally unexpected. Threat or use of force is often involved. No matter the sex of the victim, the act is one of complete dominance over a powerless child. With the male child this can result in self-esteem and masculinity doubts. This is also the first step in the child's beginning to question whether he, not the perpetrator, is "normal" (Kempe & Kempe, 1984). The clinician must also remember that the child is not acting in isolation. Even as he is feeling a loss, so are his parents. In fact the parental response is often more extreme than that of the child. The parental alarm and disproportionate intensity (e.g., need to get the situation "fixed" and put it behind the family) are very destructive. Parental reactions reveal feelings of disbelief, embarrassment, anger, fear, grief and guilt. There is a normal urge to "get" the perpetrator. Stable families work through such events, and identifications by the child with the parent's intensity are minimized. In the chaotic family, however, this parental overresponsiveness becomes the motivating force for and reason behind all family operations; this overreaction destroys the child's hope of putting the event in his or her past (Goodwin, 1982).

In essence, parental crisis mirrors the child's crisis and builds upon it. In a sense, the parental and child traumas feed upon one another. The child's sense of being overwhelmed is more critical if the parents are unable to move beyond their own crisis. It is, as DeFrancis noted (1969), an experience in which the parents are also assaulted. They feel threatened. They feel shame and guilt. Their personal self-esteem is lowered. They are anxious and fearful about what will be said about their family and their ability to protect. In the worst case, the parent who does not know how to help becomes frustrated and angry at the child victim: angry for "getting yourself into a situation in which such a thing could happen!" (DeFrancis, 1969, p. 3). The minimal treatment, then, is to provide an atmosphere in which the whole family can come to understand why sexual assault sometimes occurs and how it can be prevented from happening again (Mrazek, 1980). Beyond that, therapeutic intervention will be as different as are families and victims.

While a number of impact issues common to male and female children have been identified (Porter, Blick, & Sgroi, 1982), most treatment programs have been developed with strong ties to female impact issues associated with the father-daughter incest model. Few programs or techniques have been developed specifically for sexually abused male children. Most treatment programs which include males seem to be based upon a generic case management approach consisting of identification, crisis intervention, assessment, family therapy, group therapy, play therapy, and arts therapy (Blick & Porter, 1982; Kempe & Kempe, 1984; Naitove, 1982; Sgroi, 1978).

While most treatment programs for sexually abused children are designed for either gender, at least one exception is reported. Porter (1986) describes an overall treatment philosophy and approach he uses with young male victims of sexual assault. He recommends peer group and family therapy as the preferred and strongest treatment modalities. Individual therapy is thought by Porter to be too threatening, especially if the therapist is a male and the child was molested by a male. He also recommends that the peer group be conducted by two therapists, a male and female.

Most treatment techniques used with sexually abused male children and adolescents include group therapy (various forms), family therapy, and individual therapy. Within individual therapy, play therapy and arts therapy seem to be the preferred treatment techniques. These approaches appear to reflect a therapeutic focus on the sexual abuse itself (victimization) and on how "each child must ventilate his or her feelings about the sexual trauma in relation to: guilt and shame; positive and negative feelings toward the perpetrator; positive and negative feelings toward the nonoffending parent; feelings about the reaction of siblings; feelings about the reaction of peers and people in the community" (Porter et al., 1982, pp. 128–129). Clearly, the primary message to the child is something like this: You are a sexually abused child and you have been traumatized by this abuse. You are not responsible for your abuse, but it is vitally important that you learn to discuss the details of the abuse and then express and accept your feelings about the sexual abuse and what has happened to you since.

It is not surprising that techniques designed to foster the expression and acceptance of *feelings* associated with being a *victim* have been the mainstay of treatment plans for sexually abused young children. Interestingly, an integral part of this therapeutic approach is having the child "work through" the trauma by revealing details of the traumatic events through verbal expressions or play therapy. Yet Terr (1983) has reported that reenactment of traumatic events in play therapy does not necessarily reduce a child's anxiety associated with the event.

While we support the concept that treatment plans for the sexually abused child must include a process whereby the child can learn to express and accept his feelings about his sexual abuse, the focus of treatment should not remain on emotional responses only and the expression thereof. Wheeler and Berliner (1988) offer a somewhat different theoretical analysis of child sexual abuse and recommendations for treatment. They posit that " . . . the effects of child sexual abuse can be understood as a combination of classically conditioned responses to traumatic stress and socially learned behavioral and cognitive responses to the abuse experience" (p. 227). This analysis explains affective symptomatology, especially anxiety, as a result of pairing fear with the abuser. While the initial responses of fear and anxiety may be adaptive, they become maladaptive through the process of generalization and higher-order conditioning. For example, fear of a female abuser may generalize over time to fear of all females. Further, social learning processes mediate what the child learns from the abuse experience. Through modeling, cues and reinforcement, children develop concepts about themselves, others, and sexuality. Behavioral indices of these concepts are also learned. Treatment strategies should include, therefore, techniques for altering the maladaptive conditioned and socially acquired affective, cognitive and behavioral responses to the sexual abuse experience. Clinical experience supports this analysis, and we recommend that treatment strategies for male children be organized around the following multidimensional issues:

1. Beliefs and attitudes
2. Affective responses
3. Behavioral responses

Beliefs and Attitudes

During the normal developmental processes, children learn about themselves, others, and the world they share with others. If allowed to develop normally with the assistance of an adequate amount of nurturing, most children will form positive self-concepts, learn to trust others, and discover that the world is a reasonably safe and generally predictable place to live. These are reasonable beliefs and attitudes shared by most persons. The early introduction of adult sexuality interferes with this process and often produces beliefs and attitudes not shared with most persons. If left to grow, this belief system expands and produces maladaptive responses. It is the role of the therapist to identify and alter the child's erroneous beliefs and attitudes created as a function of the abuse of sexuality. The following areas are especially vulnerable to distorted beliefs and attitudes:

1. Responsibility for the abuse
2. Trust
3. Self-image and competency

Responsibility for the abuse. Many factors contribute to children erroneously believing that they are responsible for the abuse. Of particular importance for male victims is the culturally transmitted belief that males are expected to protect themselves; if they do not, "then they get what they deserve." Therapists treating young male victims of sexual abuse should emphasize that young males are also children, and children, even male children, cannot always be expected to protect themselves from adults who are more powerful and have greater skills at manipulating others. It is also helpful to explain why some adults become sexual with children. The explanation must be factual and informative rather than an overgeneralized statement. For example, it is usually not very helpful to the child if he is simply told that the abuser is "sick" or "perverted" because too little information is provided about how this "sickness" produced the sexual abuse. Offering an explanation containing ideas associated with the concept that some adults want to have sex with children even when they know they shouldn't helps the child understand that the abuser may have a problem but that the abuse is still the abuser's responsibility, not the child's.

In cases of incest, "apology" sessions can be helpful in resolving issues associated with responsibility. If the young victim is adequately prepared by his therapist, and, indeed, the abuser acknowledges the abuse, assumes responsibility, and assures the child that no further abuse will occur, the victim can gain considerable benefit from this type of confrontation. However, young victims are often forced into a premature confrontation with their abusers due to family pressures, an overzealous therapist, or legal requirements. In these cases, the risk for additional trauma to the victim is high. The reader is directed to the section in this volume describing confrontations for a complete discussion of the confrontational process.

Trust. Rebuilding trust with sexually abused children is difficult and may require considerable time. A good place to start is to teach children how to discriminate the untrustworthy (e.g., the actual abuser and others like him or her) from the trustworthy (e.g., the nonoffending parent, the therapist, and the other significant persons in the child's life). By assigning responsibility to the abuser in the manner just described, the child can begin to learn that *some* but not *all* adults are interested in sexual activity with children. Using the abuse experience as an example, the child can also develop skills to detect cues from persons who may be potential abusers. In this way the child not only learns that most people can be trusted, but he can also trust himself to protect himself from those few untrustworthy individuals.

Through the therapeutic relationship, the child will begin to trust again. It is important therefore that the therapist be a reliable and trustworthy person for the child. A breach of trust at this level could prove most damaging to a child. The child should also be encouraged to begin reciprocal relationships with other significant persons (e.g., teachers, relatives, coaches). If these individuals respond to the child in the usual adult-child manner, the child will begin to develop trust, improve interpersonal relationship skills, and also improve his self-concept.

Self-image and competency. Sexually abused children often develop poor self-concepts and feel incompetent. This is especially true of male children sexually abused by male adults. It seems as though their whole concept of themselves as strong and competent males is shattered by the abuse. A more positive self-image can be enhanced by providing male children with the opportunity to learn and demonstrate competency skills. The focus here is on the child's knowledge and skills, and not on his role as a victim.

Through play and other related therapeutic procedures, interpersonal relationship skills and coping skills can be modeled, cued and reinforced. Showing the male child how to be a victor again rather than a victim fits nicely into his expectations of a male. However, it is important to provide guidance for appropriate skills and not just reinforcement for any response that appears "strong and masculine." Many of the strong and masculine responses tend to be maladaptive and should be molded into more appropriate responses. For example, a male does not have to "kill his attacker" in reenactment scenes in order to learn how to protect himself from future attacks. He can learn to use other resources such as telling someone or identifying and avoiding potential abusers or high risk situations.

Young males often need reassurance that the sexual abuse from a male does not indicate that they are homosexual. Of particular concern here will be males who admit that they received some pleasure from the sexual contact. Having pleasure in a "homosexual" way is very confusing for male children and creates doubts about their masculinity. Again, ascribing the abuse to the abuser and not to the child is helpful here. The male child needs to learn that the abuse had nothing to do with his sexuality and that he will not necessarily be thrust into homosexuality because of the experience.

Affective Responses

Most sexually abused children respond with fear, anxiety, and anger. Feelings of grief are also common in cases involving the loss of a significant person such as an abusing parent. While these and other feelings are considered normal and adaptive responses to the abuse experience, these same responses become the roots for future maladaptive responses. For example, fear and anxiety may increase and generalize well beyond the abuser and the abuse experience, unresolved angry feelings can produce a generally hostile and negative person, and grief will often turn to depression and despair.

Fear and anxiety. Fear and anxiety can be seen as conditioned responses to the cues associated with the abuse experience, as well as responses to other cues through generalization. Effective treatment strategies, therefore, should include techniques for reducing anxiety in general and neutralizing the cues' power to elicit the anxiety response in particular. This approach requires some form of gradual exposure of the feared situation to the child while the child learns not to be anxious. For example, with play objects such as dolls or puppets, a child can be directed through a gradual re-enactment of the abuse experiences. The child is encouraged to discuss his thoughts and feelings about the events while the therapist models appropriate responses for the child. As the child produces approximations to the modeled responses, the therapist provides additional guidance and positive feedback. In this way the child learns to master his feelings of anxiety through a gradual desensitization of anxiety arousal cues, and by producing competing appropriate responses. (A similar play therapy procedure for abused/neglected children is described by Reams and Friedrich, 1985.) Specific anxiety reduction techniques such as relaxation training and systematic desensitization are described in detail in Chapter 6 of this volume.

While most children respond favorably to anxiety reduction techniques, some males will resist participating because they have to *admit* to being afraid. As a general rule, the older male child may appear more resistant than the younger. This seems to be a function of the older male's greater awareness of the cultural taboos against males showing fear. However, a sensitive clinician should also be able to desensitize gradually this fear of showing fear.

Anger. Often, sexually abused children have no safe place to express their anger because their abuser has not allowed the child to express any negative feelings about the sexual activities. In addition, parents and other adults tend to discourage direct expressions of anger from a child. Abused children often repress their anger and have few, if any, means of expressing it appropriately. Providing a safe environment where the child is allowed and encouraged to express his feelings is an important step in eventually teaching abused children to manage their angry feelings in constructive ways. Note that the expression of feelings is only one step in this process and not the major goal of therapy. Children should be taught the following regarding their angry feelings:

1. Their feelings are a normal outcome of the abuse.
2. They are not bad because they are angry.
3. It is OK to be mad at somebody who hurts you.
4. To be angry doesn't mean you have to hurt someone to feel better.

5. Learn to recognize when you are getting mad (e.g., tense, stomach upset, confused).
6. Learn constructive ways of venting anger (e.g., symbolic confrontation with abuser, producing stories, poems, pictures, helping other children learn to protect themselves).

Anger management techniques are especially important for sexually abused male children because they tend to express their anger in aggressive and often inappropriate ways. Research described elsewhere in this volume supports our clinical observation that males tend to externalize their angry feelings more than do females. This translates into inappropriate verbal and behavioral responses which often create additional problems for the male child.

Grief. Two types of grief are often encountered with sexually abused children: grief over the loss of an important relationship such as when the abuser was a parent or other trusted and loved individual, and grief over the loss of childhood experiences. While most children experience grief over the loss of an important relationship, older children and adolescents—understandably—appear to grieve more about their lost childhood than do younger children.

Grief associated with the loss of an important relationship often confuses sexually abused children because they often have a competing angry response as well. The therapist should accept the child's feelings and explain how he can be both grieving for the abuser and angry at him or her at the same time. Once the child understands this concept, then he can proceed to a "normal" grieving process. That is, he will be given an early introduction into how we all feel when we lose a loved one and how we begin to accept the loss and adapt to the absence of the person.

Grief associated with losing one's childhood experiences can be handled by the therapist in a manner similar to that described for adult males in this chapter.

Behavioral Responses

Sexually abused males tend to display more inappropriate behavior such as aggression and sexual acting out than do abused females. If left untreated, these behaviors can develop into a seriously dysfunctional pattern of "coping" with the abuse experience. However, inappropriate sexual behaviors can be modified by correcting the child's beliefs about sexual behavior, increasing the child's self-control skills, and shaping more appropriate and adaptable skills. The following outlines this general approach:

1. Provide age-appropriate sex education.
2. Correct misconceptions and faulty beliefs when expressed by the child, then provide the appropriate information.
3. Discourage and redirect the child's inappropriate sexual interest in the therapist and others (e.g., a male child is not permitted to fondle the therapist or other children. He is not punished for the behavior but told that the behavior is unacceptable and redirected to a more acceptable means of relating).
4. The therapist focuses on and reinforces nonsexual approaches to others.
5. The child is given guidance relating to sexual urges and the appropriate expression thereof (e.g., children are not allowed to masturbate in public simply because it feels good but are counseled that masturbation in private is a more acceptable behavior).
6. Parents are trained to respond in a reinforcing manner to appropriate expressions of sexuality by the child. Parents are also trained to redirect inappropriate expressions to more appropriate behaviors.

With older children, more cognitive self-control measures can be used such as learning how to identify the cues leading to inappropriate behavior, using a self-control internal dialogue (e.g., "I know if I do this it will lead to something worse. I need to stop now or I will be in deep trouble. I can stop and I will stop. STOP! STOP! STOP!"), and developing alternative behaviors which will prevent the inappropriate behavior (e.g., walking away, asking for help).

While most survivors appear to respond well to the overall therapeutic approach just described, many require additional treatment for specific dysfunctions. Effective treatment procedures for various dysfunctions exhibited by victims and survivors of the abuse of sexuality are described next.

5

Beyond the Path to Recovery

The Need for a Systematic Multi-Remedial Approach

More than 250 conceptually distinct approaches to psychotherapy are now available (Parloff, 1980). Psychotherapy theories are proliferating at the rate of over 13 each year (Beutler, 1983). Few of these new therapeutic approaches to psychotherapy appear to address the therapeutic needs of the male sexual abuse victim directly. Although few techniques, beyond those described in the previous chapter, have been developed specifically for male sexual abuse victims, techniques are available to treat problems experienced by male victims generally. The demand is to accommodate these therapies to the needs of the male victim or survivor.

Except for the source of the emotional problems and personal victimization issues, male victims of the abuse of sexuality present emotional and behavioral problems common to other males who enter psychotherapy. It seems reasonable to assert that if techniques exist for the successful treatment of these disorders, male sexual abuse victims will also respond favorably. It is our experience that a therapeutic focus on personal victimization issues alone will not ameliorate the array of dysfunctions experienced by many male sexual abuse victims or survivors. For example, through insight-oriented therapy, a male survivor may learn to recognize the connections between personal victimization and his anger, anxiety, and poor self-esteem. But, insight alone seldom changes deviant arousal patterns, sexual dysfunctions, or poor heterosocial skills, frequent dysfunctional outcomes of childhood sexual abuse. It has been our experience that utilizing a variety of approaches facilitates the overall recovery process for most male victims and survivors of sexually abusive childhood experiences.

Male sexual abuse victims present a multidimensional clinical challenge (Berliner & Wheeler, 1987). It is unlikely that any single theoretical/therapeutic approach will capture the emotional, cognitive and behavioral dysfunctions typically encountered clinically. We are proposing, therefore, a Systematic Multi-Remedial Evaluation and Treatment model which includes techniques associated with the path to recovery from the abuse of sexuality but also includes a number of other techniques found effective in treating males with similar emotional problems. This model presupposes no alliance with any particular theory but, rather, draws from a broad range of theoretical and therapeutic orientations. Through this process, treatment plans can be individualized and will incorporate the therapeutic methods necessary for promoting directed changes in each case.

A multidimensional therapeutic model is not a new concept. Lazarus (1971, 1976) has stressed the importance of comprehensive treatment planning. In his "multimodal" model, he proposes that ". . . durable results are in direct proportion to the number of specific modalities deliberately invoked by any therapeutic system" (p. 13).

A similar multidimensional approach is implied in Beutler's view (1983) that psychotherapy must be redefined as "a specific procedure directed at specific ends among distinct populations. This is *systematic eclectic psychotherapy*" (p. 8). Within this formulation Beutler stresses the importance of "identifying the patient, therapist, and therapeutic characteristics which facilitate patient growth and development" (p. 8). Finally, within the area of adolescent and adult sex offender treatment, an "eclectic" or multidimensional approach has naturally evolved over the past several years. Sex offender treatment programs typically are rich with a variety of treatment techniques with roots in nearly all theoretical orientations, although behavioral and cognitive-behavioral approaches predominate. Drawing from these approaches, we offer a Systematic Multi-Remedial Evaluation and Treatment model. This model consists of four overlapping processes:

1. *Multi-remedial evaluation.* Selecting from a wide variety of evaluation techniques, the clinician obtains comprehensive information along several dimensions, such as personal/developmental/sexual history, abuse of sexuality history, knowledge and attitudes regarding sexuality, areas of dysfunction, areas of strengths, support systems, and personal victimization issues. It should be noted that while the evaluation process initiates the treatment plan, evaluation remains an integral aspect throughout the treatment process.
2. *Formulating the treatment plan.* Based upon the detailed information gathered through the evaluation process, the therapist selects therapeutic methods which appear to be the most effective for the patient's dysfunctions and overall level of functioning.
3. *Explanation and implementation of the treatment plan.* The overall treatment plan, including the path to recovery and the rationale for each additional procedure, is explained in detail to the survivor. Realistic expectations of treatment are also discussed. While this step facilitates the treatment process for adolescents and adults, it may not be necessary or appropriate for the younger male.
4. *Reevaluation and modifications.* While the initial treatment plan may appear to be the best approach, ongoing evaluation information may suggest that modifications are needed. Adjustments in the treatment plan should be made accordingly.

What follows in this chapter is a catalog of therapeutic methods which either have been shown effective in or appear particularly well-suited for the treatment of the emotional, sexual, cognitive, educational, or behavioral problems experienced by most male victims or survivors of childhood sexual abuse. This listing is presented to assist therapists in selecting additional treatment techniques beyond those normally employed in the path to recovery. A combination of the approaches described in Chapter 4 with specific techniques described in this chapter can produce an effective and efficient multi-remedial treatment plan. Treatment issues and techniques are summarized in Table 5.1. In Chapter 6, a detailed discussion of the multi-remedial evaluation process is presented.

Table 5.1 Multi-Remedial Techniques

Treatment Issues	Techniques
Interpersonal Dysfunctions	Cognitive Behavior Therapy Social and Heterosocial Skills Training Assertiveness Training Relaxation Training Systematic Desensitization Depression Management Anger Management Sex Education
Sexual Dysfunctions	
Premature Ejaculation	Seman's Start-Stop Masters and Johnson's Squeeze Relaxation Training Sex Education
Erectile Disorders	Sensate Focus Steps Relaxation Training Systematic Desensitization Cognitive Behavior Therapy Sex Education
Deviant Sexual Responses	Covert Sensitization Covert Positive Reinforcement Masturbatory Satiation Organic Reconditioning Electrical Aversion Relapse Prevention Sex Education

Multi-Remedial Techniques

Personal Victimization Issues

Personal victimization issues can be a difficult challenge for any therapist. For example, males who have been sexually abused as children are often reluctant to admit to victimization, and those who do often minimize impact by focusing on the "pleasurable" aspect of the sexual activity and repressing the traumatic aspects (Freeman-Longo, 1986). Also, it is not unusual for males to enter therapy with a myriad of interpersonal and sexual problems and not reveal their childhood sexual victimization until a strong therapeutic alliance has been formed between patient and therapist. Yet, some males view themselves as chronic victims and respond accordingly. A male sexual abuse survivor can also be very confused about his actual feelings associated with the abuse. For example, he may decry his victimization on the one hand and, on the other, experience sexual arousal while describing his sexual abuse experiences (Freeman-Longo, 1986).

In order to address these issues successfully, particular attention should be given to the sexual victimization experiences and the trauma associated with the early introduction into sexual activities with an adult, without belaboring the point and exacerbating or developing a maladaptive "oh woe is me" victimization attitude. That is, personal victimization issues must be addressed openly and honestly, and resolved. However, to allow males to ascribe all past, present and future problems to their victimization experiences (without attempting adaptive approaches to their problems) is counterproductive. As Groth (1983) notes, the purpose of addressing personal victimization issues is to assist the individual to "come to grips with such unresolved life issues" (p. 172) and not to foster a self-defeating "I am a victim" attitude.

By their nature, personal victimization issues will be rather idiosyncratic. However, major issues frequently presented by sexually abused males are the following:

1. Why did it happen and was I responsible?
2. Self-perception as a chronic victim.
3. What do I do with the anger?
4. Feelings of powerlessness (feeling that his abuser still maintains some sort of power over him).
5. Relationship between his victimization experiences and his own sexual misconduct or dysfunction.
6. Damaged-goods syndrome.
7. Will I always feel this way?

Personal victimization issues can be addressed in individual sessions or in groups. Group sessions are particularly well suited for discussing these issues and receiving feedback from other victims and other males who were sexually abused as children (Giarretto,

1982). At other times victimization issues can be addressed individually, in conjunction with preparing the male victim for a specific treatment technique such as depression management, for example. Self-help aids such as survivor's manuals (e.g., Bear & Dimock, 1988) can also be helpful adjuncts to either group or individual approaches.

Techniques for Treating Interpersonal Dysfunctions

Male survivors with abuse of sexuality histories often experience difficulties in establishing positive self-concepts and healthy interpersonal relationships. Described here are several effective approaches to assist in ameliorating interpersonal dysfunctions.

Cognitive behavior therapy. While M. P. Anderson (1980) proposed that nearly all psychotherapy approaches have identifiable cognitive elements, cognitive therapies "can be conceptually differentiated from the covert or imagery based behavior therapies by their emphasis upon cognitive change as a mediator for affective rather than purely behavioral change. Likewise, they can be distinguished from the more traditional psychotherapies by their encouragement of restructuring awareness rather than acquiring it" (Beutler, 1983, p. 104). The basis for most cognitive therapies appears to rest on the proposal that irrational beliefs, not the situation, produce inappropriate emotional and behavioral responses (Ellis & Harper, 1961). However, the therapeutic approach aimed at altering irrational beliefs and maladaptive values may vary among the cognitive therapies. For example, Ellis (1962) proposes an emotional reeducation and counterpropaganda approach while Beck and Emery (1985) and Meichenbaum (1977) suggest self-evaluation and perceptual change strategies. Meichenbaum also proposes a self-instruction therapy for teaching individuals problem-solving techniques (Meichenbaum & Cameron, 1973; Meichenbaum & Goodman, 1971).

Males with abuse of sexuality histories often develop an ineffective and destructive personal belief system. They may devalue themselves by believing they are "damaged goods" or fear they are or will become homosexual. Cognitive therapy can be helpful in identifying, challenging, and "restructuring" these maladaptive cognitive distortions.

While cognitive behavior therapy can take many forms, most employ the following components:

1. Identifying cognitive distortions.
2. Explanation of how irrational beliefs lead to maladjustive emotional and behavioral consequences.
3. A challenge of the irrational belief system.
4. Self-control strategies such as teaching the individual how to identify and challenge his own irrational beliefs.

Cognitive behavior therapy can be conducted on an individual basis or in groups. Groups using a self- and peer-confrontational model have been effective in restructuring the maladaptive cognition of individuals showing a criminal pattern of behavior (Yochelson & Samenow, 1976). A cognitive/verbal mediation approach for children has also been demonstrated (e.g., Graziano, Mooney, Huber, & Ignasiak, 1979; Kanfer, Karoly, & Newman, 1975).

Social and heterosocial skills training. The purpose of social and heterosocial skills training is to ameliorate the social skills deficits often exhibited by males who have an abuse of sexuality history. In most cases, these deficits can significantly impair an individual's ability to develop satisfactory interpersonal relationships. Such impairments may also lead to inappropriate expressions of love, anger, and sex (Abel, Mittelman, & Becker, 1985; Groth, 1983). General issues such as social expectations, conversational skills, or mannerisms, as well as specific issues relating to heterosocial skills (e.g., feeling inadequate and uncomfortable when relating to age appropriate females), should be addressed.

Several social skills training packages are available for adults (e.g., Abel, Becker, Cunningham-Rathner, Rouleau, Kaplan, & Reich, 1984; Curran & Monti, 1982) and described for children (e.g., Bornstein, Bellack, & Hersen, 1977; Goldstein, Sherman, Gershaw, Sprafkin, & Glick, 1978). A core training program must begin with a complete assessment of an individual's social skills deficits, including especially troublesome situations. Identifying irrational cognitions associated with social skills deficits is an important aspect of the assessment as well. An assessment of strengths in the social arena should also be noted. Once the clinician has identified an individual's pattern of social behavior and attitudes, an intervention strategy can begin.

Most social skills training programs are based upon the skills deficit model and response acquisition approach (Bellack & Hersen, 1978; Bellack & Morrison, 1982; Hersen & Bellack, 1976). In addition to a comprehensive assessment of an individual's social deficits, this model consists of six training components: social skills deficits hierarchy construction; instructions; behavioral rehearsal through role-playing; feedback and social reinforcement; modeling; and practice. Following assessment, the first step is to order the social skills deficits so that training can begin with the least difficult situation and proceed sequentially, one deficit at a time, to the most difficult. This strategy allows the individual to achieve success on one deficit before moving to the next. However, as individuals show an ability to master the technique, more than one deficit at a time can be the focus of treatment.

The second step is to provide specific instructions and information about the skill at issue. This should always include a rationale for why the skill is important and instructions on how the response should be performed. Irrational cognitions associated with the skill should also be corrected during this phase. After instructions and information are given, the therapist engages the individual in role-playing situations associated with the specific skill deficit. In role-playing, the situation should be clear to the individual, and prompts can be used to facilitate the process. Following each role-playing scenario, the individual receives a critique (feedback) of his performance and positive social reinforcement for improvements, no matter how small they may be. Specific feedback and positive reinforcement are key elements to achieving successes with role-playing.

Modeling is also an integral part of social skills training. Modeling occurs "naturally" during the role-playing segments, but can also be used as a specific technique to demonstrate a desired response aside from role-playing. Modeling is especially helpful to children (Bandura, 1977; Bandura & Menlove, 1968). To use modeling, the therapist first describes the relevant aspects of the response to be displayed. This alerts the individual to focus on certain aspects of the modeled behavior. The therapist then models the response as described, followed again by a description of the critical aspects of the display. This process is repeated as often as necessary to achieve an understanding of what is expected of the individual regarding a specific response. The individual can then be asked to participate in a role-playing situation using the modeled response.

The final component of most social skills training programs is practice. While practice occurs through role-playing, the individual should also be encouraged to practice newly mastered responses in the natural environment. Homework assignments should be specific and include only responses the individual has mastered in the therapy sessions. For example, a survivor who has mastered the responses associated with introducing himself to a female and maintaining appropriate eye contact may be given the homework assignment to attend a social function and introduce himself, with proper eye contact, to three females at the gathering.

Social skills training can occur either in groups, on an individual basis, or in a combination of both. A nonconfrontational group setting can be most effective because it allows for greater diversification of role-playing situations, as well as increased positive social reinforcement. In addition, for individuals exhibiting deficits in heterosocial skills, behavioral rehearsal with age appropriate females is essential. Videotapes can also be very helpful in the role-playing and modeling segments of any social skills training program.

Assertiveness training. A social skills deficit frequently identified in adolescent and adult male victims or survivors of childhood sexual abuse is a lack of appropriate assertive skills. For example, many survivors report being intimidated by age appropriate interpersonal relationships and lack the assertiveness skills to correct the situation. Others may tend to be overly aggressive rather than appropriately assertive in their interpersonal relationships.

Most assertiveness training programs are based upon many of the same theoretical and training concepts as seen in social skills training (Hersen, Eisler, & Miller, 1973; Hersen, Eisler, Miller, Johnson, & Pinkston, 1973). Assertiveness training has been successfully employed with a variety of nonclinical populations (Bellack & Morrison, 1982), including marital couples (Eisler, Miller, Hersen, & Alford, 1974) and sex offenders (Abel, Becker, Cunningham-Rathner, Rouleau, Kaplan, & Reich, 1984). It is important to note that Abel et al. employ the basic concepts of social skills training, as well as variations suggested by Alberti and Emmons (1982).

A variation of the basic social skills training model for use in assertiveness training has been suggested by Kazdin (1974, 1976) and

Hersen, Kazdin, Bellack, and Turner (1979). This model is based upon covert rather than overt modeling and rehearsal procedures and begins by establishing a hierarchy of assertion scenarios. It is important that each scene contains a clear description of the situation, a model who will make an appropriate assertive response, and positive reinforcement through achieving the desired result. Once the hierarchy is completed, the individual is instructed to relax and imagine the scenes as presented to him. The therapist then describes a situation selected from the hierarchy and the individual indicates he has the image by raising a finger. The appropriate assertive response displayed by the model is then presented for the individual to imagine. When the individual acknowledges that he has an image of the modeled behavior, the therapist describes the favorable consequences of the assertive response. Each scene on the hierarchy is presented in this manner, proceeding from less to more assertive behaviors. This technique can also be used in conjunction with overt behavioral rehearsal by asking the individual to engage in role-playing following the covert presentation. As with most social skills training programs, homework assignments facilitate response acquisition.

Assertiveness training can be time consuming and tedious, and some clinicians may be tempted to speed up the process by abbreviating the procedures. This is an unwise decision. Studies conducted to evaluate the effectiveness of treatment packages suggest the importance of comprehensive skills training protocols in assertion training programs, although some combinations may be superior to others (Bellack & Morrison, 1982).

Relaxation training. Learning how to relax can assist an individual in various important ways. For example, relaxation training provides the individual with a pleasant and effective stress management technique which can be used in place of inappropriate coping strategies such as sexual acting out. A reduction of environmental stress and tension through relaxation may also provide some survivors with a rare sense of control and self-worth. Relaxation is also a valuable and, in some cases, an essential component of more complex treatment procedures (e.g., covert sensitization, systematic desensitization). And, of course, relaxation is a positive experience by itself.

The typical form of relaxation is a much abbreviated version of Jacobson's progressive relaxation training introduced in 1938. In its original form, this technique involved teaching patients to tense and release successively specific muscle groups throughout the body with few muscle groups ignored. The therapist also provided a relaxing atmosphere by providing suggestions of calmness, as well as a quiet and pleasant physical setting. While the original method was effective in producing a relaxed state, it could also be rather tedious and time consuming. It is not surprising, therefore, that several variations have been developed (Paul, 1969a). The major variation is the focus on major muscle groups, such as those in the chest, back, arms, and legs, for example. Another variation is the sequence and number of muscle groups used for training purposes. Variations can also be found regarding the use of gradual-release or abrupt-release procedures, as well as the extent to which verbal suggestions of relaxation are used. In some cases, therapists prefer to abandon Jacobson's technique completely and employ other procedures such as hypnosis or autogenic training (e.g., Luthe & Schultz, 1970; Schultz & Luthe, 1959), a combination of imaging, meditation, and breathing exercises or biofeedback (e.g., Benson, 1976; Brown, 1977; Stroebel, 1978). Similar relaxation training procedures have been used successfully with children (e.g., Anderson, 1979; Azrin & Nunn, 1974; Weil & Goldfried, 1973).

The abbreviated form of Jacobson's progressive relaxation procedures has several advantages. For example, the technique is easy to master in a rather short period of time. Once demonstrated, the individual can practice the technique at home. Relaxation training can occur on an individual basis or in a group setting. And the individual learns self-control techniques which can be applied in any setting without the assistance of drugs, hypnotic states, or feedback devices.

Systematic desensitization. Systematic desensitization is a highly structured counterconditioning procedure developed by Wolpe (1958) for eliminating maladaptive anxiety. The technique is based, in part, on the concept of conditioned inhibition (Hull, 1943) and is similar to procedures used by Jones (1924) in the treatment of children's fears. According to Wolpe, anxiety is the prominent constituent of maladaptive learned habits, and the elimination of anxiety response habits requires "the inhibition of anxiety by a competing response" (Wolpe & Lazarus, 1966, p. 12). This process is called "the reciprocal inhibition principle" (Wolpe, 1958, p. 71).

Systematic desensitization procedures for children have also been successful (e.g., Goldfried, 1971, 1973; Tasto, 1975).

While similar counterconditioning methods have been described by others (W. H. Burnham, 1924; Dollard & Miller, 1950; Frankl, 1960; Guthrie, 1962; Schultz & Luthe, 1959; Wolberg, 1954),

> Wolpe's most unique and important contribution may be in the careful clinical follow-through of stimulus analysis, means of presentation and incompatible responses. The resulting systematic desensitization package, although similar to other procedures, constituted a true innovation and the first broadly applicable and operationalized specific treatment program for maladaptive anxiety. (Paul, 1969a, p. 65)

Paul was also impressed with the high success rate reported by uncontrolled case studies, but confirmed with controlled studies:

> The findings were overwhelmingly positive, and for the first time in the history of psychological treatments a specific therapeutic package reliably produced measurable benefits for clients across a broad range of distressing problems in which anxiety was of fundamental importance. (Paul, 1969b, p. 159)

After three decades and thousands of cases, systematic desensitization continues to be an effective procedure for eliminating maladaptive anxiety (Wolpe, 1981).

Systematic desensitization consists of three sets of operations: relaxation training, anxiety hierarchy construction, and desensitization proper. The typical relaxation method used is an abbreviated version of Jacobson's (1938) progressive relaxation training, described elsewhere in this chapter.

Hierarchies are formed from a careful analysis of all situations which evoke anxiety, with particular attention given to stimulus contingencies and the duration and level of anxiety evoked. Information about the individual maladaptive anxiety can be obtained through psychological tests, fear and anxiety questionnaires, and detailed clinical interviews. Hierarchies are typically thematic (e.g., specific objects like females or abstract concepts like social criticism), spatial-temporal (e.g., a specific event in time), or a combination of the two types (e.g., a critical female arrives at a future social gathering). It is essential that hierarchies represent the central rather than peripheral sources of anxiety. Once items for the hierarchy have been identified, each item is given an anxiety rating from a Subjective Unit of Distress Scale (SUDS), normally a 0- to 100-point rating. Hierarchy construction usually begins at about the same time as relaxation training is introduced. The following is a partial hierarchy developed for a young man who developed anxiety responses to heterosexual interpersonal relationships (his history revealed an abuse of sexuality negative environment):

1. You are calling a girl on the telephone to ask her for a date.
2. You accidentally use language that is offensive to the girl you just met.
3. You meet a girl at a party and she seems very interested in you.
4. You meet a girl for the first time and ask her for her phone number.
5. You meet a girl for the first time and ask her for a date.
6. It is the day of the date.
7. You are at dinner with a girl and concerned about what you will say to her.
8. You are at her house and waiting for her to open the door.
9. When talking with a girl she looks at your receding hairline.
10. You kiss her for the first time.

Once deep relaxation (the competing response) has been achieved, hierarchies have been constructed, and the survivor has demonstrated an ability to imagine the scenes in a clear manner, desensitization proper can begin. First the survivor is instructed and assisted, if necessary, to achieve a deep state of relaxation. Once the survivor is in a relaxed state, items on the hierarchy, ranging from low to high anxiety, are presented systematically by the therapist with instructions to imagine actually engaging in the anxiety-provoking activity. The survivor is given the opportunity to reduce any anxiety the stimulus creates until the scene no longer creates tension (usually five to fifteen presentations). Upon successful completion of one item (several consecutive presentations without an increase in tension), a higher rated item is then presented until it no longer produces anxiety. The process is repeated over several sessions until all items on the hierarchy have been presented and no longer elicit anxiety. To assure success in real situations, the survivor is given instructions to attempt outside any scenes he has successfully completed in the office, but not to attempt any scene not yet desensitized. If the survivor is unable to perform successfully the scene out of the office, it should be presented again in desensitization sessions until he can successfully perform the behavior outside.

Depression management. Depression is not only one of the more common emotional dysfunctions in the general population, depression is also a common presenting problem by males with abuse of sexuality histories. While a variety of theoretical formulations has been postulated about depression and its treatment, approaches employing behavioral and cognitive concepts appear to be particularly effective (McLean & Hakatian, 1979; Rehm & Kornblith, 1979; Rush, Beck, Kovacs & Hallon, 1977). A cognitive-behavioral approach appears particularly well suited to males molested as children. For example, males who continue to experience some aspects of the "damaged goods" syndrome often display especially negative cognitions which appear full of depressive content and devoid of positive reinforcers. Lazarus (1976) suggests that "depression appears to be engendered by inadequate or insufficient reinforcers. Positive reinforcers have diminished and/or have lost their effectiveness. Above all, depressed persons seem to have little hope for future positive reinforcement" (p. 98). Beck, Rush, Shaw, and Emery (1979) and Beck and Young (1985) postulate that depression has at its core negatively based cognitions or schemes fostered through negative early childhood experiences: "The child learns to construct reality through his or her early experiences with the environment, especially with significant others. Sometimes these early experiences lead children to accept attitudes and beliefs that will later prove maladaptive" (Beck & Young, 1985, p. 207). Sexually abused males often develop survival strategies based upon their abusive experiences, only to discover that when they reach adulthood, their strategies become maladaptive.

Beck and his colleagues (1979, 1985) propose a cognitive-behavioral approach to alter depressive thinking which includes automatic thoughts (intervening thoughts between external events and the individual's emotional responses) and maladaptive assumptions (rigid, excessive, and unrealistic themes which connect the individual's automatic thoughts across situations). The major cognitive techniques used to identify and modify dysfunctional automatic thoughts and maladaptive assumptions are questioning, testing in a "scientific" manner, and reattribution. Behavioral procedures include role-playing, cognitive rehearsal, self-reliance training, diversion techniques, mastery, and pleasure activity exercises. The model calls for an active therapist who can establish and maintain a "collaborative alliance" with the patient. The therapy includes individual sessions with systematic self-help homework assignments.

Another cognitive-behavioral approach to depression management is proposed by Lewinsohn and his associates (Lewinsohn, Biglan, & Zeiss, 1976; Lewinsohn & Libet, 1972; Lewinsohn, Youngren, & Grosscup, 1980). This approach posits that depressed individuals view their environment and themselves in such a negative way that they are unable to experience pleasure even while engaging in seemingly pleasurable activities. Further, and at the core of Lewinsohn's approach, is the view that depression results from "few person-environment interactions with positive outcomes and/or an excess of such interactions with aversive or punishing outcomes" (Lewinsohn & Hoberman, 1982, p. 418). The purpose of treatment, therefore, "is to teach depressed persons skills that they can use to change problem patterns of interaction with the environment, as well as the skills needed to maintain these changes after the termination of therapy" (p. 419). Treatment consists of a highly structured array of several cognitive-behavioral techniques including but not limited to assertion training, relaxation training, planning skills training, and coping skills training. As a result, the depressed individual learns to increase the frequency of pleasurable activities and to decrease unpleasant events. A therapist manual is available (Lewinsohn & Grosscup, 1978).

Anger management. Anger management therapy is a cognitive behavioral approach developed by Novaco (1975, 1976a, 1976b, 1977) for the treatment of chronic anger. The technique is a further development of stress inoculation procedures proposed by Meichenbaum (1974, 1975). Using emotional arousal concepts presented by Konecni (1975a, 1975b), Lazarus (1967), and Schachter and Singer (1962), Novaco describes anger "as a combination of arousal and a cognitive labeling of that arousal as a function of environmental cues and one's own overt and covert behavior in the situation" (1977, p. 601). In other words, an anger response is determined by three modalities: cognitive (e.g., appraisals, attributions, expectations, and self-statements), somatic-affective (e.g., tension, agitation, ill-humor), and behavioral (e.g., withdrawal, antagonism).

Anger management therapy consists of three basic phases: cognitive preparation, skill acquisition and rehearsal, and application practice. During the initial or cognitive preparation phase, survivors are provided information about the nature and function of anger within the concept of their own personal anger pattern. General topics covered are triggering stimuli, differences between anger and aggression, understanding of the three modalities of anger with an emphasis on self-statements, appropriate versus inappropriate anger, and recognition of tension and arousal states. The management concepts as coping strategies are then introduced. The patient may also be asked to complete an anger inventory (Novaco, 1975) described in Chapter 6 of this book and maintain an anger diary.

The second phase involves skill acquisition and rehearsal. The basic procedure used by the therapist is modeling followed by rehearsal by the survivor. Three sets of coping techniques are presented in this manner. At the *cognitive* level, survivors are taught to remain task-oriented (attend to desired outcomes and use concomitant behavioral strategies) and use coping self-statements to modify the appraisal of the situation and to guide appropriate behavior. At the *somatic-affective* level, survivors are taught relaxation skills described elsewhere in this chapter, and the use of humor in the face of provocation.

During the *application practice* phase survivors are exposed to personal anger stimuli. These stimuli are the survivors' "real life" anger situations arranged on a hierarchy of arousal properties, with each scene presented through imagery followed by role-playing. During this phase, survivors have the opportunity to practice new skills until mastery is achieved.

Sex Education. It is not uncommon to find a lack of sexual knowledge plus negative attitudes toward sexuality in male victims and survivors of childhood sex abuse. These informational deficits and negative attitudes can adversely affect an individual's development of appropriate interpersonal and sexual relationships. Sex education programs can assist in ameliorating these sex-related issues. Age appropriate sex education programs for young victims of sexual abuse are recommended by Porter, Blick, and Sgroi (1982), and Wheeler and Berliner (1988).

While a plethora of sex education materials, concepts, and approaches is available, an effective program should address, depending on the age and maturity of the person, at least the following:

1. Basic information on human sexuality (e.g., what the plumbing is and how it works).
2. Sexual myths and misinformation (e.g., masturbation leads to insanity, unwanted hair, and other horrible things).
3. Identification and treatment of sexual dysfunctions (e.g., premature ejaculation, impotency).
4. Communication skills related to sexuality (e.g., learning how to discuss sexuality and sexual issues in a comfortable and effective manner).
5. Self-awareness (e.g., greater awareness of one's own sexuality).
6. Sexual attitudes (e.g., developing more positive attitudes about sexuality, in general, and appropriate sexual behavior, in particular).
7. Sexually transmitted diseases (e.g., herpes, AIDS).
8. Special topics (e.g., homosexuality, bisexuality, sex and aging).
9. Birth control (e.g., types, effectiveness, responsibility issues).

While sex education can be provided on an individual basis, group sessions can often be more effective and efficient. Material can be presented in a didactic fashion, but group discussions should be included as well. Individuals should be encouraged to discuss their own sexual concerns and listen to others as they discuss their sexuality issues. Audiovisual aids (e.g., Crooks & Baur, 1987) and written material (e.g., Strong, Wilson, Robbins, & Johns, 1981) can be used to assist in providing information and to facilitate group discussions. Structured group exercises dealing with specific issues (e.g., communication skills) and homework assignments can be used to assist further the educational process.

Techniques for Treating Sexual Dysfunctions

Sexual dysfunctions of various forms are frequently reported by adult male survivors of the abuse of sexuality. Historically, insight-oriented therapies have not been very successful in the treatment of these disorders. Described next, however, are techniques with good to excellent success rates when used to treat the most common sexual dysfunctions experienced by adult male survivors.

Premature ejaculation. In 1948 Kinsey, Pomeroy, and Martin proposed that a man's ability to ejaculate rapidly was a superior biological response, his partner's viewpoint or needs notwithstanding. While few agree with Kinsey's overly optimistic view of a man's ejaculatory prowess, disagreement among professionals about the criteria used in identifying premature ejaculation is also common. At present, however, the most widely accepted definition of a premature ejaculator is a man who is unable to delay ejaculation for a sufficient length of time during intercourse in order to satisfy a sexually responsive partner 50% of the time (Masters & Johnson, 1970). Whatever the criteria used to define premature ejaculation, Perelman (1980) suggests that men who ejaculate early "have not learned to discriminate adequately varying levels of sexual arousal and subsequently are unable to act in order to delay their orgasm" (p. 201). Effective treatment, therefore, should focus on correcting this learning deficit.

The preferred treatment for premature ejaculation employs in one form or another the basic procedures developed by Semans (1956). This technique employs a masturbatory procedure requiring a female partner to stimulate the penis manually until the man experiences sensations that are premonitory to orgasm. The masturbatory activity is then interrupted until premonitory sensations subside. Once the urge to ejaculate has abated, masturbation resumes and the process is repeated. While several variations of Semans' "pause" or "start-stop" technique have been proposed (Hastings, 1963; Johnson & Masters, 1964; Wolpe & Lazarus, 1966), the most widely accepted modification involves the "squeeze technique" recommended by Masters and Johnson (1970). This technique requires the female partner to squeeze the penis just below the coronal ridge at the moment ejaculation seems inevitable. Pressure is maintained for 15 to 30 seconds, which delays orgasm and reduces tumescence. Manual stimulation of the penis begins again and the process is repeated.

Erectile disorders. While some erectile disorders are a function of physiological causes, approximately 85% are psychogenic (Kaplan, 1975). Given the overimportance males place on their ability to have and maintain erections, it is not surprising that the psychogenic causes of erectile dysfunctions are the most common. Of all the sexual disorders, males fear "impotency" the most. Even the most secure male may have difficulty in remaining objective and calm when experiencing erectile problems. Once an erectile problem occurs, even a transitory one, most males compound the problem by becoming anxious and fearful. Anxiety to perform can build until a cycle of performance-anxiety/failure/performance-anxiety becomes well-established and seemingly intractable.

In the past, erectile disorders were viewed as expressions of severe complexes associated with sexuality. At present, however, those psychodynamic and psychoanalytic interpretations of erectile disorders have given way to theories combining factors such as culturally induced guilt about sex (Ellis, 1954, 1958; Kaplan, 1975), performance-anxiety (Annon, 1974, 1975; Ellis, 1976; Ginsberg, Frosch, & Shapiro, 1972; Kaplan, 1974, 1975; Masters & Johnson, 1970, 1976a; Zilbergeld, 1978), partnership problems (Ellis, 1960, 1976, 1980; Kaplan, 1974, 1975; Masters & Johnson, 1970; Zussman & Zussman, 1977), emotional disturbances such as general anxiety, depression, and hostility (Apfelbaum, 1977a, 1977b; Ellis, 1954, 1960, 1976, 1980; Kinder & Blakeney, 1977; Levay & Kagle, 1977), and lack of adequate information about sexual matters (Ellis, 1960, 1976, 1980; McCary 1967, 1971; Masters & Johnson, 1970, 1976a; Pomeroy, 1977).

The preferred treatment for psychogenic erectile disorders includes basic concepts proposed by Masters and Johnson (1970, 1976b) and Kaplan (1974, 1975). The procedures are as follows:

1. Sensate focus I: The couple is instructed to focus on "pleasuring" each other by caressing and exploring each others bodies and genitals. This activity occurs in the absence of intercourse and orgasm over a period of several days or weeks.

2. Sensate focus II: The couple now focus on each other's genitals and take turns stimulating each other in a teasing fashion. The prohibition of intercourse and orgasm continues throughout this phase.

3. Extravaginal orgasm: Through sensate focus exercises, performance-anxiety is reduced and the man gains confidence by having erections. The next step is to continue with extravaginal pleasuring, but the couple may now stimulate each other to orgasm if desired.

4. Vaginal containment exercises: During this step sensate focus activities continue and once erect, the man enters the woman for a short period of time, then withdraws his penis. While some thrusting may be allowed, the man is instructed not to ejaculate inside the vagina. This process should be repeated several times. If the couple decide to orgasm, the male's ejaculation must be extravaginal.

5. Coitus with an escape clause: First attempts at coitus after the preceding steps may produce a return of some anxiety and expectation that the man must now satisfy his partner. For these reasons, the couple are instructed to continue with the erotic pleasuring exercises before attempting intercourse. Once the man has entered the woman, he can decide to continue to orgasm or to withdraw if he begins to doubt himself. A return to the vaginal containment may be necessary before attempting coitus again.

As with any procedures, variations are often employed based upon the needs of the individual. For example, some males become more not less anxious with prolonged "pleasuring" exercises and may require abbreviated sensate focus steps. The extent to which a man's female partner is willing to participate in the treatment will also affect the treatment plan. Some therapists also employ adjunctive procedures such as systematic desensitization, relaxation, or cognitive restructuring to facilitate therapeutic effectiveness.

Techniques for Reducing Deviant Sexual Responses

As discussed in Chapter 4, most male sexual abuse survivors do not commit sexual offenses. Yet, some report fears of losing control over deviant sexual responses. Others may act out inappropriately in a sexual manner, but their actions are not chargeable offenses. The issues associated with deviant thoughts, sexual arousal, inappropriate behavior, and control must be addressed, lest the survivor add to his woes by eventually becoming an offender. Most survivors with deviant arousal problems experience a significant reduction in anxiety and a considerable boost in self-esteem when they master specific techniques to reduce arousal and/or increase their control over urges to act out inappropriately.

A parallel exists between the development of adult and adolescent treatment methods associated with deviant sexual responses (Abel, Becker, Cunningham-Rathner, Rouleau, Kaplan, & Reich,

1984; Brecher, 1978; Davis & Leitenberg, 1987; Groth, Hobson, Lucey, & St. Pierre, 1981; Heinz, Gargaro, & Kelly, 1987; Knopp, 1982; Lafond, Stark, & Buckley, 1979; Lane & Zamora, 1984; Margolin, 1983; Smets & Cebula, 1987). That is, the treatment approaches and goals incorporated into adolescent treatment programs bear a remarkable similarity to those associated with adults. This situation is not too surprising when you consider that most adult sex offenders were engaging in inappropriate sexual behavior in early adolescence (Longo & Groth, 1983; Longo & McFaddin, 1981). In addition, 19% (Fehrenbach et al., 1986) to 47% (Longo, 1982) of male adolescent sex offenders report histories of having been sexually abused. It seems appropriate, therefore, to employ similar techniques for the treatment of both adolescent and adult sex offenders even though an age difference exists.

Covert sensitization. In 1966, Cautela described a "new" procedure found effective in the treatment of obesity. This technique was called covert sensitization and involved the pairing through imagery of problematic behaviors with personally noxious scenes. A few years later, Cautela and Wisocki (1971) suggested that covert sensitization could also be effective in treating sexual deviations. While there have been critics of covert sensitization and questions about the process operative in the technique (e.g., Mahoney, 1974), covert sensitization has been used successfully in the treatment of a variety of inappropriate sexual behaviors (Barlow, Leitenberg, & Agras, 1969; Davison, 1968; Harbert, Barlow, Hersen, & Austin, 1973; Hayes, Brownell, & Barlow, 1978).

While several variations of the technique can be used, covert sensitization consists of three basic elements: relaxation, hierarchy construction, and the pairing of deviant responses with aversive consequences through imagery. First, the survivor is taught to relax, using techniques described elsewhere in this chapter. The purpose of this relaxation is to facilitate concentration and enhance visual imagery. The second step is to construct hierarchies of deviant sexual imagery (e.g., sexual contact with a child) and personally aversive imagery. The aversive imagery should include psychologically aversive themes (e.g., guilt, shame, detection, fear) and/or physically aversive imagery (e.g., nausea, vomiting, pain). It is also helpful, but not essential to the process, if the aversive scene is a natural consequence of the inappropriate sexual behavior. It is important that the scenes are graphic and represent the survivor's, not the therapist's, personal distress. Following hierarchy construction, the pairing process can begin. Once the survivor is in a reasonably relaxed state, an item selected from the deviant hierarchy is presented to the individual by the therapist. At some point in the scene, usually when arousal is reported or typically expected, an aversive scene is presented. Other scenes from the hierarchies are paired in a similar manner until the individual reports minimal or no arousal to all hierarchy scenes.

As mentioned before, several variations of covert sensitization are possible. One such variation is to use noxious odors, such as aromatic ammonia, ammonia sulfide, valeric or butyric acid, as an adjunct to the aversive visual imagery. This procedure is often referred to as "assisted" covert conditioning (Levin, Barry, Gambaro, Wolfinsohn, & Smith, 1977; Maletzky, 1974; Maletzky, 1973).

Another variation is to construct the deviant hierarchy in a manner depicting the chain of events leading to the actual inappropriate sexual behavior. By using this process, early antecedents, rather than just the deviant sexual acts themselves, can be paired with the aversive imagery. The major purpose of this technique is to countercondition any deviant responses which occur early in the chain of events that ultimately leads to deviant sexual behavior. The following is an example of an antecedent scene developed for an adolescent arrested for exhibitionism (his history revealed an abuse of sexuality negative and overtly sexual environment):

> You are at your parent's house. They have left for the day, but you decide to take a swim. As you change into your swimsuit you wonder if the girls next door are home. You go to the pool and sit in the sun thinking about these girls. You become excited when you think you hear them in their pool. You think about looking over the fence and begin to remove your swimsuit. You are getting very excited and as you approach the fence, your parent's best friends show up. You stand there in fear because they know what you were going to do. The man screams obscenities at you. The woman threatens to tell your parents. You are embarrassed and feeling sick. The man rushes at you and knocks you down! You are getting sicker! He begins to slap your face, then spits on you! You are very sick now and begin to vomit. The woman joins her husband in spitting on you and slapping your face. You want to hide but can't! You are violently ill and begin vomiting blood! You are certain you shall die.

Since one of the factors in effective covert sensitization is the individual's willingness to practice the technique between therapy sessions (Cautela, 1967), homework assignments are necessary adjuncts. To assist the individual, audiotapes of covert sensitization scenes can be developed and used privately. Or, the individual may be instructed to practice by presenting scenes to himself in a verbal manner.

Covert positive reinforcement. Salter (1988) describes covert positive reinforcement as a modification of the concepts and procedures used in covert sensitization. In covert sensitization, deviant arousal is reduced by pairing through imagery inappropriate sexual behavior with personally aversive scenes (Cautela & Wisocki, 1971). The purpose of covert positive reinforcement is to interrupt the chain of events leading to inappropriate sexual behavior and pair the interruption with a positive reinforcement through imagery. Through this process, the individual not only learns how to alter activities and responses during the early antecedent phase of his deviant sexual behavior, but receives a conditioning effect through positive reinforcement as well. Covert positive reinforcement consists of five basic components:

1. Relaxation
2. Identification of early antecedent behavior
3. Constructing interruption scenes
4. Establishing rewards
5. Pairing the process

First, the survivor is taught relaxation through techniques described elsewhere in this chapter. The second step is to identify early antecedents or the chains of activities which typically lead to the deviant sexual behavior. Then, realistic interruption scenes are determined for various points in the chains. Next, appropriate rewards for the interruptions are established. Salter (1988) describes three overlapping classes of rewards: cognitive (e.g., control, success, self-worth); social (e.g., positive interactions with family or others), and material (e.g., food, recreation). Once these components have been determined, the pairing process through imagery can begin.

Pairing begins with relaxation and instructing the survivor to begin verbalizing a chain of events leading to deviant sexual behavior. At a point designated for interruption, the individual begins verbalizing appropriate and realistic behavior, breaking the chain and leading him away from inappropriate sexual activities. This is followed by verbalizing a rewarding scene. While this procedure can be used in individual therapy sessions, the individual can be instructed to audiotape his verbalizations in private and the therapist can critique the tape later with the individual. As with covert sensitization, practice enhances the therapeutic effectiveness. An example of a scene developed for a man with rape fantasies follows (evaluation revealed an abuse of sexuality negative and seductive environment):

> You and your wife are having another one of your silly fights. You think she doesn't understand you and you are feeling awful. You feel rejected. You feel punished. You feel angry. You feel powerless. You leave the house before you explode and get into your car. You think about the girls at the university and start your car. As you begin to drive away you think about what will happen if you see a female alone. You know you will try to rape her but you really don't want to do that. What you really want is to feel better, and there are other ways to feel better. You know your wife loves you. You know she really does understand you. You know you will not rape anyone if you stay with her. You drive around the block and return home. You are beginning to feel better already because you stopped yourself. You go inside and your wife greets you warmly. You are now feeling much better. You are feeling loved and wanted. Your anger is subsiding. You and your wife have a good evening together, and you didn't get arrested. You are at home, not in jail. You are feeling very good about yourself.

Masturbatory satiation. Most sex offenders, especially pedophiles, report a history of masturbating while enjoying their favorite deviant sexual fantasies. Not only does this practice provide subjective pleasure for the offender, it also reinforces his sexual arousal associated with inappropriate sexual beliefs, urges, and behavior. While masturbation can increase deviant sexual impulses, it can also be used to reduce sexual arousal to deviant themes. For example, masturbatory satiation procedures were found effective in reducing sexual arousal to deviant stimuli in cases of rape (Marshall & Lippens, 1977) and pedophilia (Marshall, 1979; Rouleau, Abel, Mittelman, Becker, & Cunningham-Rathner, 1986). According to

Hull (1943), a stimulus can lose its "power" to elicit a response if presented repeatedly without reinforcing outcomes. Eventually, fatigue, habituation, and satiation occur instead of excitation.

Masturbatory satiation appears appropriate for individuals who display high sexual arousal patterns to deviant and nondeviant stimuli whether or not they have acted out their fantasies. In order to accomplish satiation, prolonged, tedious post-orgasmic masturbation while fantasizing and verbalizing deviant sexual themes is required. This technique can be used in a controlled setting or, with modifications, on an out-patient basis.

In a controlled setting, Miner and Nelson (undated) require individuals to masturbate to ejaculation while verbalizing nondeviant fantasies. Then the individual is instructed to continue to masturbate for an additional 20 minutes while "verbalizing aloud every variation the individual can produce on the themes of his deviant interest" (p. 6). Latency to ejaculation is recorded each session. Arousal levels are measured by a penile plethysmograph during weekly non-treatment sessions while the individual listens to two deviant and two nondeviant fantasies. When the individual demonstrates consistently for eight weeks average deviant arousal levels below 20% and average nondeviant arousal levels greater than 50% of maximum penile erection, the satiation process is considered successful.

Salter (1988) describes masturbatory satiation procedures employed with out-patients. This technique, called "boredom tapes," requires the individual to masturbate in the privacy of his own home to carefully selected "appropriate" (i.e., nondeviant) fantasies until orgasm. (If the individual is unable to ejaculate while masturbating to nondeviant fantasies, a time limit of about 10 minutes or less is specified for this phase of treatment.) Not only is the individual required to verbalize his fantasies, he is required to audiotape the verbalizations and the masturbatory activity. Following masturbation to nondeviant fantasies, the individual turns the tape over and, for a 45-minute period, records his masturbatory activity while verbalizing deviant fantasies. The individual is also required to satiate one portion of his deviant fantasy before masturbating to the next. Typically, an individual is required to complete about two or three boredom tapes each week for eight weeks after producing one correctly completed tape. Therapists check the tapes for appropriateness of deviant and nondeviant fantasies and proper sounds indicating masturbatory activity.

Orgasmic reconditioning. Orgasmic reconditioning is a masturbatory procedure employed to increase sexual arousal to nondeviant stimuli by pairing such stimuli with sexual arousal elicited through deviant stimuli. In its original form (Marquis, 1970), the individual was asked to masturbate while maintaining fantasies about his favorite deviant sexual activities. Just prior to orgasmic inevitability (about five seconds initially), the individual was required to switch from deviant to nondeviant themes and experience orgasm with nondeviant fantasies only. For example, a survivor with fears of molesting a child would use his fantasies involving sexual activities with a child to become aroused and masturbate. But a short time before orgasm, he would shift his fantasy content away from children to having sexual contact with a consenting adult, then ejaculate. In subsequent sessions, the survivor is slowly shaped into having shorter periods of arousal to deviant stimuli and longer periods of arousal to nondeviant stimuli by gradually moving forward in time to the point at which he is required to switch sexual themes. Eventually the survivor demonstrates increased sexual arousal to nondeviant stimuli while deviant stimuli produce decreasing amounts of sexual arousal.

A major problem with the original orgasmic reconditioning procedures is the total reliance on the individual to switch fantasy content and to orgasm only to nondeviant sexual themes. This technique has also been criticized for its failure to use physiological measures for sexual arousal. For example, Conrad and Wincze (1976) employed arousal measurements in an orgasmic reconditioning paradigm described by Marquis (1970) and found no physiological changes which could be attributed to the conditioning technique.

To address these issues, Abel, Blanchard, Barlow, and Flanagan (1975) employed a fantasy alternation technique which did not require a switch in fantasy content within each episode of masturbatory activity. Instead, blocks of trials with nondeviant fantasy content were alternated, on a weekly basis, with blocks of trials with deviant fantasy content. Physiological and self-report measures of arousal to deviant and nondeviant stimuli were used. Successful reconditioning was reported. This study was replicated with pedophiles by VanDeventer and Laws (1978), using a weekly schedule, and Foote and Laws (1981), using a daily schedule. The results of both studies suggest that the fantasy alternation variation of orgasmic reconditioning procedures is effective in cases of pedophilia in reducing sexual arousal to deviant material associated with children and increasing sexual arousal to material associated with sexual activities with consenting adults.

The theoretical foundation for orgasmic reconditioning is found in the hypothesis that a variety of seemingly deviant or novel stimuli can acquire the ability to elicit sexual arousal through an association in pairing with pleasurable orgasmic experiences (McGuire, Carlisle, & Young, 1965). However, the results of orgasmic reconditioning using fantasy alternation procedures suggest factors other than a strict conditioning paradigm. That is, an expected conditioning effect would be an increase in nondeviant sexual arousal through the pairing of nondeviant stimuli with orgasmic experiences. Unexpectedly, however, deviant arousal decreased in spite of the blocks of trials pairing deviant stimuli with orgasmic experiences. A conditioning paradigm would predict deviant arousal would remain high or increase if not asymptotic.

To explain this paradoxical effect, VanDeventer and Laws (1978), Laws and O'Neill (1981), Foote and Laws (1981), and Laws (1985) propose that cognitive mediational processes may be involved, as well as conditioning factors. They suggest that for the first time in their lives some pedophiles have learned, through orgasmic reconditioning, that they can actually experience sexual arousal to "normal" stimuli and can also learn to control sexual arousal to deviant stimuli. These successes allow them to break the pattern of devaluing themselves and to begin promoting a sense of self-worth as they master the technique of control. Thus, it is possible that reconditioning of sexual arousal patterns may include cognitive and conditioning components. In fact, Kremsdorf, Holmen, and Laws (1980) produced results similar to those found using fantasy alteration procedures by eliminating the deviant fantasy component altogether. That is, these investigators used only nondeviant fantasies to increase sexual arousal to "appropriate" stimuli, but also found the same concomitant reversal in response levels produced by using the fantasy alternation procedure. This technique appears to be the most promising for clinical settings because it is less complicated than, and solves the compliance problems associated with Marquis' original procedures. And the nondeviant fantasy-only variation apparently produced results similar to those found by using either the original technique or some form of fantasy alternation. However, it may be necessary to alternate deviant and nondeviant stimuli initially with individuals who are unable to achieve orgasm through nondeviant fantasy content alone.

A nondeviant fantasy content model of orgasmic reconditioning is described by Miner and Nelson (undated) and is summarized here. During three one-half hour sessions per week, patients are instructed to masturbate to ejaculation while verbalizing nondeviant fantasies. Fantasy content is monitored for appropriateness, and latency to ejaculation is recorded each session. To facilitate arousal, other materials (e.g., photographs, slides) with nondeviant sexual content may also be employed if needed. Treatment progress is monitored by penile plethysmograph measurements once a week throughout the treatment process. During these weekly one-hour measurement sessions, the patient's erectile responses are monitored while he listens to two deviant and two nondeviant audiotaped fantasies. Treatment is considered successful when the patient shows nondeviant arousal greater than 50% of maximum erection for eight consecutive measurement sessions.

Electrical aversion. Another technique used to suppress deviant sexual arousal is the use of response-contingent electric shock. Rachman and Teasdale (1969) characterize the electrical aversion method as "primarily a form of punishment training which almost always includes elements of classical conditioning" (p. 86). Since the 1930s, electrical aversion techniques have been used in the treatment of a wide variety of sexual disorders (Azrin & Holz, 1966; Bancroft, 1974; Blakemore, 1964; Max, 1935; McGuire & Vallance, 1964; Rachman, 1961; Rachman & Teasdale, 1969).

A typical electrical aversion session begins with instructions to the individual to recreate the inappropriate sexual activity either by verbalizing it to the therapist, through imagery, or through the presentation of slides, pictures, or similar visual stimuli. The individual then receives a nonharmful, but quite unpleasant, electric shock to the wrist when sexual arousal is reported or measured, or on a schedule predetermined by the therapist. The shock is administered through a completely safe, battery-operated device. The level of shock can be adjusted to reach the conditioning threshold of each client. Enough shock needs to be applied to overcome the pleasure which clients experience from deviant stimuli. For most individuals, a 3 to 5mA level is sufficient to eliminate arousal successfully. It should be pointed out that the purpose of the shock treatment is not to produce suffering, but to abolish the pleasure associated with, and produce an avoidance to, the sexual stimuli. Variations of this technique include aversion relief, backward conditioning procedures (Marks, 1976) and self-administered electric shocks (Wolpe, 1965).

While electrical aversion techniques can be effective in reducing deviant sexual arousal, a number of disadvantages are associated with administering painful electric shocks to humans. The most obvious is the overall unpleasantness of the process for the individual; however, Hallam, Rachman, and Falkowski (1972) reported that most "sexual deviants" rated a visit to the dentist as more unpleasant than aversion therapy. Still, an increase in aggression, anxiety, negativism, and hostility often occurs as a result of aversive therapy (Beech, 1960; Rachman & Teasdale, 1969), and this must also be addressed in the therapy sessions. For male survivors who have yet not acted out deviant fantasies, electrical aversion techniques often seem like additional victimization. As one survivor explained, "He molested me and now I have to suffer more pain to undo what he did. He should be going through this, not me."

Relapse prevention. Relapse prevention is a cognitive-behavioral intervention model developed by Marlatt (1982) to enhance control over compulsive/addictive behaviors. The model was subsequently modified for use with sexual offenders by Pithers, Marques, Gibat, and Marlatt (1983) and by Marques and Nelson (in press). While relapse prevention procedures are typically utilized in treatment programs for adolescents and adults, Wheeler and Berliner (1988) suggest that a relapse prevention approach can be adapted for use with sexually abused children as well. According to Pithers, Kashima, Cumming, and Beal (1988), "The overall goals of Relapse Prevention are to increase the clients' awareness and range of choices concerning their behavior, to develop specific coping skills and self-control capacities, and to develop a general sense of mastery or control over their lives" (p. 146). In more practical terms, the major purpose of relapse therapy is to teach sex offenders how to avoid a relapse and how to avoid a lapse when one occurs. A *lapse* is defined as the initial occurrence of the inappropriate sexual behavior and a *relapse* is defined as a complete return to the past pattern of engaging in the inappropriate sexual behavior. For example, a survivor may have a lapse if he begins again to have a fantasy about performing the inappropriate sexual activities, but a relapse does not occur until he actually has a recurrence of the inappropriate sexual behavior.

Relapse prevention begins with a complete assessment of the survivor, including an analysis of high risk situations (any situation which threatens an individual's self-control over the appropriate sexual behavior), the individual's coping skills in high risk situations, and identification of specific determinants of the individual's inappropriate sexual behavior (e.g., stress, depression, sexual dysfunction, cognitive distortions, deviant patterns of sexual arousal, needs, beliefs). Assessments are accomplished by employing several procedures and instruments. For example, self-monitoring and self-report measures can provide detailed accounts of the deviant sexual urges and behavior, including cognitive, affective, and situational antecedents. Sexual arousal patterns can be assessed by using a penile plethysmograph described elsewhere in this volume. Coping skills can be measured by self-efficacy ratings (individual "rates" his capacity to cope effectively in high risk situations), as suggested by Bandura (1977a), and/or by an appropriately modified Situational Competency Test originally developed by Chaney, O'Leary, & Marlatt (1978) for alcoholics. To assist in assessing specific determinants of the inappropriate sexual behavior, a structured interview with a focus on common determinants such as sexual dysfunction, underdeveloped social skills, hostility, and deviant patterns of sexual arousal should be used. The Clarke Sexual History Questionnaire (Langevin, 1983; Paitich, Langevin, Freeman, Mann, & Handy, 1977) can also be useful here. Information obtained from more traditional techniques, such as psychological testing, can be useful in providing information about the individual's personality characteristics, intellectual functioning, and other psychiatric disorders.

A relapse prevention treatment program is designed to be responsive to the individual's needs as determined by the assessment. It is important, therefore, that the survivor continue to provide input regarding the specific treatment procedures selected, the sequencing of the procedures, and an evaluation of the effectiveness of procedures attempted. The authors emphasize that relapse prevention therapists use firm but nonconfrontational techniques to secure the client's active participation in the program. While the relapse prevention model emphasizes individualized treatment programs, the approach can be modified for use in a small group setting as well.

Intervention procedures are selected and assigned either according to strategies associated with avoiding lapses or to strategies associated with minimizing the probability of lapses escalating into a relapse.

Several procedures are possible for assisting survivors in avoiding lapses. One of the first used in the intervention phase is a continuation of the assessment process: recognizing precursors to the inappropriate sexual behavior. That is, the survivor is taught to identify and recognize his individualized chain of events leading to engaging in inappropriate sexual activities. Important to this process is increasing an awareness of the feelings, thoughts, fantasies, urges, and behavior which "allow" the individual to move closer ultimately to perform an inappropriate act. As part of this chain are decisions which often place the survivor in a high risk situation without apparent "awareness" that the decision(s) could easily precipitate a relapse. In relapse prevention, these decisions are often the focus of treatment and are called Seemingly Unimportant Behavior That Leads To Errors (SUBTLE), formerly called Apparently Irrelevant Decisions (AIDs) (see Marlatt & Gordon, 1985). An analysis of an offender's SUBTLEs, for example, can assist in identifying a discrete point in his chain which can be designated as a lapse.

For those with experience in treating sex offenders, the notion of "warning signals," "red flags," or, in this case, lapses, is not unfamiliar. However, Pithers et al. (1988) make an important distinction between how lapses are used within relapse prevention therapy and other therapeutic models. It is their belief that most intervention strategies teach offenders to recognize warning signals but do little to teach them what they should do once they are in trouble. Although this is a debatable issue, relapse prevention does appear to be quite precise in its attempt to teach individuals how to identify, learn from, and respond to lapses.

As a survivor begins to learn how to identify his precursors and lapses, he is then taught coping strategies for use in these situations. Coping strategies come in many forms. Some of the more basic are stimulus control procedures (removing or eliminating external stimuli), avoidance strategies (avoidance of certain stimuli), and escape strategies (methods of getting out of high risk situations should they occur). In addition to the basic forms of coping strategies, the survivor also learns individualized coping skills based upon his strengths, deficits and needs. Some examples are programmed coping responses (identification and continued practice of effective coping behavior), interpersonal skills training (improving social skills via various techniques such as modeling, behavioral rehearsal, and social reinforcement, for examples), stress management, anger management, problem-solving skills, management of urges, modification of deviant sexual arousal patterns (reducing or redirecting deviant sexual arousal through various counterconditioning procedures), and modification of early antecedents (altering faulty attitudes, information, and expectancies associated with an offender's life-style in general and sexual behavior in particular).

The next step in relapse prevention therapy is to minimize the extent of lapses. A starting point in this process is to inform the survivor that it is unrealistic to expect that lapses will never occur. In this regard, it is very important for an individual to understand that some lapses may occur in spite of all the newly established coping skills. However, the occurrence of a lapse does not necessarily mean therapeutic failure or that a relapse is imminent. Rather, a recurrence of a lapse simply underscores the fact that therapy is not punctuated with self-control strategies. Specific techniques used to minimize the extent of lapses include contracting (provides specific limits on the extent to which an offender may lapse), cognitive restructuring (reduces the guilt, conflict, and negative self-concepts associated with experiencing a lapse), and lapse rehearsal imagery (provides repeated practice in using successful coping responses).

In addition to the specific program components just discussed, other procedures and consideration are important to developing a successful relapse prevention program for survivors. For example, treatment procedures designed to impact the survivor's specific sexual problems such as a deviant sexual arousal pattern or sexual dysfunction should also be included in the overall relapse prevention program. Of particular importance are sexual responses which could become critical precursors to a sexual offense.

To assist in selecting effective treatment techniques for specific dysfunctions, multi-remedial evaluation procedures are described next.

6

Formulating the Treatment Plan

A Systematic Multi-Remedial
Evaluation Approach

From our discussion of the paths to recovery in Chapter 4, it is clear that a therapist must be prepared to guide a victim or survivor through several steps or stages in order to ameliorate the multidimensional effects of the abuse of sexuality. Therapeutic guidelines for this process are presented, as well as a recommendation that the recovery can be facilitated by employing additional treatment modalities to specific areas of dysfunctions. Presented in Chapter 5 are effective therapeutic procedures to include in treatment plans for the various dysfunctions experienced by male victims of childhood sexual abuse. It is the clinician's task to determine which techniques best fit the therapeutic needs of each individual. Using the multi-remedial evaluation approach, the clinician can assess and focus on an individual's level of functioning across problem areas and select additional treatment modalities accordingly.

Before describing specific assessment procedures, it is important to note some commonalities in and differences between other diagnostic treatment approaches and the Multi-Remedial model. All approaches share the need for comprehensive information about each individual seeking treatment, and diagnosticians using any model must be trained individuals with excellent interviewing and therapeutic skills. Any approach may include traditional psychological instruments including projective devices (e.g., Rorschach, Thematic Apperception Test), assessments of intellectual functioning (e.g., Wechsler, Binet), or screening devices for organicity (e.g., Bender Visual-Motor Gestalt). While the multi-remedial evaluation approach may include evaluation procedures common to other diagnostic approaches, the Multi-Remedial model calls for a more focused, systematic and goal oriented approach than is found with most traditional assessment procedures. The focus is on general emotional problems as well as specific dysfunctions. Thus, the multi-remedial evaluation approach is guided by the following:

1. Assessments should be multidimensional. (Males with abuse of sexuality histories present with multiple and often complex symptomatology.)
2. Assessments will yield direct implications for treatment. (Assessments will assist in selecting additional techniques for specific dysfunctions.)

The multi-remedial evaluation process is begun by formulating evaluation questions related to the following areas of assessment:

1. Abuse of sexuality environment (e.g., what type of abuse of sexuality did the victim or survivor experience?)
2. Type and severity of dysfunctions (e.g., what type(s) of dysfunctions does the victim or survivor experience? How severe are the problems?)
3. Strengths and skills (e.g., what are the victim's or survivor's cognitive abilities, social skills, and coping skills?)

Multi-Remedial Evaluation of the Adult Male

While an impressive array of evaluation procedures and instruments is available, few have been developed specifically for the male survivor. Rather, as with treatment strategies for specific dysfunctions, many have been developed within treatment programs for male sexual offenders, many of whom have histories of childhood sexual abuse. Others are considered well-suited for survivors because of their relevancy to the dysfunctions many male sex abuse victims display. Some assessment techniques are multidimensional and present a broad range of evaluative information. Others focus on more specific issues and dysfunctions.

Assessment of Personal Victimization Issues

The primary method for assessing personal victimization issues associated with male victims of sexual abuse is the clinical interview. However, many males are reluctant to discuss their sexual victimization experiences, and so a series of assessment/therapy sessions may be necessary before all the information can be obtained. Some men reject the victim label. Many more may not admit that their childhood sexual experiences with an adult were "abusive." Thus, the following approach is recommended:

1. Use less offensive or controversial terms whenever possible. For example, instead of asking a male to describe his "childhood sexual experiences," request a discussion about childhood experiences in general and overall sexual experiences in particular.
2. Within the context of exploring developmentally appropriate childhood sexual experiences, access to abusive experiences may be facilitated by inquiring about any childhood sexual experiences he may have considered unusual or personally unpleasant.
3. Accept in a supportive manner whatever information he presents and look for openings into a more detailed exploration of abuse of sexuality experiences, without pressing for the information.
4. In the initial stages of the assessment process, it is important to provide the male with a comfortable, safe, nonjudgmental, understanding, and informative person with whom to discuss his sexual experiences. Remember, the clinician may be the first or among a very few persons with whom he has confided. Once a trust relationship has been established, terms like *abuse* and *victimization* may be introduced, if appropriate to clarify issues.

The following major categories of information related to personal victimization should be explored:

1. Nature of abuse of sexuality experiences, including perpetrator(s), type(s) of abuse, frequency.
2. Age during victimization.
3. Disclosure information. (Assessing responses from others following disclosure or his reasons for not disclosing can assist in identifying issues associated with breaking the silence.)

4. Feelings about the sexual activities during victimization. (Of particular importance are feelings of guilt, responsibility, anger, anxiety, and powerlessness.)
5. Overall sexual history, including developmentally appropriate and inappropriate sexual fantasies and activities.
6. Interpersonal relationship history, including friendships, dating, marriages, relationships with immediate family members, relationships with children.
7. Areas of perceived dysfunction (victimization issues).
8. Coping mechanisms and strengths.

While the above information can be obtained from an interview alone, most clinicians working with male survivors employ a wide range of assessment techniques in order to enhance the interview process. For example, overall personality characteristics can be assessed with the MMPI; sexual history information can be obtained by using a sexual autobiographical method or a questionnaire; and some victimization issues can be obtained with a structured interview format using a questionnaire designed by Groth (1979).

Assessment of Personal and Family History

Multimodal Life History Questionnaire. While the accepted method for obtaining background information remains the clinical interview, questionnaires can assist in this process. For example, the Multimodal Life History Questionnaire (Lazarus, 1976) was designed to obtain a comprehensive picture of an individual's background. The instrument is based upon Lazarus' concept of seven basic modalities: behavior, affect, sensation, imagery, cognition, interpersonal relationships, and drugs—the BASIC ID. Within this context, the questionnaire covers the following major categories of information about an individual:

1. General information (e.g., name, marital status, employment, living arrangements, etc.)
2. Description of presenting problem
3. Personal and social history
4. Behavior
5. Feelings
6. Physical sensations

7. Images
8. Thoughts
9. Expectation regarding therapy
10. Interpersonal relationships
11. Biological factors
12. Sequential history

Multidimensional Assessment of Personality Characteristics and Emotional Dysfunctions

Adult Nowicki-Strickland Internal/External Locus of Control Scale. The Nowicki-Strickland Internal/External Locus of Control Scale (Nowicki & Duke, 1974) was designed to measure the extent to which an individual feels that he is in personal control of his life (internal locus of control) versus the extent to which he feels that power resides outside of himself in the form of fate, luck, chance, other people, or events (external locus of control). The scale consists of 40 questions reflecting either an internal locus of control orientation (e.g., do you feel that you can change what might happen tomorrow by what you do today?) or an external locus of control orientation (e.g., when you get punished, does it usually seem it's for no good reason at all?). Respondents are instructed to answer either "yes" or "no" to each question based upon the way they feel the item relates to them personally.

The MMPI consists of 566 statements to which the individual responds in a "true" or "false" format. Four validity and ten clinical scales make up the standard MMPI profile. The validity indicators measure the individual's test taking attitude, while the clinical scales assess personality characteristics along the following dimensions:

1. Hypochondriasis (complaint scale about bodily functions)
2. Depression (clinical symptom pattern of depression)
3. Hysteria (neurotic defenses)
4. Psychopathic deviate (amoral and asocial personality characteristics)
5. Masculinity-femininity (male sexual inversion)
6. Paranoia (delusional beliefs, suspicions, guarded, overly sensitive)

7. Psychasthenia (anxiety, ruminations, preoccupations, obsessions, phobias, rigidity)
8. Schizophrenia (poor reality contact, bizarre sensory experiences, delusions, hallucinations, confusion)
9. Mania (overactivity, emotional excitement, flight of ideas, overoptimism, impulsivity)
10. Social introversion extroversion (interest and satisfaction associated with social contacts)

In addition to the standard MMPI profile, a number of supplemental MMPI scales and indexes have been developed and researched. Many of these scales can be helpful in enhancing the basic MMPI interpretation.

While the victim of childhood sexual abuse has been the focus of several studies using the MMPI, none has included the male victim. However, research on female sexual abuse victims found 4-8/8-4, 8-9/9-8, and 6-8/8-6 MMPI code types to be the common mean profile for victims in psychotherapy (Scott & Stone, 1986a, 1986b; Tsai, Feldman-Summers, & Edgar, 1979).

A search for a "sex offender profile" has produced an extensive body of literature using the MMPI, but no such profile (Friedrich, 1988). While some studies found that some child sexual offenders produce a 4-8/8-4 mean MMPI profile (Armentrout & Hauer, 1978; Hall, Maiuro, Vitaliano, & Proctor, 1986; Panton, 1979), most studies found a diversity of MMPI code types (Friedrich, 1988; Hall et al., 1986). Groth (1979) and Lanning (1986) suggest that this diversity of profile types merely reflects the diversity among offender types and the sexual offenses they commit.

While the use of the MMPI in child sexual abuse cases has its shortcomings, individual profiles can be helpful in assessing the male survivor's personality characteristics and dysfunctional areas. The MMPI can provide valuable information about a person's level of emotional distress, such as the degree of his anxiety and depression, for example, as well as numerous other indexes of the person's overall level of functioning. The clinician is cautioned, however, to be aware of the heterogeneity of the impact of childhood sexual abuse on victims and to employ additional assessment techniques (Friedrich, 1988; Lanyon, 1986; Tsai et al., 1979).

Millon Clinical Multiaxial Inventory-II (MCMI-II). As discussed in Chapter 4, male adult survivors often exhibit symptoms of emotional distress which reflect a number of diagnostic categories. The Millon Clinical Multiaxial Inventory-II (MCMI-II) (Millon, 1987) can be helpful in this regard because it is the only clinical assessment instrument currently available which has been explicitly coordinated with the nosological format of the *Diagnostic and Statistical Manual of Mental Disorders-III-R (DSM-III-R)* (American Psychiatric Association, 1987). The MCMI-II consists of 175 statements associated with a wide variety of personality and clinical symptoms to which the respondent answers "true" or "false." Normative data are based entirely on clinical samples (e.g., persons who have already exhibited symptoms of emotional or interpersonal difficulties). Twenty-two clinical scales and three correction scales are divided into five categories:

1. Modifier indexes (correction scales)
2. Clinical personality pattern scales (DSM-III-R/Axis II)
3. Severe personality pathology scales (schizotypal, borderline, paranoid)
4. Clinical syndrome scales (DSM-III-R/Axis I)
5. Severe clinical syndrome scales (thought disorder, major depression, delusional disorder)

Assessment of Anxiety, Anger, and Depression

Most adult male survivors exhibit problems associated with the "big three": anxiety, anger, and depression. Assessments in these areas can be helpful in determining if additional techniques beyond those ordinarily used in the path to recovery should be implemented. For example, a specific evaluation of a survivor's level and pattern of anger can assist in formulating an effective anger management program. Assessments of anxiety and depression will also assist the therapist in developing treatment strategies for these areas important for the survivor's successful recovery.

The State-Trait Anxiety Inventory. The primary purpose of the State-Trait Anxiety Inventory (Spielberger, Gorsuch, & Lushene, 1970) is to measure anxiety along two dimensions: fluctuation anxiety associated with situational stress factors (A-State) and an overall pattern of anxiety proneness (A-Trait). The inventory consists of 40 items equally divided into A-State and A-Trait categories. Respondents are instructed to rate items which best describe their present feelings (A-State) and how they perceive their overall or general feelings (A-Trait).

Novaco Anger Inventory. The Novaco Anger Inventory (Novaco, 1975) was designed to assess the degree of anger an individual would experience in provocative situations. It was developed in conjunction with Novaco's cognitive-behavioral program for the treatment of chronic anger. The inventory is composed of 90 statements of provocation incidents for which the individual rates his degree of personal anger or provocation on a five-point scale ranging from "not at all" to "very much."

Beck Depression Inventory. The Beck Depression Inventory (Beck, Ward, Mendelson, Mock, & Erbaugh, 1961) is a multiple choice inventory comprised of 21 groups of statements. Respondents are instructed to choose one statement from each group which best describes them at the present time. Several dimensions of depression often described by survivors, such as self-dislike, guilt, pessimism, sadness, sleep disorders, and social withdrawal are covered by the Beck. A shorter version of this instrument contains 13 items and correlates well with the original inventory (Beck & Beck, 1972).

Assessment of Interpersonal Dysfunctions

Attitudes Toward Women Scale. The original Attitudes toward Women Scale (Spence & Helmreich, 1972) is a 55-item scale designed to measure an individual's attitudes toward women and their roles associated with several areas, including vocational, educational, intellectual, freedom and independence, dating, sexual behavior, and marital relationships. A 15-item version of the original is also available (Spence & Helmreich, 1978a, 1978b). Using a four-point scale ranging from "agree strongly" to disagree strongly," respondents are instructed to express their feelings about each statement. Higher scorers reflect a more egalitarian attitude toward women.

A measure of attitudes toward women is useful with survivors, given the tendency of some survivors to hold very rigid and conservative views of women. This viewpoint often manifests itself as inappropriate and dysfunctional interactions with females. Research with a nonclinical population supports the notion that this scale does differentiate between a respondent's traditional versus his egalitarian attitudes toward women. In addition, Koss, Leonard,

Berzley, and Oros (1981) found that males with conservative attitudes toward women also tended to be more sexually aggressive than were males who expressed more egalitarian attitudes.

Interpersonal Behavior Survey. The Interpersonal Behavior Survey (Groth, 1979, 1983) is an inventory designed to measure an individual's interpersonal behaviors, with an emphasis on assertive and aggressive behavior. The survey consists of 272 items to which the individual responds in a "true" or "false" format. Four components are delineated: validity scales, aggressiveness scales, assertiveness scales, and relationship scales. This is an excellent instrument to assist in the measurement of changes in a survivor's inappropriate aggressive behaviors to more appropriate assertive behaviors.

Social Avoidance and Distress Scale. The Social Avoidance and Distress Scale (Watson & Friend, 1969) was designed to assess an individual's level of personal distress experienced in social interactions. It also assesses the individual's level of avoidance associated with social situations. The scale consists of 28 statements to which the individual responds in a "true" or "false" format. This scale is helpful in assessing the survivor's level of social anxiety and his tendency to avoid potentially positive and nurturing social interactions. High scorers tend to experience anxiety and fear in social situations and may require anxiety reduction and/or social skills training.

Fear of Negative Evaluation Scale. The Fear of Negative Evaluation Scale (Watson & Friend, 1969) was designed to measure anxiety related to being evaluated by others in interpersonal situations. Within this context, the scale also measures expectations and avoidance of negative evaluations. High scorers tend to be overly sensitive to possible criticism, defensive, self-effacing, and anxious. They also tend to seek approval and avoid situations where possible criticism is perceived. The scale consists of 30 items to which the respondent answers "true" or "false" insofar as each statement pertains to him personally.

This scale is recommended because it is an excellent measure of survivors' misconceptions about themselves and others regarding interpersonal relationships. For example, many survivors are especially sensitive to criticism, anticipate negative responses from people, misinterpret responses as negative, and often isolate themselves out of fear of rejection and personal criticism.

Adult Nowicki-Strickland Internal/External Locus of Control Scale. The Nowicki-Strickland Internal/External Locus of Control Scale (Nowicki & Duke, 1974) was designed to measure the extent to which an individual feels that he is in personal control of his life (internal locus of control) versus the extent to which he feels that power resides outside of himself in the form of fate, luck, chance, other people, or events (external locus of control). The scale consists of 40 questions reflecting either an internal locus of control orientation (e.g., do you feel that you can change what might happen tomorrow by what you do today?) or an external locus of control orientation (e.g., when you get punished, does it usually seem it's for no good reason at all?). Respondents are instructed to answer either "yes" or "no" to each question based upon the way they feel the item relates to them personally.

This scale assists in assessing the survivor's feelings about his power to direct his life. It has been our experience that many survivors begin therapy with negative feelings associated with disempowerment (external locus of control), but as they work toward recovery, the feeling of empowerment increases (internal locus of control).

Assessment of Sexual Dysfunctions

Sexual autobiography. In order to obtain a detailed history of an individual's sexual history, a written sexual autobiography can be requested. To obtain this information, some clinicians provide few instructions other than "cover everything in sequence"; others offer suggestions about content areas and format, while still others provide a printed outline as a guide. Our experience indicates that most males need guidance in this task. A structured format is useful in preparing a sexual autobiography because males often assume, erroneously, that some abuse of sexuality events are unimportant or irrelevant. Also, many males are reluctant to reveal sexual experiences they consider "unmanly" or embarrassing and need encouragement and structure to do so.

We have found it helpful to request sexual information in six segments, starting with an early childhood period and proceeding sequentially into the individual's present age category. The age segments are as follows:

Early Childhood   (0 through 5 years)
Middle Childhood   (6 through 10 years)
Early Adolescence   (11 through 14 years)
Adolescence   (15 through 18 years)
Young Adult   (19 through 24 years)
Adult   (25 and beyond)

Within this age format, the male is instructed to provide personal information about the following, somewhat overlapping content areas:

1. First awareness of anything "sexual" including feelings, observations and experiences.
2. The development of feelings about sexual matters.
3. Sexual activities, including those related to early childhood curiosity and exploration.
4. Masturbation, including age of first experience, fantasies, feelings, and frequency.
5. Dating experiences, including first dates, feelings, activities, courtship, marriage, infidelity.
6. First heterosexual sexual experiences.
7. First homosexual sexual experiences.
8. Sexual attitudes and behavior exhibited by family members and other persons important to you.
9. Sources for and type of information about sexuality.
10. Sexual fantasies.
11. Sexually transmitted diseases.
12. Sexual problems, such as premature ejaculation, impotency, low or high sexual desire.
13. Sexual satisfaction and preference.
14. Self-concept as it relates to your sexuality.
15. "Unusual" sexual experiences either initiated by another or you. Include your feelings about the experiences.
16. Counseling for sex related matters.

Sexual Adjustment Inventory. The Sexual Adjustment Inventory (Stuart, Stuart, Maurice, & Szasz, 1975) was designed to obtain information from couples in preparation for a marital and/or sexual treatment plan. Each individual completes the questionnaire separately but some items require each indivdiual to provide not only his/her own response, but an indication of what he/she thinks his/her partner's response will be. The inventory contains a wide range of response formats within the following major categories:

1. General information and household composition.
2. Information about physical and mental health.
3. Mood.
4. Birth control methods and issues.
5. Present sexual experiences.
6. Sexual satisfaction.
7. Sexual functioning.
8. Masturbation.
9. Frequency and pleasure associated with a wide variety of sexual activities.
10. Decision-making practices associated with sexual behavior.
11. Verbal communication about sexual relationships.
12. Attitudes toward sex.

This inventory is helpful in assessing the suvivor's overall sexual adjustment and is especially useful when treating a survivor and his partner for sexual problems.

Assessment of Deviant Sexual Responses

In our earlier discussion about treatment issues associated with survivors, we stated that most survivors do not become sexual offenders, but many express concerns regarding deviant fantasies about children. At times, survivors also complain of deviant fantasies about other adults. Not to address these issues in therapy would be a gross error because fantasies and urges may eventually be expressed in inappropriate behavioral responses, some of which could be chargeable offenses. Taking their cue from treatment programs designed for sex offenders, a number of excellent evaluation procedures and instruments are available. The ones selected for presentation here are especially useful for survivors because the major focus is on fantasies, urges, and behavior associated with assessing the probability of engaging in inappropriate sexual behavior. High probability survivors may need specialized treatment plans designed to reduce deviant covert responses before they become overt sexual responses.

Penile plethysmograph. The penile plethysmograph is a physiological recording technique for measuring male sexual arousal. It consists of two basic components: a sensing device and a recording device. The sensing device, called a penile transducer, is attached to the midshaft of the individual's penis. Two different types of transducers are available. The first is a Barlow-type strain gauge (Barlow, Becker, Leitenberg, & Agras, 1970) which is a ring-shaped piece of metal open at the bottom and flat on the top. The second is a mercury-in-rubber strain gauge (Bancroft, Jones, & Pullan, 1966) which is a loop of silicone tubing filled with mercury. Each device, in its own way, senses vascular changes in the penis and sends the information to a recording device. Recording devices are available in a variety of models ranging from portable machines to highly sophisticated, multidimensional, laboratory-type physiological recorders. While more expensive, recorders which produce a hard copy readout of the responses are desirable.

After receiving instructions on how to attach the strain gauge, the individual, in private, places the device around his penis. Depending on the purpose of the assessment, sexually arousing stimuli are presented to the person, and changes in tumescence are recorded. Three major types of stimuli are typically used: video, audio, or slides. Videotape and motion pictures are considered the most powerful stimuli (Abel, Barlow, Blanchard, & Mavissakalian, 1975). Research has shown that male sexual arousal states can be reliably and validly assessed with the penile plethysmograph (Abel, 1976; Barlow, 1977; Freund, 1963; Rosen & Keefe, 1978; Zuckerman, 1971).

Abel and Becker Cognition Scale. The Abel and Becker Cognition Scale (Abel, Becker, Cunningham-Rathner, Rouleau, Kaplan, & Reich, 1984) was designed to measure an individual's cognitive distortions regarding sexual activity with children. This scale consists of 29 statements actually made by sex offenders. The individual indicates his level of agreement with each statement by selecting a response from 1 (strongly agree) to 5 (strongly disagree).

Wilson Sexual Fantasy Questionnaire. The Wilson Sexual Fantasy Questionnaire (Gosselin & Wilson, 1980; Wilson, 1978) was designed to assess an individual's fantasies associated with a wide range of sexual activity categorized within four major themes:

1. Exploratory sex (e.g., mate-swapping, being seduced as an "innocent," being promiscuous).
2. Intimate sex (e.g., having intercourse with a loved partner, giving oral sex, kissing passionately).
3. Impersonal sex (e.g., intercourse with an anonymous stranger, watching others have sex, looking at obscene pictures or films).
4. Sado-masochistic sex (e.g., whipping or spanking someone, being hurt by a partner, being tied up).

On a 5-point scale ranging from 0 (never) to 5 (regularly), the respondent indicates how frequently each of 40 fantasies occurs to him. Each major theme contains 10 items producing total theme scores from 0 to 50.

Burt Rape Myth Acceptance Scale. The Burt Rape Myth Acceptance Scale (Burt, 1980, 1983; Burt & Albin, 1981) was designed to measure the acceptance of myths associated with rape. A popular myth, for example, suggests that women secretly wish to be raped and that they find the experience positive in spite of their protestations. This self-report questionnaire consists of 19 items with which the respondent agrees or disagrees. A seven-point scale ranging from "strongly agree" to "strongly disagree" is used for scoring. The research literature associated with the Burt Rape Myth Acceptance Scale suggests a relationship between high acceptance of rape myths and the justification of violence against women (Burt, 1983), reluctance to define sexual coercive situations as rape (Burt & Albin, 1981), and an increase in aggressive behavior (Check & Malamuth, 1985).

The Multiphasic Sex Inventory. The Multiphasic Sex Inventory (Nichols & Molinder, 1984) consists of 300 true/false items divided into 20 scales and a 50-item sex history component. While most self-report instruments designed to assess deviant sexual responses do not contain validity scales, the Multiphasic Sex Inventory contains six validity scales. The clinical subtests are:

1. The Paraphilia-Sexual Deviation Subtest (measures cognitions and behaviors associated with child molestation, rape, and exhibitionism).
2. The Paraphilia-Atypical Sexual Outlet Subtest (measures behaviors associated with fetishes, obscene calls, voyeurism, bondage and discipline, and sado-masochism).

3. The Sexual Dysfunction Subtest (measures nondeviant but dysfunctional sexual behavior).
4. Sexual Knowledge Scale.
5. Treatment Attitude Scale.

The Inventory, a user's manual, and information about validity studies using the Inventory can be obtained from Nichols and Molinder (1984).

Clarke Sexual History Questionnaire. The Clarke Sexual History Questionnaire (Paitich, Langevin, Freeman, Mann, & Handy, 1977) consists of 225 items associated with the respondent's frequency and type of erotic preferences and behavior. Through factor-analyses, 27 clusters for deviant and nondeviant areas have been identified.

The Thorne Sex Inventory. The Thorne Sex Inventory (Thorne, 1966) consists of 40 subtle-indirect and 160 obvious-direct items relating to nearly all aspects of sexuality. This self-report measure was specifically designed to assess deviant sexual responses and has eight factor analytically derived scales:

1. Sex drive and interests
2. Sex frustrations and maladjustment
3. Neurotic conflict associated with sex
4. Sexual fixations and cathexes
5. Repression of sexuality
6. Loss of sex controls
7. Homosexuality
8. Promiscuity-sociopathy

The application of multi-remedial evaluation procedures to adult males with abuse of sexuality histories is summarized in Table 6.1.

Table 6.1 Application of Multi-Remedial Evaluation Procedures to Adult Males with Abuse of Sexuality Histories

	Abuse of Sexuality Environment	Personal Victimization Issues	Personal and Family History	Personality Characteristics	Emotional Dysfunctions	Interpersonal Dysfunctions	Sexual Dysfunctions	Deviant Sexual Responses
Clinical Interview	o	o	o		o	o	o	o
Multimodal Life History Questionnaire	o		o					
MMPI				o	o			
Millon (MCMI-II)					o			
State-Trait Anxiety Inventory					o			
Novaco Anger Inventory					o			
Beck Depression Inventory					o			
Attitudes Toward Women Scale						o		
Interpersonal Behavior Survey						o		
Social Avoidance and Distress Scale						o		
Fear of Negative Evaluation Scale						o		
Nowicki-Strickland I/E Scale						o		
Sexual Autobiography	o	o					o	o
Sexual Adjustment Inventory						o	o	
Penile Plethysmograph								o
Abel and Becker Cognition Scale								o
Wilson Sexual Fantasy Questionnaire								o
Burt Rape Myth Acceptance Scale								o
Multiphasic Sex Inventory								o
Clarke Sexual History Questionnaire								o
Thorne Sex Inventory								o

Assessment Categories span the eight columns; the rows are grouped under *Multi-Remedial Evaluation Procedures*.

Multi-Remedial Evaluation of Male Children

According to Seidner and Calhoun (1984), the child victim's response to a sexually abusive encounter is directly related to the attributions given to the act, his role, his physical response, and the reactions of the persons surrounding the act. These are all descriptive elements which must be explored in depth by the clinician before a treatment plan is constructed. As we have seen, the attributions associated with the abuse of sexuality are likely to be wide and require a broad rather than narrow evaluation approach.

The National Center on Child Abuse and Neglect has offered that both the initial and long-term effects of sexual abuse upon a child are related to the child's age, relative maturity, relationship to the offender, degree of force or violence experienced, familial and societal reactions, preexisting family pathology, and the legal process. Also cited by others is the length of time between the act and disclosure (Brandt & Tisza, 1977) and whether the event took place within the family circle or somewhere beyond it (DeJong, Hervada, & Emmett, 1983). Sexual assaults involving family members and caretakers are thought to hold the possibility of greater trauma as a result of the degree of violation implied and the power the assailant has held over the child (Finkelhor & Hotaling, 1984). Treatment plans should be built upon an accurate assessment of these factors. For example, some clinicians suggest that differential approaches depending upon the child's age, developmental status, sex, diagnosis, and family situation, and the availability of services. Kempe and Kempe (1984) offer some critical commonalities in evaluation and treatment strategies. First, the clinician must assess and understand the nature of the specific act to which the child victim was subjected. Uniquely important in this is the degree of coercion or violence incorporated into the act. Next, the clinician must conduct an assessment of the victim's emotional age, emotional vulnerability, developmental and physical susceptibility to negative consequences, and his ability both to understand and cope with the event. Consideration must be given to assessing the child's relationship with and knowledge of the perpetrator as well as the role the perpetrator played in the child's social environment. Demographically speaking, the length of time the sexualized behavior took place, the chronicity of the behavior, and the frequency of the sexual assault(s) must be determined and plugged into the treatment formula. The reactions of the adults surrounding the child must also be considered, as must the secondary victimization experienced through the legal system's intervention. Finally, all of this information must be weighed carefully against a full understanding of the child victim's personal strengths and weaknesses. It is only through a careful evaluation of these clinical underpinnings that hope will be offered toward successful treatment—no matter the gender of the victim.

Certainly, the child's treatment needs should be primary, but many evaluations are conducted chiefly for the purposes of documenting sexual abuse for legal matters and secondarily for assessing the child's needs for therapeutic intervention. Assessment scales, or guides, to obtaining or determining a child's truthfulness about his/her sexual abuse are well-known to child welfare workers, legal professionals, and mental health professionals involved in forensic work. For example, the Sex Abuse Legitimizing Scale developed by Gardner (1987) purports to differentiate between bona fide cases and fabricated cases of child sexual abuse. Bolton and Bolton (1987) recommend that clinicians attend during the child sexual abuse interview to a number of critical issues suggested by the work of Berliner and Barbieri (1984), Fote (1985), Loftus and Davies (1984), Goodman (1984a, 1984b), Johnson and Foley (1984), Steller (1986), Steller and Raskin (1986), and Yuille and King (1986). And anatomically correct dolls have been used to obtain details about sexual abuse to be used in court proceedings even though studies only recently suggest this procedure may have merit (Jampole & Weber, 1987; White, Strom, & Santilli, in press). However, Adams-Tucker (1984) reminds us:

> While portions of an initial interview may be used by law enforcement professionals for criminal prosecution of the offender, the primary purpose for our assessment time with a child is not to play "gum shoe" or detective, but to achieve a psychiatric understanding of the child; to learn about the incest and the girl's [or boy's] reactions to it, as well as coping strategies, and to learn what has gone on *before* incest in her life and what has occurred *since* she told of her victimization. (p. 508)

While treatment and legal issues appear multidimensional, assessment techniques appear less so. In fact, our review of treatment programs for sexually abused children revealed a heavy reliance on the assessment interview to document sexual abuse, assess the negative impact on the child, and formulate a treatment plan. However, the techniques within the assessment interview did vary somewhat, depending upon the age of the child. For example, Adams-Tucker (1984) recommends "play" as the best mode for the interview with preschool aged children, "play" plus drawings for school-aged children, and for the adolescent, the interview is the primary mode, but other "tools" such as dolls, dollhouses, and drawing materials may also be available. While anatomically correct dolls may be used in assessing the adolescent, this technique appears better suited for younger children. In addition, few procedures other than a standard psychological testing battery and an interview are available for young sexually abused children. As the need becomes more apparent, we expect new instruments and procedures to be developed, researched, and put into practice. For the present, however, the only additional techniques that show promise are behavioral checklists such as those developed by Achenbach and Edelbrock (1983a), and Miller (1981).

Thus, other than anatomically correct dolls, various interview procedures, and a couple of checklists, few techniques have been developed for evaluating the treatment needs of the sexually abused child of either gender. And nothing other than a somewhat different focus in an interview situation has been proposed specifically for the male victim. Yet, nearly all researchers and clinicians working in the area of childhood sexual abuse describe a wide array of emotional and behavioral problems and emphasize a need to address all of these issues in treatment. Perhaps a more systematic and multidimensional approach could be helpful in this regard rather than the heavy reliance on "traditional" interviewing techniques. While recognizing that little is available, we propose that a multi-remedial evaluation approach should be considered. More traditional approaches to evaluate children, such as projective devices (e.g., Rorschach, Children's Apperception Test and Drawings) and intelligence tests (e.g., Wechsler, Binet), are not described below but may be included as part of the multi-remedial evaluation process if desired or needed.

While not as impressive as the array of evaluation procedures and instruments available to assess the adult male, a number of procedures should be given consideration when evaluating a male child with an abuse of sexuality history. However, it should be noted that few have been developed specifically for males who are victims of child sexual abuse. Most have been found useful in other areas, especially with adolescent sexual offenders with a history of sexual abuse or, in some cases, with adult sex offenders.

Assessment of Personal Victimization Issues

As with adults, the clinical interview is the primary method for assessing personal victimization issues associated with male children with abuse of sexuality experiences. Depending upon the age and maturity of the child, adjunctive materials may be used. Toys, dolls, and drawing materials, for example, may be helpful when assessing a young male. However, only minor modifications in the procedures and major categories of information for assessing the adult male as described elsewhere in this chapter may be required with adolescents.

Assessment of Personal and Family History

Again, the clinical interview is the major technique for obtaining a history from sexually abused children. With young males, historical information may also be obtained from the child's parents or primary caretaker. Although the Multimodal Life History Questionnaire, described elsewhere in this chapter, was not designed for children, this instrument can be a useful adjunct with older or mature adolescents. Also, the following is helpful in assessing the level of family dysfunction:

Family Adaptability and Cohesion Scale (FACES). The Family Adaptability and Cohesion Scale (Olson, Portner, & Lavee, 1985; Olson, Sprenkle, & Russell, 1979) was designed to assess the level of dysfunction within an individual's family unit. The scale consists of 20 items associated with family adaptability and cohesion. "Perceived" as well as "ideal" family functioning can be assessed. The individual is instructed to indicate the frequency of his family's conformance to each statement by choosing one of five possible choices ranging from "almost never" to "almost always."

Four levels of family cohesion can be identified: disengaged, separated, connected, and enmeshed. Likewise, four levels of adaptability can be identified: flexible, structured, rigid, and chaotic. Sixteen different family types can be identified by combining the four levels of adaptability. In this way, families can be classified as functional or dysfunctional types. A mid-range is also possible. Olson et al. (1985) report that sex offenders, alcoholics, adolescent juvenile offenders, and runaways tend to score in the direction of more severe family dysfunction than do control families.

Treatment plans for children and adolescent victims of incest usually include some form of family intervention. An assessment of the family's level of dysfunction can be helpful in formulating the treatment plan.

Assessment of Personality Characteristics

Minnesota Multiphasic Personality Inventory (MMPI). The MMPI is one of the most widely used clinical instruments for the objective assessment of personality characteristics and psychological problems. While the MMPI is not designed for use with young children, its use with adolescents is common. More detailed information about the MMPI can be found elsewhere in this chapter.

Millon Adolescent Personality Inventory (MAPI). The MAPI (Millon, Green, & Meagher, 1982) is designed to evaluate a wide range of personality characteristics, not just problem areas. The MAPI can be used with adolescents aged 13 through 18 years and contains 150 items. Interpretations are made from scores on 22 scales within four major categories:

1. Personality styles (introversive, inhibited, cooperative, sociable, confident, forceful, respectful, sensitive)
2. Expressed concerns (self-concept, personal esteem, body comfort, sexual acceptance, peer security, social tolerance, family rapport, academic confidence)
3. Behavioral correlates (impulse control, social conformity, scholastic achievement, attendance consistency)
4. Reliability and validity indexes (test-taking attitudes, confused or random responding)

Children's Personality Questionnaire (CPQ). The CPQ (Porter & Cattell, 1988) is a standardized personality test for children aged 9 through 12 years. The CPQ contains 140 items and assists in evaluating social, personal, and academic development. Potential emotional problems may also be detected by using the CPQ.

Assessment of Emotional and Interpersonal Dysfunctions

In addition to a clinical interview, the following instruments, described elsewhere in this chapter, can be used with most older or mature adolescents:

1. Novaco Anger Inventory
2. Beck Depression Inventory
3. Social Avoidance and Distress Scale
4. Fear of Negative Evaluation Scale
5. Nowicki-Strickland Internal/External Loss of Control Scale (Adolescent Form)
6. FACES

For younger children, behavior checklists can be useful in assessing emotional and interpersonal problems. Two of the most widely used checklists are described below.

Child Behavior Checklist (CBCL). The CBCL (Achenbach & Edelbrock, 1983a, 1983b) is a 118-item checklist that measures a child's overall social competence. Items relating to depression, social withdrawal, aggression, hyperactivity, delinquency, immaturity, obesity, schizoid processes, somatic complaints, and sex problems are grouped under two major categories: internalizing and externalizing. The CBCL is completed by a parent or the child's primary caretaker. A teacher's version is also available. The typical age range for the CBCL is 4 to 12 years old.

Louisville Behavior Checklist (LBC). The LBC (Miller, 1981) is a true-false questionnaire completed by the child's parents or primary caretaker. This instrument measures childhood behavioral problems along several dimensions including aggression, hyperactivity, social, fears, cognitive, neuroticism, psychoticism, somatic, and sexual. Factor analyses of normative data have produced 18 scales and an overall measure of severity. Depending upon the age of the child, three versions of the LBC are available: E-1 (4 to 6 years); E-2 (7 to 13 years); and E-3 (14 to 18 years).

Assessment of Sexual Dysfunctions

Younger adolescents may have difficulty with this task and may be too inexperienced to recognize or understand the nature of a sexual dysfunction. However, older or more mature adolescents may be able, with assistance from the therapist, to prepare a sexual autobiography as outlined elsewhere in this chapter. If necessary, the therapist can use the outline in an interview format and assist the adolescent in providing the information. The CBCL and the LBC, just described, have sections addressing sexual problems. These measures can be useful adjuncts to the clinical interview.

Assessment of Deviant Sexual Responses

For adolescent survivors who express concerns about deviant sexual feelings and fantasies but who have not yet acted out, an assessment of deviant sexual responses is important for planning a treatment program. While most of the instruments and procedures designed specifically for this purpose were developed for the adult male sexual offender, some have been adapted for use with the older or more mature adolescent. Consideration should be given to the following procedures described in this chapter:

1. Sexual autobiography
2. Penile plethysmograph
3. Abel and Becker Cognition Scale
4. Burt Rape Myth Acceptance Scale

The application of the multi-remedial evaluation procedures to adolescents and younger males with abuse of sexuality histories is summarized in Table 6.2.

The Process: A Guide for the Clinician

The process of evaluating and treating emotional and behavioral problems related to abusive childhood sexual experiences rests upon two basic assumptions:

1. The Abuse of Sexuality model increases the clinician's understanding of childhood sexual environments and their impact on the development of male sexuality.
2. The impact often is multidimensional and will require a multidimensional evaluation and treatment approach.

Table 6.3 summarizes the six-step process described next. It should be noted that the multi-remedial evaluation and treatment process is presented only as a guide. The steps are suggestions, not rigid rules. Some clinicians may find, for example, that steps one and two occur together or in reverse order. And, with males, identifying the abuse of sexuality environment (step one) may not occur until a treatment plan has been developed (step three) or later. How-

Table 6.2 Application of Multi-Remedial Evaluation Procedures to Adolescents (A) and Younger Males (Y) with Abuse of Sexuality Histories

Multi-Remedial Evaluation Procedures

	Abuse of Sexuality Environment	Personal Victimization Issues	Personal and Family History	Personality Characteristics	Emotional Dysfunctions	Interpersonal Dysfunctions	Sexual Dysfunctions	Deviant Sexual Responses
Clinical Interview	A,Y	A,Y	A,Y		A,Y	A,Y	A	A,Y
Multimodal Life History Questionnaire	A		A					
MMPI				A	A			
Millon (MAPI)				A	A			
Children's Personality Questionnaire				Y	Y	Y		
Navaco Anger Inventory					A			
Beck Depression Inventory					A			
Social Avoidance and Distress Scale						A		
Fear of Negative Evaluation Scale						A		
Internal/External Locus of Control Scale						A		
FACES						A		
Child Behavior Checklist					Y	Y	Y	
Louisville Behavior Checklist					A,Y	A,Y	A,Y	
Sexual Autobiography	A	A					A	A
Penile Plethysmograph								A
Abel and Becker Cognition Scale								A
Burt Rape Myth Acceptance Scale								A

Assessment Categories

ever, the steps have a logical progression found useful by clinicians who employ the basic procedures posited by the multi-remedial approach.

Step One: Identify the Abuse of Sexuality Environment

To evaluate a male's childhood history as it relates to sexually abusive experiences, the clinician needs a working knowledge of the

Table 6.3 The Multi-Remedial Evaluation and Treatment Process

Step One: Identify the Abuse of Sexuality Environment
 1. The Evasive Environment
 2. The Environmental Vacuum
 3. The Permissive Environment
 4. The Negative Environment
 5. The Seductive Environment
 6. The Overtly Sexual Environment

Step Two: Evaluate the Impact
 1. Assessment of Dysfunctional Areas
    Personal Victimization Issues
    Emotional Dysfunctions
    Interpersonal Relationship Dysfunctions
    Sexual Dysfunctions
    Deviant Sexual Responses

Step Three: Develop and Implement Treatment Plan
 1. Establish Goals for Treatment
 2. Establish Priorities for Treatment
 3. Select Treatment Techniques for Each Goal
 4. Discuss Treatment Plan with Patient
 5. Implement Treatment Plan

Step Four: Evaluate Progress

Step Five: Termination

Step Six: Follow-Up

---

abuse of sexuality environments described in Chapter 1. The environmental descriptors can assist the clinician in recognizing abuse of sexuality experiences presented by a victim or survivor even if the patient does not identify the experiences as abusive. Some critical areas to be assessed are:

1. How did the members of the family respond to the child's requests for information about sex?

2. What type of information about sex did family members offer to the child without a request by the child?

3. How did family members respond to the child's sexual exploratory behavior typical for his developmental period (e.g., touching his penis, looking at other children's genitalia)?

4. How was love and affection shown among family members (e.g., verbal expression, hugs, kisses)?

5. Did family members engage in sexual activities in the presence of children? If so, what were the circumstances, frequency, and type of sexual behavior observed?

6. Did any family member or other adult engage the child in any form of sexual contact? Who?

7. Was the child exposed to any sexual materials in the family setting? By whom? What kind? How frequently? For what purpose?

8. What were the sleeping and bathing arrangements in the family?

9. What about nudity?

10. What appears to be the overall attitude about sex as displayed by the child's father? His mother? Other adult family members?

11. How does the patient feel about his childhood experiences related to his sexuality?

Step Two: Evaluate the Impact

Step two actually consists of two components: an assessment of the patient's dysfunctional areas, and an assessment of the relationship between the dysfunctions and his childhood sexual environment.

Assessment of dysfunctional areas. As mentioned, males often do not offer an accurate presenting problem. It is important, therefore, to employ a broad rather than a narrow approach to assessing males' emotional and behavioral dysfunctions. This is especially important in cases of abuse of sexuality because of the wide range of dysfunctions possible and the male's tendency toward denial and minimization.

While the list of procedures is lengthy, few clinicians find it necessary to administer all the tests. Generally speaking, an initial screening battery for an adult or adolescent consists of a clinical interview, personality assessment inventories, and written autobiographical procedures. For the younger male, the initial battery typically includes a clinical interview (with adjunctive materials and procedures appropriate for the child's age), personality assessment inventories, and behavior checklists. Additional instruments and procedures are added depending upon the information obtained by the initial evaluation or other sources. However, some clinicians prefer to assess the entire range of dysfunctional areas initially by administering at least one instrument from each area.

Relationship between sexual environment and dysfunctions.
While it is tempting to ascribe most of the patient's problems to an
abuse of sexuality, resist the temptation. Other factors may have
contributed to his problems as well. On the other hand, it is also a
mistake to deny that an abuse of sexuality environment could be the
major source of the patient's difficulties. Unfortunately for the therapist, a linear function does not exist between a particular environment and a particular dysfunction. Since individual differences are
the norm, predictions about specific outcomes from any of the
abuse of sexuality environments are risky business. It is important,
however, to assess the relationship between the sexual environment
and the dysfunction in order to facilitate a treatment plan. For example, if a patient's overall level of dysfunction is found to be related more to other variables (e.g., learning disability, intellectual
deficits) than to abuse of sexuality, it would be a therapeutic blun-
der to focus on personal victimization issues rather than on the actual contributing factors. And if the major source of a patient's
distress is an abuse of sexuality, the treatment plan should focus on
this area.

The level of impact can be assessed by addressing the following
critical issues:

1. When did the dysfunction first appear?
2. Has the dysfunction changed over time? How? Under what circumstances?
3. What seems to be the most important factors associated with the
   dysfunction? Are these factors closely related to an abuse of sexuality environment?
4. Was an abuse of sexuality environment only part of a generally
   abusive and/or chaotic family environment?
5. What is the patient's assessment of other factors related to his dysfunction?
6. What is the patient's assessment of his childhood environment?
7. Does the patient objectively evaluate factors affecting himself and
   his dysfunction?

Step Three: Develop and Implement Treatment Plan

Establish goals for treatment. Using the multi-remedial approach, evaluation information is gathered in a fashion leading di-

rectly to therapeutic intervention. Goals for treatment, therefore, become natural outcomes of the assessment process. For example, evaluation information revealing severe heterosocial anxiety, an erectile dysfunction, and rape fantasies would suggest treatment goals related to reducing anxiety, increasing heterosocial skills, increasing erectile functioning, and reducing (controlling, eliminating) fantasies associated with rape.

Establish priorities for treatment. Typically, several goals for treatment emerge from a multi-remedial evaluation. It is helpful, therefore, to arrange the goals in a sequence consistent with the victim's or survivor's needs for treatment, with the more urgent problems assigned higher priority ratings. What differentiates an urgent from a less urgent problem rests with each individual case. For one, deviant sexual urges may be the most urgent problem because the patient is on the verge of acting out his fantasies. For another, premature ejaculation could be the urgent problem due to severe marital discord associated with this sexual dysfunction. As a general rule, the more complete the evaluation, the easier it is to produce a hierarchy of goals which accurately represents the patient's treatment needs.

Select treatment techniques for each goal. With goals in hand, the clinician can now select treatment techniques. Starting with the top priority, treatment techniques should be selected for each goal. As the clinician moves from goal to goal, an overall treatment plan unfolds. Treatment techniques categorized by dysfunctional areas are described in Chapter 5. Table 6.4 presents an example of treatment goals by priority and techniques selected for each goal.

Discuss treatment plan with patient (and other family members if appropriate). Psychotherapy appears a strange and mystical process for most people, especially for males. Males typically experience difficulty in accepting the notion that they need help. Most also find it difficult to believe that "talking about problems" (which they probably don't have anyway) will help. An important part of the multi-remedial system is to demystify the therapeutic process. Overall, it is wise for the clinician to explain the path to recovery treatment process and provide information about the additional techniques selected for the treatment plan. And for some treatment procedures, such as aversive conditioning techniques, a written, informed consent is required. In addition to parental consent to treat a child, an informed family can be a valuable addition to the overall

Table 6.4   Examples of Treatment Goals, Priority Ratings, and Treatment Techniques Using the Multi-Remedial Evaluation and Treatment Process

Priority	Treatment Goal	Treatment Technique
1.	Reduce deviant sexual urges associated with young girls.	Covert Sensitization Electrical Aversion
2.	Reduce anxiety associated with heterosocial behavior.	Relaxation Systematic Desensitization
3.	Reduce inappropriate expression of anger.	Relaxation Anger Management
4.	Increase level of knowledge and understanding of sexuality.	Sex Education
5.	Increase length of time before ejaculation from five seconds to twelve minutes after penetration.	Sensate Focus Squeeze Relaxation

treatment strategy. At the very least, the clinician and patient should agree on the treatment plan before implementation. Understanding, acceptance, and cooperation can facilitate reaching treatment goals.

Implement treatment plan. Once goals are established and prioritized, treatment techniques are selected for each goal, and the victim or survivor understands and agrees to the treatment plan, the treatment can begin.

Step Four: Evaluate Progress

An ongoing accurate assessment of progress is important with any patient; however, it seems especially so for males with childhood abuse of sexuality histories. As mentioned previously, males tend to reject the victim role and minimize or deny the negative impact of sexual experiences. Also, while it may not be "masculine" to enter therapy, it is within the "masculine role" to demonstrate strength through strong recuperative powers. So, once in treatment, males often inflate their ratings of progress. Some clues to this process can be found in statements like, "Well, that used to bother me some, but it doesn't bother me at all now!" The clinician should be aware that the impact rating is minimal ("bother me some") and the progress rating rather unrealistic ("doesn't bother me at all now!"). A more objective and reliable assessment of progress by a male would be, "Well, that used to bother me a lot, but it doesn't bother me nearly as much now." In this example, the impact is not minimized ("used to bother me a lot") and the progress rating appears more reasonable ("doesn't bother me nearly as much now"). Of course, as with any subjective evaluation of progress, the clinician is concerned about the reliability of the male's assessment of himself. It is wise, therefore, always to employ other, more objective assessment measures when evaluating progress in therapy. For example, the penile plethysmograph can be used to measure progress in decreasing sexual arousal to deviant stimuli. Corroboration of progress by family members or other significant persons can be helpful. And, of course, other objective testing devices described in this chapter are effective in measuring progress in treatment.

Progress is always measured against the treatment goals. Thus, if a treatment goal calls for a reduction or increase in some entity, the level of progress is rated by a reduction or increase in that entity. A reduction in anxiety, an increase in the frequency of dating, an increase in length of time before ejaculation, fewer episodes of inappropriate expressions of anger, and a reduction in the frequency of negative self-comments are but a few examples of measures of progress applied directly to the goals for treatment.

If reasonable progress is not shown, the clinician should be concerned about the treatment plan. It may be necessary to reevaluate impact areas, treatment goals, and techniques before pressing on with the original treatment plan. Adjustments in the treatment strategy should be made accordingly.

Step Five: Termination

Termination is just the final step in measuring progress in treatment. That is, if the goals for treatment accurately represent the patient's needs for therapy, termination can be considered once the goals have been accomplished. In order to document progress and validate the decision to terminate, a final evaluation is recommended.

Step Six: Follow-Up

In any treatment program for sexually abused males, the clinician is concerned with the potential for relapses. It seems judicious, therefore, to schedule follow-up contacts. The initial two to four contacts should be office visits. This allows the clinician the opportunity to conduct a "face-to-face" assessment of the patient not possible via telephone. Additional contacts can be made either through office visits or by telephone. To provide adequate coverage, follow-up contacts should be scheduled at one- to four-month intervals for a period of one to three years, logistics permitting. At any point, a patient should be encouraged to reenter therapy if he appears to be at risk from or exhibits the symptoms of a relapse. Some critical areas to assess during follow-up contacts are:

1. Have there been relapses? In what areas? How severe?
2. Does the patient display or describe other problems not included in the treatment plan?
3. What is his overall level of functioning now compared to the initial visit and last contact?
4. Has he progressed on his own since last contact?
5. Does he require additional treatment?

Clinical Issues Within the Use of This Model: Today and Tomorrow

This book began with a proposal to expand our thinking about males and their childhood sexual abuse experiences. We suggested that our current definitions of child sexual abuse, with their focus on overt sexual contact, are too narrow for clinical utility. Missing for the clinician was the notion that males could have their sexuality abused by events other than those operationally defined for research or legal purposes. A rationale for accepting covert as well as overt sexual events as potentially harmful to the sexual development of males is found in the clinical picture presented by many males who have experienced a covert, noncontact form of abuse. The range of emotional and behavioral dysfunctions displayed by these males can be remarkably similar to that displayed by males with contact forms of sexual victimization experiences. The demands of "growing up male" also play an important role in how males view their sexuality, in general, and their abuse of sexuality experiences, in particular. One challenge for the clinician is to understand the relationship between covert sexually abusive events and a male's developing view of sexuality. Another is to treat the dysfunctions produced by the abuse.

To assist the clinician in achieving a full understanding of these noncontact activities, an Abuse of Sexuality model was presented. The model rests upon the assumptions that sexuality develops from infancy forward and, like other developmental areas, may be either nurtured or hindered (abused) in numerous ways. Childhood learning environments containing evasive, deficient, overly permissive, punitive, or seductive approaches to sexual matters are examples of noncontact activities which can hinder, misdirect, or otherwise abuse a child's developing sexuality. Of course, the overtly sexual environment is included as an abuse of sexuality.

Also proposed in this work was a process for the evaluation and treatment of the multiple adverse effects of child sexual abuse. While the multi-remedial process is not conceptualized from any one theoretical or therapeutic framework, behavioral and cognitive-behavioral concepts predominate. The approach is broad and thought to encompass the critical therapeutic issues brought to the clinician by males with abuse of sexuality histories. Guidelines for using the multi-remedial approach are straightforward. The general position taken here is that the multifaceted adverse effects of child sexual abuse require an expanded definition of sexual abuse and a multidimensional approach to understanding, evaluating and treating the male victim.

Understood are the risks associated with proposing "new" definitional models and therapeutic processes. However, clinicians thirst for information about the treatment needs of sexually abused males. What is known must be gathered in a framework suitable for testing, so more can be learned.

The challenge for clinicians and researchers alike is to take this theoretical formulation and go forward. Some of the content of this theoretical formulation will be confirmed repeatedly. Perhaps, as more is learned, some of it will be rejected. For the purpose of this work, however, this study should draw attention to a vital problem. If this attention is motivated, this theoretical offering will have been a success.

References

Abel, G.G. (1976). Assessment of sexual deviation in the male. In M. Hersen & A.S. Bellack (Eds.), *Behavioral assessment: A practical handbook* (pp. 437-457). Elmsford, NY: Pergamon.

Abel, G.G., Barlow, D.H., Blanchard, E.B., & Mavissakalian, M. (1975). Identifying specific erotic cues in sexual deviations by audio-taped descriptions. *Journal of Applied Behavior Analysis, 8,* 247-260.

Abel, G.G., Becker, J.V., Cunningham-Rathner, J., Rouleau, J., Kaplan, M., & Reich, J. (1984). *The treatment of child molesters: A manual* (Available from G.G. Able, Emory University, Atlanta, GA).

Abel, G.G., Becker, J.V., Murphy, W.D., & Flanagan, B. (1981). Identifying dangerous child molesters. In R.B. Stuart (Ed.), *Violent behavior.* New York: Brunner/Mazel.

Abel, G.G., Blanchard, E.B., Barlow, D.H., & Flanagan, B. (1975, December). *A case report of the behavioral treatment of a sadistic rapist.* Paper presented at the meeting of the Association of Behavior Therapy, San Francisco.

Abel, G.G., Blanchard, E.B., & Becker, J.V. (1978). An integrated treatment program for rapists. In R. Rada (Ed.), *Clinical aspects of the rapist.* New York: Grune and Stratton.

Abel, G.G., Mittelman, M.S., & Becker, J.V. (1985). Sexual offenders: Results of assessment and recommendation for treatment. In M.H. Ben-Aron, S.J. Huckle, & C.D. Webster (Eds.), *Clinical Criminology: The assessment and treatment of criminal behavior* (pp. 191–205). Toronto: M & M Graphic.

Achenbach, T.M. & Edelbrock, C. (1983a). *The child behavior checklist and revised child behavior profile.* New York: Queen City Printers.

Achenbach, T.M. & Edelbrock, C. (1983b). *Manual for the child behavior checklist.* Burlington: University of Vermont.

Adams-Tucker, C. (1982). Proximate effects of sexual abuse in children. *American Journal of Psychiatry, 139,* 1252–1256.

Adams-Tucker, C. (1984). The unmet psychiatric needs of sexually abused youths: Referrals from a child protection agency and clinical evaluations. *Journal of the American Academy of Child Psychiatry, 23* (6), 659–667.

Ageton, S.S. (1983). *Sexual assault among adolescents.* Lexington, MA: Lexington Books.

Alberti, R.E., & Emmons, M.L. (1982). *Your perfect right: A guide to assertive living.* San Luis Obispo, CA: Impact Publishers.

American Humane Association. (1978). *National analysis of official child abuse and neglect reporting.* Denver: Author.

American Psychiatric Association. (1980). *Diagnostic and statistical manual of mental disorders* (3rd ed.). Washington, DC: Author.

American Psychiatric Association (1987). *Diagnostic and statistical manual of mental disorders (Third Edition-Revised).* Washington, DC: Author.

Anderson, D.R. (1979). Treatment of insomnia in a 13-year old boy by relaxation training and reduction of parental attention. *Journal of Behavior Therapy and Experimental Psychiatry, 10,* 263–265.

Anderson, L.M., & Shafer, G. (1979). The character-disordered family: A community treatment model for family sexual abuse. *American Journal of Orthopsychiatry, 49,* 453–458.

Anderson, M.P. (1980). Imaginal process: Therapeutic applications and theoretical models. In M.J. Mahoney (Ed.), *Psychotherapy Process.* New York: Plenum.

Annon, J.S. (1974). *The behavioral treatment of sexual problems: Vol. 1.* Honolulu: Enabling Systems. (Also: New York: Harper & Row, 1977).

Annon, J.S. (1975). *The behavioral treatment of sexual problems: Vol. 2.* Honolulu: Enabling Systems.

Apfelbaum, B. (1977a). A contribution to the development of the behavioral-analytic sex therapy model. *Journal of Sex and Marital Therapy, 3,* 128–138.

Apfelbaum, B. (1977b). On the etiology of sexual dysfunctions. *Journal of Sex and Marital Therapy, 3,* 50–62.

Armentrout, J.A. & Hauer, A.L. (1978). MMPIs of rapists of adults, rapists of children, and non-rapist sex offenders. *Journal of Clinical Psychology, 34* (2), 330–332.

Arroyo, W., Eth, S., & Pynoos, R. (1984). Sexual assault of a mother by her preadolescent son. *American Journal of Psychiatry, 141,* 1107–1108.

Awad, G.A. (1976). Father-son incest: A case report. *Journal of Nervous and Mental Disease, 162,* 135–139.

Azrin, N.H., & Holz, W.C. (1966). Punishment. In W.K. Honig (Ed.), *Operant behavior.* New York: Appleton-Century-Crofts.

Azrin, N.H., & Nunn, R.G. (1974). A rapid method of eliminating stuttering by a regulated breathing approach. *Behavior Research and Therapy, 12,* 279–286.

Baker, A.W. (1985). Child sexual abuse: A study of prevalence in Great Britain. *Child Abuse and Neglect, 9,* 457–467.

Baker, J.M., & Morris, L.A. (1984). Parents anonymous children's treatment project/self help for abused children and their parents: Evaluation report. Tucson: Behavior Associates.

Bancroft, J., Jones, H.G., & Pullan, B.R. (1966). A simple transducer for measuring penile erection, with comments on its use in the treatment of sexual disorders. *Behavior Research and Therapy, 4,* 239–241.

Bancroft, K. (1974). *Deviant sexual behavior: Modification and assessment.* Oxford: Clarendon.

Bandura, A. (1977a). Self-efficacy: Toward a unifying theory of behavior change. *Psychological Review, 84,* 191–215.

Bandura, A. (1977b). *Social learning theory.* Englewood Cliffs, NJ: Prentice-Hall.

Bandura, A., & Menlove, F.L. (1968). Factors determining vicarious extinction of avoidance behavior through symbolic modeling. *Journal of Personality and Social Psychology, 8,* 99–108.

Barlow, D.H. (1977). Assessment of sexual behavior. In A.B. Criminero, K.S. Calhoun, & H.E. Adams (Eds.), *Handbook of behavioral assessment* (pp. 461–508). New York: John Wiley.

Barlow, D.H., Becker, R., Leitenberg, H., & Agras, W.S. (1970). A mechanical strain gauge for recording penile circumference change. *Journal of Applied Behavior Analysis, 3,* 73–76.

Barlow, D.H., Leitenberg, H., & Agras, W.S. (1969). The experimental control of sexual deviation through manipulation of the noxious scene in covert sensitization. *Journal of Abnormal Psychology, 74,* 596–601.

Bauman, R.C., Kaspar, C.J., & Alford, J.M. (1983). The child sex abusers. *Journal of Social and Correctional Psychiatry, 3,* 76–80.

Bear, E., & Dimock, P.T. (1988). *Adults molested as children: A survivor's manual for women and men.* Orwell, VT: Safer Society Press.

Beck, A.T., & Beck, R.W. (1972). Screening depressed patients in family practice—A rapid technique. *Postgraduate Medicine, 52,* 81–85.

Beck, A.T., & Emery, G. (1985). *Anxiety disorders and phobias: A cognitive perspective.* New York: Basic Books.

Beck, A.T., Rush, A.J., Shaw, B.F., & Emery, G. (1979). *Cognitive therapy for depression.* New York: Basic Books.

Beck, A.T., Ward, C.H., Mendelson, M., Mock, J., & Erbaugh, J. (1961). An inventory for measuring depression. *Archives of General Psychiatry, 4,* 561–571.

Beck, A.T., & Young, J.E. (1985). Depression. In D.H. Barlow (Ed.), *Clinical handbook of psychological disorders* (206–244). New York: Guilford.

Becker, J.V., Kaplan, M.S. Cunningham-Rathner, J., & Kavoussi, R. (1986). Characteristics of adolescent incest sexual perpetrators: Preliminary findings. *Journal of Family Violence, 1,* 85–97.

Beech, R.H. (1960). The symptomatic treatment of writer's cramp. In H. Eysenck (Ed.), *Behavior therapy and the neuroses.* New York: Pergamon.

Bell, A., & Weinberg, M. (1978). *Homosexualities.* New York: Simon & Schuster.

Bell, A. & Weinberg, M. (1981). *Sexual preference: Its development among men and women.* Bloomington: Indiana University Press.

Bell, A.P. & Hall, C.S. (1971). *The personality of a child molester: An analysis of dreams.* Chicago: Aldine and Atherton.

Bellack, A.S., & Hersen, M. (1978). Chronic psychiatric patients: Social skills training. In M. Hersen & A.S. Bellack (Eds.), *Behavior therapy in the psychiatric setting.* Baltimore: Williams & Williams.

Bellack, A.S, & Morrison, R.L. (1982). Interpersonal dysfunction. In A.S. Bellack, M. Hersen, & A.E. Kazdin (Eds.), *International handbook of behavior modification and therapy* (pp. 717–747). Baltimore: Williams & Williams.

Bender, L. (1954). *A dynamic psychopathology of childhood.* Springfield, IL: Charles C Thomas.

Bender, L., & Blau, A. (1937). The reaction of children to sexual relations with adults. *American Journal of Orthopsychiatry, 7,* 500–518.

Bender, L., & Grugett, A. (1952). A follow-up report on children who had atypical sexual experiences. *American Journal of Orthopsychiatry, 22,* 825–837.

Benson, H. (1976). *The relaxation response.* New York: William Morrow.

Berliner, L., & Barbieri, M.K. (1984). The testimony of the child victim of sexual assault. *Journal of Social Issues, 40,* 125–134.

Berliner, L., & Wheeler, J.R. (1987). Treating the effects of sexual abuse on children. *Journal of Interpersonal Violence, 2,* (4), 415–434.

Bernard, F. (1975). An enquiry among a group of pedophiles. *The Journal of Sex Research, 11,* 242–255.

Beutler, L.E. (1983). *Eclectic psychotherapy: A systematic approach.* New York: Pergamon.

Blakemore, C.B. (1964). The application of behavior therapy to a sexual disorder. In H.J. Eysenck (Ed.), *Experiments in behavior therapy.* New York: Pergamon.

Blake-White, J., & Kline, C.M. (1984, September). Treating the dissociative process in adult victims of childhood incest. *Social Casework: The Journal of Contemporary Social Work,* 394–402.

Blick, L.C., & Porter, F.S. (1982). Group therapy with female adolescent incest victims. In S.M. Sgroi (Ed.), *Handbook of clinical intervention in child sexual abuse* (pp. 147–276). Lexington, MA: Lexington Books.

Block, J.H. (1983). Differential premises arising from differential socialization of the sexes: Some conjectures. *Child Development, 54,* 1335–1354.

Blumberg, M.L. (1979). Character disorders in traumatized and handicapped children. *American Journal of Psychotherapy, 33* (2), 201–213.

Bolton, F.G., Jr. (1983). *When bonding fails: Clinical assessment of the high-risk family.* Beverly Hills, CA: Sage.

Bolton, F.G., & Bolton, S.R. (1987). *Working with violent families: A guide in clinical and legal practitioners.* Beverly Hills, CA: Sage.

Bornstein, M.R., Bellack, A.S., & Hersen, M. (1977). Social-skills training for unassertive children: A multiple baseline analysis. *Journal of Applied Behavior Analysis, 10,* 183–195.

Bourne, R., & Newberger, E.H. (Eds.). (1979). *Critical perspectives on child abuse.* Lexington, MA: DC Heath.

Brandt, R.S.T., & Tisza, V.B. (1977). The sexually misused child. *American Journal of Orthopsychiatry, 47,* 80–90.

Brassard, M.R., Germain, R., & Hart, S.N. (1987). *Psychological maltreatment of children and youth.* New York: Pergamon.

Brecher, E.M. (1978). *Treatment programs for sex offenders.* Washington, DC: National Institute of Law Enforcement and Criminal Justice.

Briere, J. (1985, April). *The effects of childhood sexual abuse on later psychological functioning: Defining a post-sexual abuse syndrome.* Paper presented at the Third National Conference on Sexual Victimization of Children, Washington, DC.

Briere, J., & Runtz, M. (1988). Post sexual abuse trauma. In G.E. Wyatt & G.J. Powell (Eds.), *Lasting effects of child sexual abuse* (pp. 85–99). Newbury Park, CA: Sage.

Brown, B.B. (1977). *Stress and the art of biofeedback.* New York: Harper & Row.

Brown, L., & Holder, W. (1980). The nature and extent of sexual abuse in contemporary American society. In W. Holder (Ed.), *Sexual abuse of children.* Denver: American Humane Association.

Brown, M.E., Hull, L.A., & Panesis, S.K. (1984). *Women who rape.* Boston, MA: Massachusetts Trial Court.

Browne, A., & Finkelhor, D. (1986). The impact of child sexual abuse: A review of the research. *Psychological Bulletin, 99* (1). (prepublication mimeo copy)

Brownmiller, S. (1975). *Against our will: Men, women and rape.* New York: Bantam.

Brunold, H. (1964). Observations after sexual traumata suffered in childhood. *Excerpta Criminologica, 4,* 5–8.

Burgess, A.W. (Ed.). (1984). *Child pornography and sex rings* (pp. 111–126). Lexington, MA: Lexington Books.

Burgess, A.W., Groth, A.N., Holmstrom, L.L., & Sgroi, S.M. (1978). *Sexual assault of children and adolescents.* Lexington, MA: Lexington Books.

Burgess, A.W., Groth, A., & McCausland, M.P. (1981). Child sex initiation rings. *American Journal of Orthopsychiatry, 51,* 110–118.

Burgess, A.W., Hartman, C.R., McCousland, M.P., & Powers, P. (1984). Impact of child pornography and sex rings on child victims and their families. In A.W. Burgess (Ed.), *Child pornography and sex rings.* (pp. 111–126). Lexington, MA: Lexington Books.

Burgess, A.W., & Holmstrom, L.L. (1979). Sexual disruption and recovery. *American Journal of Orthopsychiatry, 49,* 648–657.

Burnam, A. (1986) [1985]. Personal communication concerning the Los Angeles Epidemiological Catchment Area Study. Reported in D. Finkelhor & associates, *A sourcebook on child sexual abuse.* Beverly Hills, CA: Sage.

Burnham, W.H. (1924). *The normal mind.* New York: Appleton.

Burt, M.R. (1980). Cultural myths and supports for rape. *Journal of Personality and Social Psychology, 38* (2), 217–230.

Burt, M.R. (1983). Justifying personal violence: A comparison of rapists and the general public. *Victimology: An International Journal, 8* (3–4), 131–150.

Burt, M.R., & Albin, R.S. (1981). Rape myths, rape definitions, and probability of conviction. *Journal of Applied Social Psychology, 11*(3), 212–230.

Byrne, J.P., & Valdiserri, E.V. (1982). Victims of childhood sexual abuse: A follow-up study of noncompliant population. *Hospital and Community Psychiatry,* 938–940.

Calderone, M.S. (1985). Adolescent sexuality: Elements and genesis. *Pediatrics, 76* (4), 699–703.

Cautela, J.R. (1966). Treatment of compulsive behavior by covert sensitization. *Psychological Record, 16,* 33–41.

Cautela, J.R. (1967). Covert sensitization. *Psychological Reports, 20,* 459–508.

Cautela, J.R., & Wisocki, P.A. (1971). Covert sensitization for the treatment of sexual deviation. *Psychological Record, 21,* 37–48.

Chaney, E.F., O'Leary, M.R., & Marlatt, G.A. (1978). Skill training with alcoholics. *Journal of Consulting and Clinical Psychology, 46,* 1092–1104.

Chasnoff, I.J., Burns, W.J., Schnoll, S.H., Burns, K., Chisum, G., & Kyle-Spore, L. (1986). Maternal-neonatal incest. *American Journal of Orthopsychiatry, 56,* 577–580.

Chatz, T.L. (1972). Recognizing and treating dangerous sex offenders. *International Journal of Offender Therapy and Comparative Criminology, 16,* 109–115.

Check, J.B., & Malamuth, N. (1985). An empirical assessment of some feminist hypotheses about rape. *International Journal of Women's Studies, 8,* 414–423.

Clark, M., & Grier, P.E. (1987). *Female sexual offenders in a prison setting.* St. Louis: Behavioral Science Institute.

Cohen, M.T., Seghorn, T., & Calmas, W. (1969). Sociometric study of the sex offender. *Journal of Abnormal Psychology, 1,* 74–85.

Conrad, S.R. & Wincze, J.P. (1976). Orgasmic reconditioning: A controlled study of its effects upon sexual arousal and behavior of adult male homosexuals. *Behavior Therapy, 7,* 155–166.

Conte, J.R. (1984, November). *The effects of sexual abuse on children: A critique and suggestions for future research.* Paper presented to the Third International Institute of Victimology, Lisbon, Portugal.

Conte, J.R. (1985). The effects of sexual abuse on children: A critique and suggestions for future research. *Victimology: An International Journal, 10,* 110–130.

Conte, J.R., & Schuerman, J.R. (1987a). Factors associated with an increased impact of child sexual abuse. *Child Abuse and Neglect, 11,* 201–211.

Conte, J.R., & Schuerman, J.R. (1987b). The effects of sexual abuse on children: A multidimensional view. *Journal of Interpersonal Violence, 2* (4), 380–390.

Costell, R.M. (1980). The nature and treatment of male sex offenders. In B. Jones (Ed.), *Sexual abuse of children: Selected readings,* Washington, DC: National Center on Child Abuse and Neglect (OHDS), 78-30161.

Courtois, C. (1986, May). *Treatment for serious mental health sequelae of child sexual abuse: Post-traumatic stress disorder in children and adults.* Paper presented at the Fourth National Conference on Sexual Victimization of Children, New Orleans.

Crooks, R., & Baur, K. (1987). *Our sexuality.* Menlo Park, CA: Benjamin Publishing.

Curran, J.P., & Monti, P.M. (1982). *Social skills training: A practical handbook for assessment and treatment.* New York: Guilford Press.

Dahlstrom, W.G., Welsh, G.S., & Dahlstrom, L.E. (1972). *An MMPI handbook: Vol. 1. Clinical interpretation.* Minneapolis: University of Minnesota Press.

Davis, G.E., & Leitenberg, H. (1987). Adolescent sex offenders. *Psychological Bulletin, 101,* 417–427.

Davison, G.C. (1968). Elimination of a sadistic fantasy by a client-centered counterconditioning technique. *Journal of Abnormal Psychology, 73,* 84–89.

DeFrancis, V. (1969). *Protecting the child victim of sex crimes committed by adults.* Denver: American Humane Association.

DeJong, A., Hervada, A., & Emmett, G. (1983). Epidemiological variations in childhood sexual abuse. *Child Abuse and Neglect, 7,* 155–162.

DeJong, A.R., Emmett, G.A., and Hervada, A.A. (1982). Epidemiologic factors in sexual abuse of boys. *American Journal of Diseases of Children, 136* (11), 990–993.

deYoung, M. (1982). *Sexual victimization of children.* Jefferson, NC: McFarland.

Dixon, K.N., Arnold, L.E., & Calestro, K. (1978). Father-son incest: Underreported psychiatric problem? *American Journal of Psychiatry, 135,* 835–838.

Dollard, J., & Miller, N.E. (1950). *Personality and psychotherapy.* New York: McGraw-Hill.

Donaldson, M.A., & Gardner, R., Jr. (1985). Diagnosis and treatment of traumatic stress among women after childhood incest. In C.R. Figley (Ed.), *Trauma and its wake: The study and treatment of post-traumatic stress disorder* (pp. 356–377). New York: Brunner/Mazel.

Eisenberg, N., Owens, R.G., & Dewey, M.E. (1987). Attitudes of health professionals to child sexual abuse and incest. *Child Abuse and Neglect, 11,* 109–116.

Eisler, R.M., Miller, P.M., Hersen, M., & Alford, H.A. (1974). Effects of assertive training on marital interaction. *Archives of General Psychiatry, 30,* 643–649.

Ellerstein, N., & Canavan, W. (1980). Sexual abuse of boys. *American Journal of Diseases of Children, 134,* 255–257.

Ellis, A. (1954). *The American sexual tragedy.* New York: Twayne. (Revised edition, 1961. New York: Lyle Stuart & Grone.)

Ellis, A. (1958). *Sex without guilt.* New York: Lyle Stuart. (Revised edition, 1965. New York: Lyle Stuart & Hollywood).

Ellis, A. (1960). *The art and science of love.* New York: Lyle Stuart. (Revised edition, 1969. New York: Lyle Stuart & Bantam.)

Ellis, A. (1962). *Reason and emotion in psychotherapy.* New York: Lyle Stuart.

Ellis, A. (1976). *Sex and the liberated man.* New York: Lyle Stuart.

Ellis, A. (1980). Treatment of erectile dysfunction. In S.R. Leiblum & L.A. Pervin (Eds.), *Principles and practice of sex tragedy.* New York: Twayne. (Revised edition, 1961. New York: Lyle Stuart & Grone.)

Ellis, A., & Harper, R.A. (1961). *A Guide to rational living.* Englewood Cliffs, NJ: Prentice-Hall.

Eth, S., & Pynoos, R.S. (1985). *Post-traumatic stress disorder in children.* Los Angeles: American Psychiatric Association.

Farber, E.D., Showers, J.C., Johnson, C.F., Joseph, J.A., & Oshins, L. (1984). The sexual abuse of children: A comparison of male and female victims. *Journal of Clinical Child Psychology, 13,* 294–297.

Fehrenbach, P.A., Smith, W., Monastersky, C., & Deisher, R.W. (1986). Adolescent sexual offenders: Offender and offense characteristics. *American Journal of Orthopsychiatry, 56,* 225–233.

Finch, S.M. (1967). Sexual activity of children with other children and adults (commentaries). *Clinical Pediatrics, 3,* 1–2.

Finkelhor, D. (1979). *Sexually victimized children.* New York: Free Press.

Finkelhor, D. (1980). Sex among siblings: A survey of prevalence, variety, and effects. *Archives of Sexual Behavior, 9,* 171–194.

Finkelhor, D. (1983). Common features of family abuse. In D. Finkelhor, R.J. Gelles, G.T. Hotaling, & M.A. Straus (Eds.), *The dark side of families: Current family violence research* (pp. 11–17). Beverly Hills, CA: Sage.

Finkelhor, D. (1984a). Child sexual abuse: New theory and research. New York: Free Press.

Finkelhor, D. (1984b). Sexual abuse of boys. In A.W. Burgess (Ed.), *Research handbook on rape and sexual assault.* New York: Garland.

Finklehor, D. (1986). Designing new studies. In D. Finklehor (Ed.), *A sourcebook on child sexual abuse.* (pp. 199–223). Beverly Hills, CA: Sage.

Finkelhor, D. (1988). The trauma of child sexual abuse: Two models. In G.E. Wyatt & G.J. Powell (Eds.), *Lasting effects of child sexual abuse* (pp. 61–82). Newbury Park, CA: Sage.

Finklehor, D. & Baron, L. (1986). High-risk children. In D. Finklehor (ed.), *A Sourcebook on Child Sexual Abuse.* (pp. 60–88). Beverly Hills, CA: Sage.

Finklehor, D., & Browne, A. (1985). The traumatic impact of child sexual abuse: A conceptualization. *American Journal of Orthopsychiatry, 55,* 530–541.

Finkelhor, D., & Browne, A. (1986). Initial and long-term effects: A conceptual framework. In D. Finkelhor, *A sourcebook on child sexual abuse.* (pp. 180–198). Beverly Hills, CA: Sage Publications.

Finkelhor, D., & Hotaling, G. (1983). *Sexual abuse in the national incidence study of abuse and neglect.* Report to National Center on Child Abuse and Neglect. Washington, DC.

Finkelhor, D., & Hotaling, G. (1984). Sexual abuse in the national incidence study of child abuse and neglect. *Child Abuse and Neglect, 8,* 22–32.

Foote, W.E., & Laws, D.R. (1981). A daily alteration procedure for orgasmic reconditioning with a pedophile. *Journal of Behavioral Therapy and Experimental Psychiatry, 12,* 267–273.

Fortenberry, J.D., & Hill, R.F. (1986). Sister-sister incest as a manifestation of multigeneration sexual abuse. *Journal of Adolescent Health Care, 7,* 202–204.

Fote, D.J. (1985). Child witness in sexual abuse criminal proceedings: Their capabilities, special problems, and proposals for reforms. *Pepperdine Law Review, 13* (1), 157–184.

Frankl, V.W. (1960). Paradoxical intention: A logotherapeutic technique. *American Journal of Psychotherapy, 14,* 520–535.

Franklin, C.W., II (1984). *The changing definition of masculinity.* New York: Plenum.

Frederick, C.J. (1986). Post-traumatic stress disorder and child molestation. In A. Burgess & C. Hartman (Eds.), *Sexual exploitation of clients by mental health professionals.* New York: Praeger.

Freeman-Longo, R.E. (1986). The impact of sexual victimization on males. *Child Abuse and Neglect, 10,* 411–414.

Freund, K. (1963). A laboratory method for diagnosing predominance of homo or hetero-erotic interest in the male. *Behavior Research and Therapy, 1,* 85–93.

Freund, K., Heasman, G., Racansky, I.G., & Glancy, G. (1984). Pedophilia and heterosexuality vs. homosexuality. *Journal of Sex and Marital Therapy, 10,* 193–200.

Friedrich, W.N. (1988). Child abuse and sex abuse. In R.L. Green (Ed.), *The MMPI: Use in specific diagnostic groups.* New York: Grune and Stratton.

Friedrich, W.N., Beilke, R.L., & Urquiza, A.J. (1987). Sexually abusive families: A behavioral comparison. *Journal of Interpersonal Violence, 2,* 391–402.

Friedrich, W.N., Beilke, R.L., & Urquiza, A.J. (1988). Behavior problems in young sexually abused boys. *Journal of Interpersonal Violence, 3,* 21–28.

Friedrich, W.N., & Borishin, J.A. (1976). The role of the child in abuse: A review of the literature. *American Journal of Orthopsychiatry, 46,* 580–590.

Friedrich, W.N., & Luecke, W.J. (1988). Young school-age sexually aggressive children: Assessment and comparison. *Professional Psychology, 19,* 153–164.

Friedrich, W.N., Urquiza, A.J., & Beilke, R.L. (1986). Behavior problems in sexually abused young children. *Journal of Pediatric Psychology, 11,* 47–57.

Fritz, G.S., Stoll, K., & Wagner, N.A. (1981). A comparison of males and females who were sexually molested as children. *Journal of Sex and Marital Therapy, 7,* 54–59.

Fromuth, M.E. (1983). *The long term psychological impact of childhood sexual abuse.* Unpublished doctoral dissertation, Auburn University, Auburn, AL.

Gaffney, G.R., & Berlin, F.S. (1984). Is there hypothalamic-pituitary-gonadal dysfunction in pedophilia? *British Journal of Psychiatry, 145,* 657–660.

Gaffney, G.R., Laurie, S.F., & Berlin, F.S. (1984). Is there familial transmission of pedophilia? *Journal of Nervous and Mental Disease, 172,* 546–548.

Gagnon, J.H. (1965). Female victims of sex offenses. *Social Problems, 13,* 176–192.

Gardner, A. (1987). *The parental alienation syndrome and the differentiation between genuine and fabricated child sex abuse.* Cresskill, NJ: Creative Therapeutics.

Gebhard, P.H., & Gagnon, J.H. (1964). Male sex offenders against very young children. *American Journal of Psychiatry, 121,* 576–579.

Gebhard, P.H., Gagnon, J.H., Pomeroy, W.B., & Christenson, C.V. (1965). *Sex offenders: An analysis of types.* New York: Harper & Row.

Giarretto, H. (1982). Comprehensive child sexual abuse treatment program. *Child Abuse and Neglect, 6* (3), 263–278.

Gilligan, C. (1982). *In a different voice: Psychological theory and women's development.* Cambridge, MA: Harvard University Press.

Ginsberg, F.L., Frosch, W.A., & Shapiro, T. (1972). The new impotence. *Archives of General Psychiatry, 26,* 218–220.

Giovannoni, J.M., & Bercerra, R.M. (1979). *Defining child abuse.* New York: Free Press.

Glasner, A.J. (1981). The incidence of adult sexual dysfunction in people who were sexually molested during childhood. *Dissertation Abstracts International, 41* (8), 3158–3159.

Goldfried, M.R. (1971). Systematic desensitization as training in self-control. *Journal of Consulting and Clinical Psychology, 37,* 228–234.

Goldfried, M.R. (1973). Reduction of generalized anxiety through a variant of systematic desensitization. In M.R. Goldfried & M. Merbaum (Eds.), *Behavior change through self-control.* New York: Holt, Rinehart, & Winston.

Goldman, R., & Goldman, J. (1982). *Children's sexual thinking.* Boston: Routledge and Kegan Paul.

Goldstein, A.P., Sherman, B., Gershaw, N.J., Sprafkin, R.P., & Glick, B. (1978). Training aggressive adolescents in pro-social behavior. *Journal of Youth and Adolescence, 7,* 73–92.

Gomes-Schwartz, B. (1984). Juvenile sexual offenders. In *Sexually exploited children: Service and research project.* Washington, DC: U.S. Department of Justice.

Gomes-Schwartz, B., Horowitz, J., & Sauzier, M. (1985). Severity of emotional distress among sexually abused preschool, school-age and adolescent children. *Hospital & Community Psychiatry, 30* (5), 503–508.

Goodman, G.S. (1984a). Children's testimony in historical perspective. *Journal of Social Issues, 40* (2), 9–32.

Goodman, G.S. (1984b). The child witness: Conclusions and future directions for research and legal practice. *Journal of Social Issues, 40* (2), 157–176.

Goodwin, J. (1982). *Sexual abuse: Incest victims and their families.* Boston: John Wright PSG.

Goodwin, J. (1984). Incest victims exhibit Post Traumatic Stress Disorder. *Clinical Psychiatry News, 12,* 13.

Goodwin, J., McCarthy, T., & DiVasto, P. (1981). Prior incest in mothers of abused children. *Child Abuse and Neglect, 5,* 87–95.

Gosselin, C., & Wilson, G. (1980). *Sexual variations: Fetishism, sado-masochism, and transvestism.* New York: Simon & Schuster.

Graziano, A.M., Mooney, K.C., Huber, C., & Ignasiak, D. (1979). Self-instruction for children's fear reduction. *Journal of Behavior Therapy and Experimental Psychiatry, 10,* 221–227.

Green, A.H. (1984). Child abuse by siblings. *Child Abuse and Neglect, 8,* 311–317.

Green, V. (1985). Experiential factors in childhood and adolescent sexual behavior: Family interactions and previous sexual experiences. *The Journal of Sex Research, 21* (2), 157–182.

Groth, A.N. (1979). *Men who rape: The psychology of the offender.* New York: Plenum.

Groth, A.N. (1983). Treatment of sexual offenders in a correctional institution. In J. Greer & I. Stuart (Eds.), *The sexual aggressor: Current perspective on treatment.* New York: Van Nostrand Reinhold.

Groth, A.N., & Birnbaum, H.J. (1978). Adult sexual orientation and attraction to underage persons. *Archives of Sexual Behavior, 7* (3), 175–181.

Groth, A.N., & Burgess, A.W. (1979). Sexual trauma in the life histories of rapists and child molesters. *Victimology, 4,* 10–16.

Groth, A.N., Hobson, W.F., & Gary, T. (1982). The child molester: Clinical observations. In J. Conte & D. Shore (Eds.), *Social work and child sexual abuse* (pp. 129–144). New York: Haworth.

Groth, A.N., Hobson, W.F., Lucey, K.P., & St. Pierre, J. (1981). Juvenile sex offenders: Guidelines for treatment. *International Journal of Offender Therapy and Comparative Criminology, 25,* 265–272.

Groth, A.N., & Loredo, C.M. (1981). Juvenile sex offenders: Guidelines for assessment. *International Journal of Offender Therapy and Comparative Criminology, 25,* 31–39.

Guthrie, E.R. (1962). *The psychology of human conflict.* Boston: Beacon.

Haas, A. (1979). *Teenage sexuality: A survey of teenage sexual behavior.* New York: Macmillan.

Hall, G.C.N., Maiuro, R.D., Vitaliano, P.P., & Proctor, W.C. (1986). The utility of the MMPI with men who have sexually assaulted children. *Journal of Consulting and Clinical Psychology, 54,* 493–496.

Hallam, R., Rachman, S., & Falkowski, W. (1972). Subjective attitudinal and physiological effects of electrical aversion therapy. *Behavior Research and Therapy, 10,* 1–14.

Hamilton, G.V. (1929). *A research in marriage.* New York: Albert & Charles Boni.

Harbert, T.L., Barlow, D.H., Hersen, M., & Austin, J.B. (1973). Measurement and modification of incestuous behavior: A case study. *Psychological Reports, 34,* 79–86.

Hartley, R.E. (1959). Sex-role pressures in the socialization of the male child. *Psychological Reports, 5,* 459–468.

Hastings, D.W. (1963). *Impotence and frigidity.* Boston: Little, Brown.

Hathaway, S.R. (1960). Foreword. In W.G. Dahlstrom & G.S. Welsh, *An MMPI handbook: A guide to use in clinical practice and research* (pp. vii–xi). Minneapolis: University of Minnesota Press.

Hayes, S.H., Brownell, K.D., & Barlow, D.H. (1978). The use of self-administered covert sensitization in the treatment of exhibitionism and sadism. *Behavior Therapy, 9*, 283–289.

Haynes, C.F. (1985). *Review of the literature on child abuse and neglect.* Presentation at the Fourteenth Annual Child Abuse and Neglect Symposium, Keystone, CO.

Heinz, J.W., Gargaro, S., & Kelly, K.G. (1987). *A model residential juvenile sex-offender treatment program: The Hennepin County home school.* Syracuse, NY: Safer Society Press.

Helfer, R.E., & Kempe, C.H. (1968). *The battered child* (3rd. ed.). Chicago: University of Chicago Press.

Henderson, J. (1972). Incest: A synthesis of data. *Canadian Psychiatric Association Journal, 17*, 299–313.

Henn, F.A., Herjanic, M., & Vanderpearl, R.H. (1976). Forensic psychiatry: Profiles of two types of sex offenders. *American Journal of Psychiatry, 133*, 694–696.

Herman, J. (1981). *Father-daughter incest.* Cambridge, MA: Harvard University Press.

Herman, J., & Hirschman, L. (1977). Father-daugher incest. *Signs, 2*, 1–22.

Hersen, M., & Bellack, A.S. (1976). Social skills training for chronic psychiatric patients: Rationale, research findings and future directions. *Comprehensive Psychiatry, 17*, 559–580.

Hersen, M., Eisler, R.M., & Miller, P.M. (1973). Development of assertive responses: Clinical measurement and research considerations. *Behavior Research and Therapy, 11*, 505–521.

Hersen, M., Eisler, R.M., Miller, P.M., Johnson, M.B., & Pinkston, S.G. (1973). Effect of practice, instructions and modeling on components of assertive behavior. *Behavior Research and Therapy, 11*, 442–451.

Hersen, M., Kazdin, A.E., Bellack, A.S., & Turner, S.M. (1979). Effects of live modeling, covert modeling, and rehearsal on assertiveness in psychiatric patients. *Behavior Research and Therapy, 17*, 369–377.

Howells, K. (1979). Some meanings of children for pedophiles. In M. Cook & G. Wilson (Eds.), *Love and attraction: An international conference* (pp. 55–92). Oxford: Pergamon.

Howells, K. (1981). Adult sexual interest in children: Considerations relevant to theories of etiology. In M. Cook & K. Howells (Eds.), *Adult sexual interest in children.* New York: Academic Press.

Hoyenga, K.B., & Hoyenga, K.T. (1979). *The question of sex differences: psychological, cultural and biological issues.* Boston: Little, Brown.

Hull, C.L. (1943). *Principles of behavior.* New York: Appleton-Century-Crofts.

Hunter, R.S., & Kilstrom, N. (1979). Breaking the cycle in abusive families. *American Journal of Psychiatry, 136*, 1320–1322.

Hunter, R.S., Kilstrom, N., & Loda, F. (1985). Sexually abused children: Identifying masked presentations in a medical setting. *Child Abuse and Neglect, 9*, 17–25.

Ingham, M. (1984). *Men: The male myth exposed.* London: Century.

Jacobson, E. (1938). *Progressive relaxation.* Chicago: University of Chicago Press.

Jampole, L., & Weber, M.K. (1987). An assessment of the behavior of sexually abused and nonsexually abused children with anatomically correct dolls. *Child Abuse and Neglect, 11*, 187–192.

Janas, C. (1983). Family violence and child sexual abuse. *Medical Hypnoanalysis, 4* (2), 68–76.

Janus, M-D., Scanlon, B., & Price, V. (1984). Youth prostitution. In A.W. Burgess (Ed.), *Child pornography and sex rings* (pp. 127–146). Lexington, MA: Lexington Books.

Johnson, M.K., & Foley, M.A. (1984). Differentiating fact from fantasy: The reliability of children's memory. *Journal of Social Issues, 40* (2), 33–50.

Johnson, R.L., & Shrier, D.K. (1985). Sexual victimization of boys: Experience at an adolescent medicine clinic. *Journal of Adolescent Health Care, 6,* 372–376.

Johnson, R.L., & Shrier, D.K. (1987). Past sexual victimization by females in an adolescent medicine clinic population. *American Journal of Psychiatry, 144* (5), 650–652.

Johnson, V.E., & Masters, W.H. (1964). A team approach to the rapid diagnosis and treatment of sexual incompatibility. *Western Journal of Surgery, Obstetrics and Gynecology, 72* (6), 371–375.

Jones, M.C. (1924). The elimination of children's fears. *Journal of Experimental Psychology, 7,* 382–390.

Justice, B., & Justice, R. (1979). *The broken taboo: Sex in the family.* New York: Human Sciences Press.

Kagan, J. (1976). Psychology of sex differences. In F. Beach (Ed.), *Human sexuality in four perspectives* (pp. 87–114). Baltimore: Johns Hopkins University Press.

Kallen, D.J., Stephenson, J.J., & Doughty, A. (1983). The need to know: Recalled adolescent sources of sexual and contraceptive information and sexual behavior. *Journal of Sex Research, 19,* 137–159.

Kanfer, F.H., Karoly, P., & Newman, A. (1975). Reduction of children's fear of the dark by competence-related and situational threat-related verbal cues. *Journal of Consulting and Clinical Psychology, 43,* 251–258.

Kaplan, H.S. (1974). *The new sex therapy.* New York: Brunner/Mazel.

Kaplan, H.S. (1975). *The illustrated manual of sex therapy.* New York: Quadrangle, The New York Times Book Co.

Karpman, B. (1954). *The sexual offender and his offenses.* New York: Julian.

Kaufman, A., DiVasto, P., Jackson, R., Voorhees, D. & Christy, J. (1980). Male rape victims: Noninstitutionalized assault. *American Journal of Psychiatry, 137* (2), 221–223.

Kaufman, J., & Zigler, E. (1987). Do abused children become abusive parents? *American Journal of Orthopsychiatry, 57,* 186–192.

Kazdin, A.E. (1974). Effects of covert modeling and model reinforcement on assertive behavior. *Journal of Abnormal Psychology, 83,* 240–252.

Kazdin, A.E. (1976). Effects of covert modeling, multiple models, and model reinforcement on assertive behavior. *Behavior Therapy, 7,* 211–222.

Kempe, R.S., & Kempe, C.H. (1984). *The common secret: Sexual abuse of children and adolescents.* New York: Freeman.

Kercher, G., & McShane, M. (1984). The prevalence of child sexual abuse victimization in an adult sample of Texas residents. *Child Abuse and Neglect, 8,* 485–502.

Kinder, B.N., & Blakeney, P. (1977). Treatment of sexual dysfunction: A review of outcome studies. *Journal of Clinical Psychology, 33,* 523–530.

Kinsey, A.C., Pomeroy, W.B., & Martin, C.E. (1948). *Sexual behavior in the human male.* Philadelphia: W.B. Saunders.

Kinsey, A.C., Pomeroy, W.B., Martin, C.E., & Gebhard, P.H. (1953). *Sexual behavior in the human female.* Philadelphia: W.B. Saunders.

Kirby, D., Alter, J., & Scales, P. (1979). *An analysis of U.S. sex education programs and evaluation methods.* (HEW Report No. CDC-2021-79-DK FR). Atlanta: U.S. Department of Health, Education and Welfare, Public Health Service, Center for Disease Control, Bureau of Health Education.

Knopp, F.H. (1982). *Remedial intervention in adolescent sex offenses: Nine program descriptions.* Syracuse, NY: Safer Society Press.

Knopp, F.H., & Lackey, L.B. (1987). *Female sexual abusers: A summary of data from 44 treatment providers.* Orwell, VT: Safer Society Press.

Koch, M. (1980). Sexual abuse in children. *Adolescence, 15* (59), 643–648.

Kohan, M.J., Pothier, P., & Norbeck, J.S. (1987). Hospitalized children with history of sexual abuse: Incidence and care issues. *American Journal of Orthopsychiatry, 57,* 258–264.

Kohlberg, L. (1966). A cognitive-developmental analysis of children's sex-role concepts and attitudes. In E. Maccoby (Ed.), *The development of sex differences* (pp. 82–166). Stanford: Stanford University Press.

Konecni, V.J. (1975a). Annoyance, type and duration of post annoyance activity, and aggression: The "cathartic effect." *Journal of Experimental Psychology: General, 104,* 76–104.

Konecni, V.J. (1975b). The mediation of aggressive behavior: Arousal level in anger and cognitive labeling. *Journal of Personality and Social Psychology, 31,* 706–712.

Koss, M.P., Leonard, K.E., Berzley, D.A., & Oros, C.J. (1981, August). *Personality and attitudinal characteristics of sexually aggressive men.* Paper presented at the annual meeting of the American Psychological Association, Los Angeles.

Krafft-Ebing, R. (1950) [1886]. *Psychopathia sexualis: A medico-forensic study.* New York: Pioneer.

Kremsdorf, R.B., Holmen, M.L., & Laws, D.R. (1980). Orgasmic reconditioning without deviant imagery: A case report with a pedophile. *Behavior Research and Therapy, 18,* 203–207.

Lafond, M., Stark, B., & Buckley, C. (1979). *Echo Glen Children's Center sex offender program.* (Microfiche). Rockville, MD: National Criminal Justice Reference Service.

Landis, J. (1956). Experiences of 500 children with adult sexual deviants. *Psychiatric Quarterly Supplement, 30,* 91–109.

Lane, S., & Zamora, P. (1984). A method for treating the adolescent sex offender. In R.A. Matias, P. DeMuro, & R.S. Allinson (Eds.), *Violent juvenile offenders: An anthology* (pp. 347–363). San Francisco: National Council on Crime and Delinquency.

Langevin, R. (1983). *Sexual strands: Understanding and treating sex anomalies in men.* Hillsdale, NJ: Lawrence Erlbaum

Langevin, R., Handy, L., Hook, H., Day, D., & Russon, A. (1985). Are incestuous fathers pedophilic and aggressive? In R. Langevin (Ed.), *Erotic preference gender identity and aggression.* New York: Lawrence Erlbaum.

Lanning, K.V. (1986). *Child molesters: A behavioral analysis.* Washington, DC: National Center for Missing and Exploited Children.

Lanyon, R. (1985). Theory and treatment in child molestation. *Journal of Consulting and Clinical Psychology, 54* (2), 176–182.

Lanyon, R. (1986). Psychological assessment procedures in court-related settings. *Professional Psychology, 17,* 260–268.

Laws, D.R. (1985). Sexual fantasy alteration: Procedural considerations. *Journal of Behavior Therapy and Experimental Psychiatry, 16,* 39–44.

Laws, D.R., & O'Neill, J.A. (1981). Variations on masturbatory conditioning. *Behavior Psychotherapy, 9,* 23–31.

Lazarus, A.A. (1971). *Behavior therapy and beyond.* New York: McGraw-Hill.

Lazarus, A.A. (1976). *Multi-modal behavior therapy.* New York: Springer.

Lazarus, R. (1967). Cognitive and personality factors underlying threat and coping. In M. Apple & R. Trumbell (Eds.), *Psychological stress.* New York: Appleton-Century-Crofts.

Levay, A.N., & Kagle, S. (1977). Ego deficiencies in the areas of pleasure, intimacy and cooperation. *Journal of Sex and Marital Therapy, 3,* 10–18.

Levin, S.M., Barry, S.M., Gambaro, S., Wolfinsohn, L., & Smith, A. (1977). Variations of covert sensitization in the treatment of pedophilic behavior: A case study. *Journal of Consulting and Clinical Psychology, 45,* 896–907.

Lew, M. (1988). *Victims no longer: Men recovering from incest and other sexual child abuse.* New York: Nevraumont.

Lewinsohn, P.M., Biglan, A., & Zeiss, A.M. (1976). Behavioral treatment of depression. In P.O. Davidson (Ed.), *The behavioral management of anxiety, depression and pain.* New York: Brunner/Mazel.

Lewinsohn, P.M., & Grosscup, S.L. (1978). *Decreasing unpleasant events and increasing pleasant events: A treatment manual for depression.* Unpublished manuscript, University of Oregon.

Lewinsohn, P.M., & Hoberman, H.M. (1982). Depression. In A.S. Bellack, M. Hersen, & A.E. Kazdin (Eds.), *International handbook of behavior modification and therapy* (pp. 397–431). New York: Plenum.

Lewinsohn, P.M. & Libet, J. (1972). Pleasant events, activity schedules and depression. *Journal of Abnormal Psychology, 79,* 291–295.

Lewinsohn, P.M., Youngren, M.A., & Grosscup, S.L. (1980). Reinforcement and depression. In R.A. Depue (Ed.), *The psychobiology of the depressive disorders: Implications for the effects of stress.* New York: Academic Press.

Lewis, I.A. (1985). *Los Angeles Times Poll #98.* Unpublished raw data.

Lindberg, F.H., & Distad, L.H. (1985). Post-traumatic stress disorder in women who experienced childhood incest. *Child Abuse and Neglect, 9,* 329–334.

Loftus, E.F., & Davies, G.M. (1984). Distortions in the memory of children. *Journal of Social Issues, 40* (2), 51–68.

Longo, R.E. (1982). Sexual learning experiences among adolescent sexual offenders. *International Journal of Offender Therapy and Comparative Criminology, 26,* 235–241.

Longo, R.E., & Groth, A.N. (1983). Juvenile sexual offenses in the histories of adult rapists and child molesters. *International Journal of Offender Therapy and Comparative Criminology, 27,* 150–155.

Longo, R.E., & McFaddin, B. (1981). Sexually inappropriate behavior: Development of the sexual offender. *Law and Order,* 21–23.

Lukianowicz, N. (1983). Incest. *British Journal of Psychiatry, 12,* 301–313.

Luthe, W., & Schultz, J.H. (1970). *Autogenic therapy: Applications in psychotherapy.* New York: Grune & Stratton.

Maas, P. (1986). *Male sexual abuse and the pedophile.* Unpublished manuscript, Arizona State University, Counselor Education Department, Tempe, AZ.

Maccoby, E.E., & Jacklin, C.N. (1974). *The psychology of sex differences.* Stanford: Stanford University Press.

Maccoby, E.E., & Jacklin, C.N. (1987). Gender segregation in childhood. *Advances in Child Development and Behavior, 20,* 239–87.

MacFarlane, K., & Korbin, J.E. (1983). Confronting the incest secret long after the fact: A family study of multiple victimization with strategies for intervention. *Child Abuse and Neglect, 17* (2), 225–238.

Maddock, J.W. (1983). Sex in the family system. *Marriage and Family Review, 6* (3/4), 9–19.

Mahoney, M.J. (1974). *Cognition and behavior modification.* Cambridge, MA: Ballinger.

Maletzky, B.M. (1973). "Assisted" covert sensitization: A preliminary report. *Behavior Therapy, 4,* 117–119.

Maletzky, B.M. (1974). Assisted covert sensitization in the treatment of exhibitionism. *Journal of Consulting and Clinical Psychology, 42,* 34–40.

Margolin, L. (1983). A treatment model for the adolescent sex offender. *Journal of Offender Counseling Services and Rehabilitation, 8,* 1–12.

Marks, I.M. (1976). Management of sexual disorders. In H. Leitenberg (Ed.), *Handbook of behavior modification and behavior therapy* (255–300). Englewood Cliffs, NJ: Prentice-Hall.

Marlatt, G.A. (1982). Relapse prevention: A self-control program for the treatment of addictive behavior. In R. B. Stuart (Ed.), *Adherence, compliance, and generalization in behavioral medicine.* New York: Brunner/Mazel.

Marlatt, G.A., & Gordon, J.R. (Eds.). (1985). *Relapse prevention: Maintenance strategies in the treatment of addictive behaviors.* New York: Guilford.

Marquis, J.N. (1970). Orgasmic reconditioning: Changing sexual object choice through controlling masturbation fantasies. *Journal of Behavior Therapy and Experimental Psychiatry, 1,* 263–271.

Marshall, W.L. (1979). Satiation therapy: A procedure for reducing deviant arousal. *Journal of Applied Behavior Analysis, 12,* 377–389.

Marshall, W.L., & Lippens, K. (1977). The clinical value of boredom: A procedure for reducing inappropriate sexual interests. *Journal of Nervous and Mental Diseases, 165,* 283–287.

Marvasti, J. (1986). Incestuous mothers. *American Journal of Forensic Psychiatry, 1,* 63–69.

Masson, J.M. (1984). *The assault on truth: Freud's suppression of the seduction theory.* New York: Farrar, Straus & Giroux.

Masters, R. (1970). *Patterns of incest.* New York: Ace Book.

Masters, W.H., & Johnson, V.E. (1966). *Human sexual response.* Boston: Little, Brown.

Masters, W.H., & Johnson, V.E. (1970). *Human sexual inadequacy.* Boston: Little, Brown.

Masters, W.H., & Johnson, V.E. (1976a). *The pleasure bond.* New York: Bantam.

Masters, W.H., & Johnson, V.E. (1976b). Principles of the new sex therapy. *American Journal of Psychiatry, 133,* 548–554.

Masters, W.H., Johnson, V.E., & Kolodny, R.C. (1985). *Human sexuality* (2nd ed.). Boston: Little, Brown.

Mathews, R. (1987). *Preliminary typology of female sex offenders.* MN: PHASE and Genesis II for Women. (Available from The Safer Society Program, Shoreham Depot Road, Orwell, VT 05760)

Mavissakalian, M., Blanchard, E.B., Abel, G.G., & Barlow, D.H. (1975). Responses to complex erotic stimuli in homosexual and heterosexual males. *British Journal of Psychiatry, 126,* 252–257.

Max, L. (1935). Breaking up a homosexual fixation by the conditional reaction technique. *Psychological Bulletin, 32,* 734.

McCaghy, C.H. (1971). Child molesting. *Sexual Behavior, 1,* 16–24.

McCary, J.L. (1967). *Human sexuality.* Princeton: Van Nostrand.

McCary, J.L. (1971). *Sexual myths and fallacies.* New York: Van Nostrand.

McCreary, C.P. (1975a). Personality profiles of persons convicted of indecent exposure. *Journal of Clinical Psychology, 31,* 260–262.

McCreary, C.P. (1975b). Personality differences among child molesters. *Journal of Personality Assessment, 39,* 591–593.

McGuire, R.J., Carlisle, J.M., & Young, B.G. (1965). Sexual deviations as conditional behavior. *Behavior Research and Therapy, 2,* 185–190.

McGuire, R., & Vallance, M. (1964). Aversion therapy by electric shock: A simple technique. *British Medical Journal, 1,* 151–152.

McLean, P.D., & Hakatian, A.R. (1979). Clinical depression: Comparative efficacy of outpatient treatments. *Journal of Consulting and Clinical Psychology, 47,* 818–836.

Meichenbaum, D. (1974). *Cognitive behavior modification.* Morristown, NJ: General Learning Press.

Meichenbaum, D. (1975). A self-instructional approach to stress management: A proposal for stress inoculation training. In C. Spielberger & I. Sarason (Eds.), *Stress and Anxiety: Vol. 2.* New York: John Wiley.

Meichenbaum, D. (1977). *Cognitive behavior modification: An integrative approach.* New York: Plenum.

Meichenbaum, D., & Cameron, R. (1973). Training schizophrenics to talk to themselves: A means of developing self-control. *Behavior Therapy, 4,* 515–534.

Meichenbaum, D., & Goodman, J. (1971). Training impulsive children to talk to themselves: A means of developing self-control. *Journal of Abnormal Psychology, 77,* 115–126.

Metcalf, A., & Humphries, M. (Eds.). (1985). *The sexuality of men.* London: Pluto Press.

Miller, L. (1981). *Louisville behavior checklist.* Los Angeles: Western Psychological Services.

Millon T. (1987). *Millon clinical multiaxial inventory—II.* Minneapolis: National Computer Systems.

Millon, T., Green, C.J., & Meagher, Jr., R.B. (1982). *Millon adolescent personality inventory.* Minneapolis: National Computer Systems.

Miner, M., & Nelson, C. (undated). *The modification of deviant sexual arousal patterns through the use of various behavioral techniques.* Sex Offender Treatment and Evaluation Project, Atascadero State Hospital, Atascadero, CA.

Mohr, J.W. (1962). The pedophilias: Their clinical, social and legal implications. *Canadian Psychiatric Association Journal, 7,* 225–260.

Mohr, J.W., Turner, R.E., & Jerry, M.B. (1964). *Pedophilia and exhibitionism.* Toronto: University of Toronto.

Money, J. (1977). Paraphilias. In J. Money & H. Musaph (Eds.), *Handbook of sexology.* San Diego: College-Hill.

Money, J., & Wiedeking, C. (1980). Gender identity/role: Normal differentiation and its transpositions. In B.B. Wolman & J. Money (Eds.), *Handbook of human sexuality* (pp. 269–284). Englewood Cliffs, NJ: Prentice-Hall.

Morgan, S.R. (1985). *Children in crises: A team approach in the schools.* San Diego: College-Hill.

Mrazek, P.B. (1980). Annotation: Sexual abuse of children. *Journal of Child Psychology and Psychiatry, 21* (10), 91–94.

Naitove, E.E. (1982). Arts therapy with sexually abused children. In S.M. Sgroi (Ed.), *Handbook of clinical intervention in child sexual abuse* (269–308). Lexington, MA: Lexington Books.

National Center on Child Abuse and Neglect. (1981). *Study findings: National study of incidence and severity of child abuse and neglect.* Washington, DC: Department of Health Education and Welfare.

Nichols, H.R., & Molinder, I. (1984). *Multiphasic sex inventory manual.* (Available from Nichols and Molinder, 437 Bowes Drive, Tacoma, WA 98466).

Nielsen, T., (1983). Sexual abuse of boys: Current perspectives. *Personnel and Guidance Journal, 62,* 139–142.

Novaco, R.W. (1975). *Anger control: The development and evaluation of an experimental treatment.* Lexington, MA: Lexington Books.

Novaco, R.W. (1976a). The functions and regulation of the arousal of anger. *American Journal of Psychiatry, 133,* 1124–1128.

Novaco, R.W. (1976b). The treatment of anger through cognitive and relaxation controls. *Journal of Consulting and Clinical Psychology, 44,* 681.

Novaco, R.W. (1977). Stress inoculation: A cognitive therapy for anger and its application to a case of depression. *Journal of Consulting and Clinical Psychology, 45,* 600–608.

Nowicki, S., & Duke, M.P. (1974). A locus of control scale for college as well as non-college adults. *Journal of Personality Assessment, 38,* 136–137.

O'Carroll, T. (1980). *Pedophile: The radical case.* London: Peter Owen.

O'Connor, A.A. (1987). Female sex offenders. *British Journal of Psychiatry, 150,* 615–620.

Oliver, B.J. (1967). *Sexual deviations in American society.* New Haven, CT: United Printing.

Olson, D.H., Portner, J., & Lavee, Y. (1985). *FACES III.* (Available from Family Social Science, University of Minnesota, 290 McNeal Hall, St. Paul, MN 55108).

Olson, D.H., Sprenkle, D.H., & Russell, C.S. (1979). Circumplex model of marital and family systems: Cohesion and adaptability dimensions, family types, and clinical applications. *Family Process, 16,* 3–28.

Orr, D.P., & Prietto, S.V. (1979). Emergency management of sexually abused children. *American Journal of Diseases of Children, 133,* 628–631.

Paitich, D., Langevin, R., Freeman, R., Mann, K., & Handy, L. (1977). The Clark sexual history questionnaire: A clinical sex history questionnaire for males. *Archives of Sexual Behavior, 6,* 421–435.

Panton, J.H. (1979). MMPI profile configurations associated with incestuous and non-incestuous child molesting. *Psychological Reports, 45,* 335–338.

Parke, R., & Collmer, C. (1975). Child abuse: An interdisciplinary analysis. In E.M. Hetherington (Ed.). *Review of child development research* (Vol 5). Chicago: University of Chicago Press.

Parloff, M.B. (1980, April) *Psychotherapy and research: An anaclitic depression.* Frieda Fromm-Reichman Memorial Lecture, Washington School of Psychiatry, St. Louis.

Paul, G.L. (1969a). Outcome of systematic desensitization I: Background, procedures, and uncontrolled reports of individual treatment. In C.M. Franks (Ed.), *Behavior therapy: Appraisal and status* (pp. 63–104). New York: McGraw-Hill.

Paul, G.L. (1969b). Outcome of systematic desensitization II: Controlled investigations of individual treatment, technique variations, and current status. In C.M. Franks (Ed.), *Behavior therapy: Appraisal and status* (pp. 105–159). New York: McGraw-Hill.

Perelman, M.A. (1980). Treatment of premature ejaculation. In S.R. Leiblum & L.A. Pervin (Eds.), *Principles and practice of sex therapy* (pp. 195–233) New York: Guilford Press.

Peters, S.D., Wyatt, G.E., & Finklehor, D. (1986). Prevalence. In D. Finklehor (Ed.), *A sourcebook on child sexual abuse* (pp. 15–59). Beverly Hills, CA: Sage.

Petrovich, M., & Templer, D. (1984). Heterosexual molestation of children who later become rapists. *Psychological Reports, 54,* 810.

Pierce, L.H., & Pierce, R.L. (1984, August). *Race as a factor in childhood sexual abuse.* Paper presented at the Second National Conference for Family Violence Researchers, Durham, NH.

Pithers, W.D., Kashima, K.M., Cumming, G.F., & Beal, L.S. (1988). Relapse prevention: A method of enhancing maintenance of change in sex offenders. In A. Salter (Ed.), *Treating child sex offenders and victims* (pp. 131–170). Beverly Hills, CA: Sage.

Pithers, W.D., Marques, J.K., Gibat, C.C., & Marlatt, G.A. (1983). Relapse prevention with sexual aggressives: A self control model of treatment and maintenance of change. In J.G. Greer & J.R. Stuart (Eds.), *The sexual aggressor: Current perspectives on treatment.* New York: Van Nostrand Reinhold.

Plummer, K. (1981). Pedophilia: Constructing a sociological baseline. In M. Cook & K. Howells (Eds.), *Adult sexual interest in children.* London: Academic Press.

Pomeroy, J.C., Behar, D., & Steward, M.A. (1981). Abnormal sexual behavior in prepubescent children. *British Journal of Psychiatry, 138,* 11–125.

Pomeroy, W.B. (1977). The new sexual myths of the 1970's. *Siecus Report, 5* (6), 1, 14–15.

Porter, E. (1986). *Treating the young male victim of sexual assault: Issues & intervention strategies.* Syracuse, NY: Safer Society Press.

Porter, F.S., Blick, I.C., & Sgroi, S.M. (1982). Treatment of the sexually abused child. In S.M. Sgroi (Ed.), *Handbook of clinical intervention in child sexual abuse* (pp. 109–145). Lexington, MA: Lexington Books.

Porter, R.B., & Cattell, R.B. (1988). *Children's personality questionnaire.* Odessa, FL: Psychological Assessment Resources, Inc.

Prentky, P. (1984, August). *Childhood physical and sexual abuse in the lives of sexually aggressive offenders.* Paper presented at the Second National Conference for Family Violence Researchers, Durham, NH.

Quinsey, V.L. (1977). The assessment and treatment of child molesters: A review. *Canadian Psychological Review, 18* (3), 204–220.

Rachman, S. (1961). Sexual disorder and behavior therapy. *American Journal of Psychiatry, 118,* 235–240.

Rachman, S., & Teasdale, J. (1969). *Aversion therapy with behavior disorders: An analysis.* Coral Gables, FL: University of Miami Press.

Rada, R., Laws, D., & Kellner, R. (1976). Plasma testosterone levels in the rapist. *Psychosomatic Medicine, 38* (4), 257–268.

Rascovsky, M., & Rascovsky, A. (1950). On consummated incest. *International Journal of Psychoanalysis, 31,* 42–47.

Raybin, J. (1969). Homosexual incest. *Journal of Nervous and Mental Disease, 148,* 105–110.

Reams, R., & Friedrich, W. (1985). *A manual for time-limited play therapy with abused/neglected children.* Unpublished manuscript. University of Washington, Seattle.

Rehm, L.P., & Kornblith, S.J. (1979). Behavior therapy for depression: A review of recent developments. In M. Hersen, R.M. Eisler, & P.M. Miller (Eds.), *Progress in behavior modification: Vol. 7.* New York: Academic Press.

Reiss, I.C. (1969). *The social context of premarital sexual permissiveness.* New York: Holt, Rinehart & Winston.

Rhinehart, J. (1961). Genesis of overt incest. *Comparative Psychiatry, 2,* 338–349.

Richardson, L.W. (1981). *The dynamics of gender* (2nd ed.). Boston: Houghton Mifflin.

Roberts, R.E., Abrams, L., & Finch, J.R. (1973). Delinquent sexual behavior among adolescents. *Medical Aspects of Human Sexuality, 7,* 162–183.

Romanik, R.L., & Goodwin, J. (1982). Adaptation to pregnancy due to childhood sexual abuse. *Birth Psychology Bulletin, 3* (2), 2–9.

Rosen, R.C., & Keefe, F.J. (1978). The measurement of human penile tumescence. *Psychophysiology, 15,* 366–367.

Rosenfeld, A.A. (1976). The clinical management of incest and sexual abuse of children. *Journal of the American Medical Association, 242,* 1761–1764.

Rossman, P. (1980). The pederasts. In L.G. Schultz (Ed.), *The sexual victimology of youth* (pp. 335–349). Springfield, IL: Charles C Thomas.

Rouleau, J.L., Abel, G.G., Mittelman, M.S., Becker, J.V., & Cunningham-Rathner, J. (1986 February). *Effectiveness of each component of a treatment program for nonincarcerated pedophiles.* Paper presented at NIGH Conference on sex offenders, Tampa, FL.

Rush, A.J., Beck, A.T., Kovacs, M., & Hallon, S. (1977). Comparative efficiency of cognitive therapy and imipramine in the treatment of depressed outpatients. *Cognitive Therapy and Research, 1,* 17–37.

Russell, D.E.H. (Ed.). (1983). The incidence and prevalence of intrafamilial and extrafamilial sexual abuse of female children. *Child Abuse and Neglect, 7,* 133–146.

Russell, D.E.H. (1984). *Sexual exploitation: Rape, child sexual abuse, and workplace harassment.* Beverly Hills, CA: Sage.

Russell, D.E.H., & Finkelhor, D. (1984). The gender gap among perpetrators of sexual abuse. In D.E.H. Russell (Ed.), *Sexual exploitation: Rape, child sexual abuse and workplace harassment* (pp. 215–231). Beverly Hills, CA: Sage.

Ryan, G., Lane, S., Davis, J., & Isaac, C. (1987). Juvenile sexual offenders: Development and correction. *Child Abuse and Neglect, 11,* 385–395.

Salter, A. (1988). *Treating child sex offenders and victims.* Beverly Hills, CA: Sage.

Sandfort, T.G.M. (1979). *Pedosexual contacts and pedophiliac relationships.* The Netherlands: Netherlands Institute for Social-Sexological Research.

Sandfort, T.G.M. (1984). Sex in pedophiliac relationships: An empirical investigation among a nonrepresentative group of boys. *The Journal of Sex Research, 20,* 123–142.

Sarrell, P., & Masters, W. (1982). Sexual molestation of men and women. *Archives of Sexual Behavior, 11,* 117–131.

Scacco, A.M., Jr. (Ed.). (1982). *Male rape: A casebook of sexual aggressions.* New York: AMS Press.

Schachter, S., & Singer, J.E. (1962). Cognitive, social, and physiological determinants of emotional state. *Psychological Review, 69,* 379–399.

Schultz, J.H., & Luthe, W. (1959). *Autogenic training.* New York: Grune and Straton.

Schultz, L.G. (Ed.). (1975). *Rape victimology.* Springfield, IL: Charles C Thomas.

Schultz, L.G. (1980). *The sexual victimology of youth.* Springfield, IL: Charles C Thomas.

Scott, R.L., & Stone, D.A. (1986a). MMPI measures of psychological disturbance and adult victims of father-daughter incest. *Journal of Clinical Psychology, 42,* 251–259.

Scott, R.L., & Stone, D.A. (1986b). MMPI profile constellations in incest families. *Journal of Consulting and Clinical Psychology, 54,* 364–368.

Seghorn, T.K. (1981, August). *The decision tree: Factors in the clinical subtyping of sexually dangerous persons.* Presented at the American Psychological Association annual meeting, Los Angeles.

Seghorn, T.K., & Boucher, R.J. (1980). Sexual abuse in childhood as a factor in adult sexually dangerous criminal offenses. In J.M. Samson (Ed.), *Childhood and sexuality: Proceedings of the international symposium.* Montreal: Editions Etudes Vivantes.

Seidner, A.L., & Calhoun, D.S. (1984, August). *Childhood sexual abuse: Factors related to differential adult adjustment.* Paper presented at the Second National Conference for Family Violence Researchers, Durham, NH.

Semans, J.H. (1956). Premature ejaculation: A new approach. *Southern Medical Journal, 49,* 353–358.

Serrill, M.S. (1974). Treating sex offenders in New Jersey. *Corrections Magazine,* November-December, 13–24.

Sgroi, S.M. (1975). Child sexual molestation: The last frontier in child abuse. *Children Today, 44,* 18–21.

Sgroi, S.M. (1978). Child sexual assault: Some guidelines for intervention and assessment. In A.W. Burgess, A.N. Groth, L.L. Holmstrom, & S.M. Sgroi (Eds.), *Sexual assault of children and adolescents* (pp. 129–142). Lexington, MA: Lexington Books.

Sgroi, S.M., Blick, L.C., & Porter, F.S. (1982). A conceptual framework for child sexual abuse. In S.M. Sgroi (Ed.), *Handbook of clinical intervention in child sexual abuse* (pp. 9–37). Lexington, MA: Lexington Books.

Shah, F., & Zelnik, M. (1981). Parent and peer influence on sexual behavior, contraceptive use, and pregnancy experience of young women. *Journal of Marriage and the Family, 43,* 339–348.

Sharabany, R., Gershoni, R., & Hofman, J.E. (1981). Girlfriend, boyfriend: Age and sex differences in intimate friendship. *Developmental Psychology, 17*(6), 800–808.

Shengold, L. (1980). Some reflections on a case of mother/adolescent son incest. *International Journal of Psychoanalysis, 61,* 461–476.

Showers, J., Farber, E., Joseph, J., Oshins, L., & Johnson, C. (1983). The sexual victimization of boys: A three-year survey. *Health Values, 7,* 15–18.

Silbert, M., & Pines, A. (1981). Sexual child abuse as an antecedent to prostitution. *Child Abuse and Neglect, 5,* 407–411.

Sloane, P., & Karpinski, E. (1942). Effects of incest on the participants. *American Journal of Orthopsychiatry, 13,* 666–673.

Smets, A.C., & Cebula, C.M. (1987). A group treatment program for adolescent sex offenders: Five steps toward resolution. *Child Abuse and Neglect, 11,* 247–254.

Smith, E.A., Udry, J.R., & Morris, N.A. (1985). Pubertal development and friends: A biosocial explanation of adolescent sexual behavior. *Journal of Health and Social Behavior, 26,* 183–192.

Spence, J.T., & Helmreich, R.L. (1972). The attitudes toward women scale: An objective instrument to measure attitudes toward the rights and roles of women in contemporary society. *Psychological Documents, 2,* 153.

Spence, J.T., & Helmreich, R.L. (1978a). *Attitudes toward women.* Austin: University of Texas Press.

Spence, J.T., & Helmreich, R.L. (1978b). *Masculinity & femininity: Their psychological dimensions, correlates and antecedents.* Austin: University of Texas Press.

Spielberger, C.D., Gorsuch, R.L., & Lushene, R.G. (1970). *The state-trait anxiety inventory.* Palo Alto, CA: Consulting Psychologists Press.

Steller, M. (1986, February). *Statement reality analysis.* Paper presented to the Assessing the Credibility of the Child Witness in the Sexual Abuse Case Seminar, St. Luke's Hospital Center for Behavioral Health and the Law, Scottsdale, AZ.

Steller, M., & Raskin, D.C. (1986, February). *Credibility assessment procedure.* Paper presented to the Assessing the Credibility of the Child Witness in the Sexual Abuse Case Seminar, St. Luke's Hospital Center for Behavioral Health and the Law, Scottsdale, AZ.

Stroebel, C.F. (1978). *Biofeedback procedures.* New York: Grune and Stratton.

Strong, B., Wilson, S., Robbins, M., & Johns, T. (1981). *Human sexuality: Essentials* (2nd ed.). St. Paul: West Publishing.

Stuart, F., Stuart, R.B., Maurice, W.L., & Szasz, G. (1975). *Sexual adjustment inventory.* Champaign, IL: Research Press.

Summit, R.C. (1983). The child sexual abuse accommodation syndrome. *Child Abuse and Neglect, 7,* 177–193.

Summit, R.C., & Kryso, J. (1978). Sexual abuse of children: A clinical spectrum. *American Journal of Orthopsychiatry, 48,* 237–251.

Swanson, D.W. (1971). Who violates children sexually? *Medical Aspects of Human Sexuality, 5,* 184–197.

Swift, C. (1980). *Sexual victimology of youth.* Springfield, IL: Charles C Thomas.

Tasto, D.L. (1969). Systematic desensitization, muscle relaxation and visual imagery in the counter conditioning of a four-year-old phobic child. *Behavior Research and Therapy, 1,* 409–411.

Terr, L.C. (1983). Coachella revisited: The effects of psychic trauma four years after a school-bus kidnapping. *American Journal of Psychiatry, 140,* 1543–1550.

Thorne, F.C. (1966). The sex inventory. *Journal of Clinical Psychology, 22,* 367–374.

Tierney, K., & Corwin, D. (1983). Exploring intra-familial child sexual abuse. A systems approach. In D. Finkelhor, R.J. Gelles, G.T. Hotaling, & M.A. Straus (Eds.), *The dark side of families* (pp. 102–116). Beverly Hills, CA: Sage.

Tobias, J.L., & Gordon, R. (1977). *Operation lure* (mimeo). Michigan State Police.

Tsai, M., Feldman-Summers, S., & Edgar, M. (1979). Childhood molestation: Variables related to differential impacts on psychosexual functioning in adult women. *Journal of Abnormal Psychology, 88,* 407–417.

Tsai, M., & Wagner, N.W. (1979). Therapy groups for women sexually molested as children. *Archives of Sexual Behavior, 7,* 417–427.

Tufts New England Medical Center, Division of Child Psychiatry. (1984). *Sexually exploited children: Service and research project: Final Report.* Washington, DC: Office of Juvenile Justice and Delinquency Prevention, U.S. Department of Justice.

VanDeventer, A.D., & Laws, D.R. (1978). Orgasmic reconditioning to redirect sexual arousal in pedophiles. *Behavior Therapy, 9,* 748–765.

Virkunnen, M. (1974). Incest offenses and alcoholism. *Medicine, Science, and the Law, 14,* 124–128.

Virkkunen, M. (1976). The pedophilic offender with antisocial character. *Acta Psychiatrica Scandinavica, 53,* 401–405.

Wahl, C. (1960). The psychodynamics of consummated maternal incest. *Archives of General Psychiatry, 3,* 188–193.

Watson, D. & Friend, R. (1969). Measurement of social-evaluative anxiety. *Journal of Consulting and Clinical Psychology, 33,* 448–457.

Weil, G., & Goldfried, M.R. (1973). Treatment of insomnia in an eleven year old child by self-relaxation. *Behavior Therapy, 4,* 282–294.

Weinberg, S.K. (1955). *Incest behavior.* New York: Citadel Press.

Wheeler, J.R., & Berliner, L. (1988). Treating the effects of sexual abuse on children. In G.E. Wyatt & G.J. Powell (Eds.), *Lasting effects of child sexual abuse* (pp. 227–247). Newbury Park, CA: Sage Publications.

White, S., Strom, G.A., & Santilli, G. (in press). *Child abuse and neglect.* Pergamon Journals.

Wilson, G. (1978). *The secrets of sexual fantasy.* London: J.M. Dent.

Wilson, G.D., & Gosselin, C.C. (1980). Personality characteristics of fetishists, transvestites, and sadomasochists. *Personality and Individual Differences, 1,* 289–295.

Wilson, G.D., & Gosselin, C.C. (1983). Personality characteristics of pedophile club members. *Personality and Individual Differences, 4,* 323–329.

Wolberg, L.R. (1954). *The techniques of psychotherapy.* New York: Pergamon.

Wolfe, F.A. (1985, March). *Twelve female sexual offenders*. Presentation to "Next Steps in Research on the Assessment and Treatment of Sexually Aggressive Persons (Paraphiliacs)," St. Louis, MO.

Wolpe, J. (1958). *Psychotherapy by reciprocal inhibition*. Stanford: Stanford University Press.

Wolpe, J. (1965). Conditioned inhibition of craving in drug addiction. *Behavior Research and Therapy, 2*, 285–287.

Wolpe, J. (1981). *Our useless fears*. Boston: Houghton Mifflin.

Wolpe, J., & Lazarus, A.A. (1966). *Behavior Therapy Techniques*. New York: Pergamon.

Woods, S.C., & Dean, K.S. (1984). *Final report: Sexual abuse of males research project* (NCCAN Report No. 90-CA-812). Washington, DC: National Center on Child Abuse and Neglect.

Wyatt, G.E. (1985). The sexual abuse of Afro-American and White American women in childhood. *Child Abuse and Neglect, 9*, 507–520.

Yates, A. (1982). Children eroticized by incest. *American Journal of Psychiatry, 139*, 482–485.

Yochelson, S., & Samenow, S. (1976). *The criminal personality: A profile for change: Vol. 1*. New York: Jason Aronson.

Yuille, J.C., & King, M.A. (1986). *Children and witnesses*. (Mimeo). Vancouver: University of British Columbia Eyewitness Research Project.

Zilbergeld, B. (1978). *Male sexuality*. Boston: Little, Brown.

Zuckerman, M. (1971). Physiological measures of sexual arousal in the human. *Physiological Bulletin, 75*, 297–329.

Zussman, L., & Zussman, S. (1977). The treatment of sexual dysfunction: Some theoretical considerations. *Journal of Contemporary Psychotherapy, 8*, 83–90.

About the Authors

Frank G. Bolton, Jr., is currently in private practice in Phoenix, Arizona. He is the author of more than forty articles and five books. His other Sage books in family violence and related areas are *The Pregnant Adolescent: Problems of Premature Parenthood, When Bonding Fails: Clinical Assessment of the High Risk Family,* and *Working with Violent Families: A Guide for Clinical and Legal Practitioners.*

Larry A. Morris is a clinical psychologist with a private practice in Tucson, Arizona. He has specialized in the evaluation and treatment of victims of childhood sexual abuse as well as sex offenders for nearly two decades. He has also served as consultant to or evaluation project director of several federally funded social action programs designed to increase the informational base and skills of prospective parents, to expand self-help programs for abusive parents, and to foster the cognitive and emotional growth of young children through family education programs. He has conducted training seminars for child protective services staff, and has served as an expert witness in cases involving physical and sexual child abuse. He is author of a series of books in the area of early childhood learning experiences, *Teach Me* (Aztex, 1982) and over twenty articles and reports.

Ann E. MacEachron, B.A. (Cornell University), M.S.W. (University of Pittsburgh), Ph.D. (Cornell University), was formerly the Samuel and Rose Gingold Associate Professor of Human Development at Brandeis University and is currently Professor of Social Work Research at the Arizona State University School of Social Work. She has published in the areas of developmental disabilities, family violence, Indian Child Welfare, and the management of effective human services.